IMAGES
of America

AFRICAN AMERICANS IN VALLEJO

On the Cover: In the spring of 1964, this lovely group of young women was presented to Vallejo society by the It Club, a local social organization. Standing in front of the historic Kyles Temple African Methodist Episcopal Zion Church, then located on the corner of Illinois Street and Sonoma Boulevard, the young women include (in no particular order) Nona Cohen, Ollie Ware, Sherry Foundoe, Janice Colbert, Deborah Williams, Shirley Scott, Faye Williams, Faye Burris, Irma Higgins, and Norma Husband. For a number of years, the It Club sponsored cotillion balls that were the highlight of the Vallejo African American social season. (Courtesy of the Vallejo Naval and Historical Museum.)

IMAGES
of America

AFRICAN AMERICANS IN VALLEJO

Sharon McGriff-Payne

ARCADIA
PUBLISHING

ISBN 978-0-7385-9581-8

Published by Arcadia Publishing
Charleston, South Carolina

Printed in the United States of America

Library of Congress Control Number: 2012935708

For all general information, please contact Arcadia Publishing:
Telephone 843-853-2070
Fax 843-853-0044
E-mail sales@arcadiapublishing.com
For customer service and orders:
Toll-Free 1-888-313-2665

Visit us on the Internet at www.arcadiapublishing.com

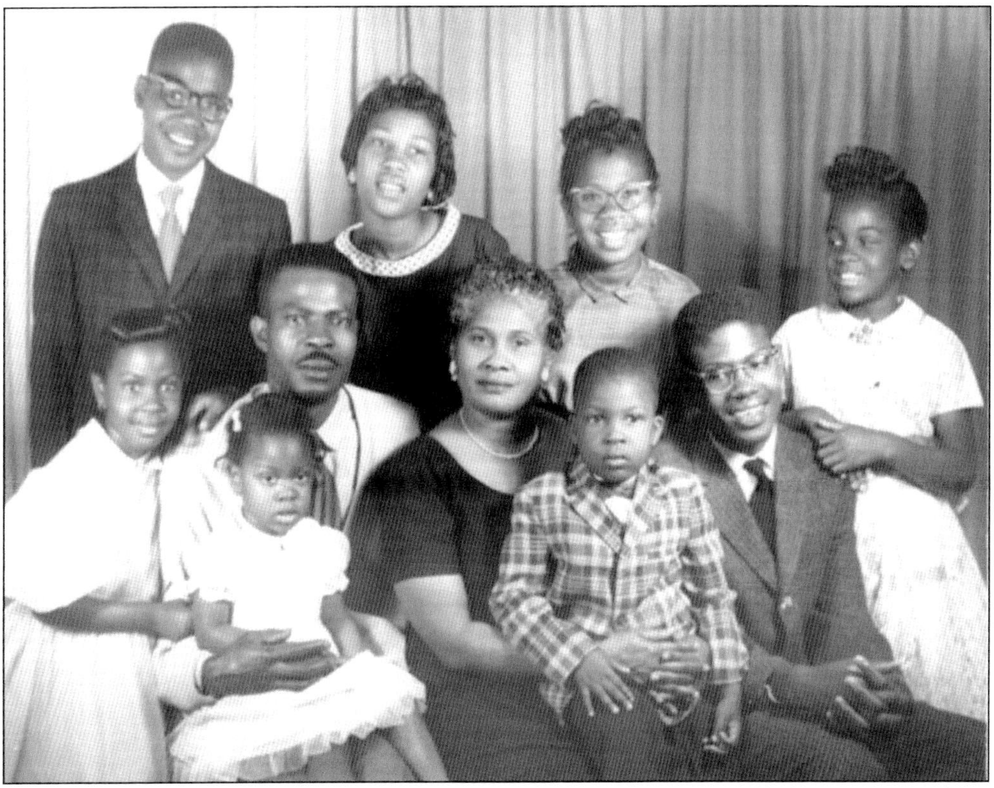

This book is dedicated to my parents, the late Marshall and Bernice McGriff, who were the authors of my Great Migration story, and is in loving memory of my siblings, Robert Leon Robinson, Melody Ann McGriff, Erica Dawn McGriff, and Patricia Alice McGriff. Pictured from left to right in 1961 are (first row) Erica, Marshall, Patricia, Bernice, Gregory, and Marshall Jr.; (second row) Michael, Melody, Sharon (author), and Crystal. (Courtesy of the author.)

Contents

ACKNOWLEDGMENTS

Writing is largely a singular effort; it is the writer, his or her thoughts, and a pen, pencil, or computer. But when a book deals with history as well as the added task of compiling photographs, like *African Americans in Vallejo*, creating a book turns into a community effort. Thankfully, I had a wonderful, supportive community to lend a hand in the making of this book. My gratitude for all those people—especially those of my parents' generation, who made the Great Migration to Vallejo so many years ago—runs deep. A thanks goes to my husband, Clarence Payne, for supporting me with all my projects. None of this would work without him. I want to thank Lauren Coodley, retired Napa Valley Community College professor, for connecting me to Arcadia Publishing, which published this book. A thank-you also goes to Jim Kern, executive director of the Vallejo Naval and Historical Museum, who pointed me to photographs and historical information stored there. I am grateful to all those people who contributed photographs and information about the period between 1910 and 1970. Thanks go to James "Jimmy" and John "Chocqui" Boyden. Their wonderful family photo album helped me tremendously. Also, many thanks go to attorney Lewis F. Brown for sharing stories and photographs. A special thank-you goes to Haskell Forte, who shared wonderful photographs of the 1940s and 1950s. Others who helped include the following: the late James Williams and his wife, Ursula; the late Mary Johnson; Ruth Love; James and Jackie Brown; Emma and Ruth Etta Perry; Catherine Fulcher; Bradis McGriff; Linnie Bell Joiner; Yvonne Johnson; Cherubim "Jake" Speaks; Betty Johnson; Cris Arriola; Ray Calip; Joe Jones; Gertrude Jones Williams; Beatrice Brown; the John F. Kennedy Library; the Greater Vallejo Recreation District; Richard Whitesides; Charles Joiner; and Thomas "Jerry" Kea of Solano Community College and the National Archives. Very special thanks goes to Sgt. Herman Robinson of the Vallejo Police Department for sharing his poignant story of his father, the late Alfred Robinson, who, for a short period in the late 1940s, was Vallejo's first African American police officer.

In the creation of this book, I used social media to help spread the word about the Great Migration and Vallejo. I created a Great Migration page on Facebook. Many members on the page are the children, grandchildren, and great-grandchildren of those involved in the Great Migration. From the start, they shared their own Great Migration stories—thank you, all. My love and thanks goes to my nephew Charles E. Oliver, who, when called upon, served as my chauffeur, typist, photographer, and general assistant during this project.

Last, but certainly not least, my biggest thanks must go to my parents, the late Marshall and Bernice McGriff, who, as a young couple fresh out of the Lake Wales, Florida, fell in love with Vallejo so many years ago. That love was passed on to me and my siblings, and we are forever grateful.

INTRODUCTION

A few years back, I wrote a book on the early African Americans who settled in Vallejo and surrounding areas during the 19th and early 20th centuries. The book, *John Grider's Century—African Americans in Solano, Napa, and Sonoma Counties from 1845 to 1925*, explored the lives of men, women, and children who came West as part of an early migration.

My book dealt with earlier regional African American history during the life of John Grider, a black veteran of the California Bear Flag Revolt of 1846. Grider came to California in bondage in 1845, moved to Vallejo following the Gold Rush, and purchased his freedom with money he had earned in the gold fields of Calaveras County. Grider lived in Vallejo for more than 65 years. He moved to a county hospital in Fairfield for the last 10 years of his life and died in December 1924 at the age of 98.

After finishing that book, I realized that I had more work to do. I knew that I needed to expand the story of those black folks who came to Vallejo around the turn of the 20th century. I knew that Vallejo's African American community had grown substantially between 1910 and 1970. That growth was part of a larger phenomenon that historians call the Great Migration, a period of 60 years in which more than six million African Americans left the South, headed for states in the Northeast, Midwest, and West.

The Great Migration did not bypass Vallejo. In fact, Vallejo was one of cities in California that benefitted from this huge influx, especially during the 1940s, when thousands of African Americans moved to the city.

I'm a child of the Great Migration. My parents, Marshall and Bernice McGriff, moved to Vallejo in 1941. My father was in the Navy and was stationed at Mare Island. My parents were raised in Lake Wales, Florida, but fell in love with Vallejo at first sight. Although they returned to Florida not long after World War II, within five years they were back in Vallejo to settle down. They brought five of their children with them and had three more over the next 10 years.

While my Great Migration story is typical of many of the families who came here during the 1940s, there were earlier journeys. Right before the start of the Great Migration in 1910, Vallejo had already seen a small growth in its black population. Former Buffalo Soldiers, who had once been stationed at the Presidio in San Francisco, moved to Vallejo en masse around the early 1900s. These former soldiers brought leadership skills to Vallejo; they helped start churches, organizations, and businesses and constructed buildings that are still a part of Vallejo. They helped start the Vallejo branch of the National Association for the Advancement of Colored People (NAACP) and Prince Hall Masons.

But it was the 1940s—the height of the Great Migration—that brought huge numbers of African Americans to Vallejo. They were lured by readily available jobs at Mare Island Navy Yard, which were created as a result of World War II.

These new transplants largely came from all parts of the South. They came from small farms in Alabama, the cotton fields of Texas, large cities in Louisiana, and from tenant farms in Mississippi.

They came by car and train, with some even jumping freight cars to get to Vallejo and what they hoped was a better life.

They sought more lucrative jobs and freedom from the unrelenting bigotry of the South. Once in Vallejo, they built on the black community that was already here. These new transplants and their numbers expanded the churches that were already here and started new congregations, businesses, and organizations. They brought their music and strong sense of community and built a business and entertainment community in Vallejo's downtown.

The 1940s brought a number of social changes to Vallejo. Crowded conditions created tensions, and black folks soon learned that the racial prejudice they thought they had left behind in the South was present in Vallejo.

With strong organizations like the NAACP—Vallejo had the third largest NAACP in California during the 1940s—they fought, sometimes successfully, discrimination wherever it reared its ugly head. When blacks were denied access to government housing, they fought back and filed grievances. When the Vallejo school district refused to hire black teachers, they pushed until Grace Logan, Vallejo's first black schoolteacher, was hired in 1949. And when black men and women were turned away from jobs at department stores and other businesses during the 1950s and early 1960s, they mounted boycotts of those businesses.

This book, which is largely photographs and some documents, does not pretend to tell the whole story of Vallejo's Great Migration; there are not enough books to tell that story.

My hope is that *African Americans in Vallejo* will allow a glimpse into the lives of some of the people, like my parents, who courageously stepped out on faith and moved clear across country into the unknown.

We owe them—and we can continue to repay them by telling their stories and never forgetting their courageous journeys.

One

They Came Early

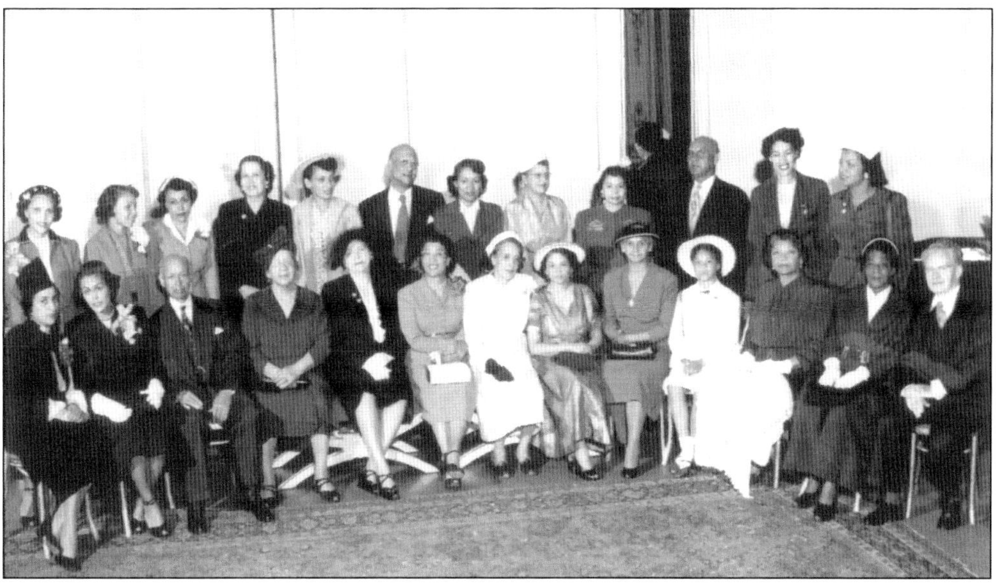

The roots of many Vallejo residents run deep in California history. This photograph, which appeared in the August 2, 1952, edition of the *Sun Reporter*, is perhaps one of the most important images in African American California history. Pictured are the descendants of the California Gold Rush. Two Vallejo residents, Grace Logan (Patterson), sitting sixth from the right, and Peter Williams, standing third from the right, were descendants of pioneer Alfred Coffey, who came to California in the late 1840s. (Courtesy of Jeannette Mohlson.)

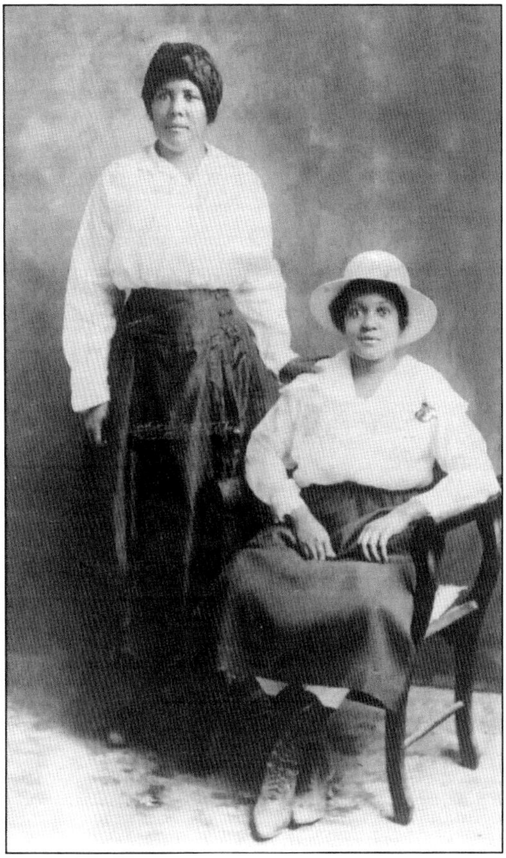

Johnnie Malcolm Thomas, standing next to her mother, came to Vallejo in the early 1900s. Johnnie lived at 1133 Louisiana Street, one of Vallejo's early African American neighborhoods. (Courtesy of the Boyden collection.)

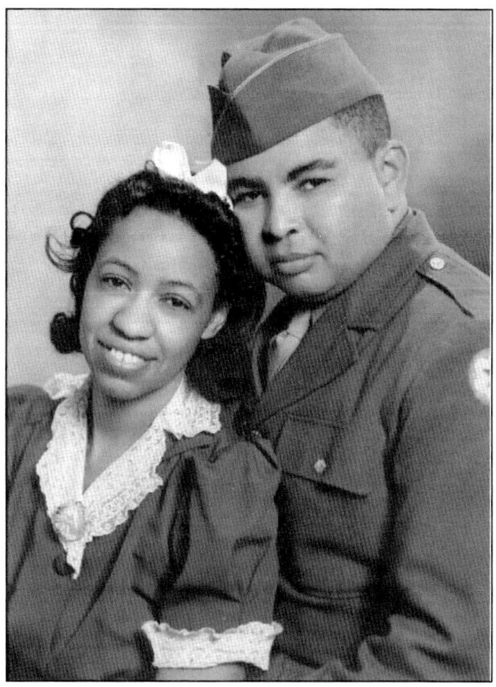

Ruth and Alvin Logan were members of two pioneer African American families from California who moved to Vallejo in the late 1940s. Alvin Logan was born on Guinda Summit in the Capay Valley in 1908, and Ruth was born in Colusa, Sutter County. The couple moved to Vallejo in the early 1950s and was among the original residents of Lofas-Lakeside neighborhood. (Courtesy of Jeannette Mohlson.)

Shortly after he was discharged from the US Army, James Owens, a native of Mississippi, arrived in Vallejo around 1902. A Buffalo Soldier, he was assigned to the 9th Cavalry while in service. Owens helped start the Vallejo branch of the National Association for the Advancement of Colored People, Kyles Temple AME Zion Church, and the Spanish-American War veterans association for African Americans in Vallejo. It is believed that he helped in the construction of the Masonic Lodge at 1209 Georgia Street. Erected around 1914–1915, the lodge was originally the meeting hall for African American Spanish-American War veterans.

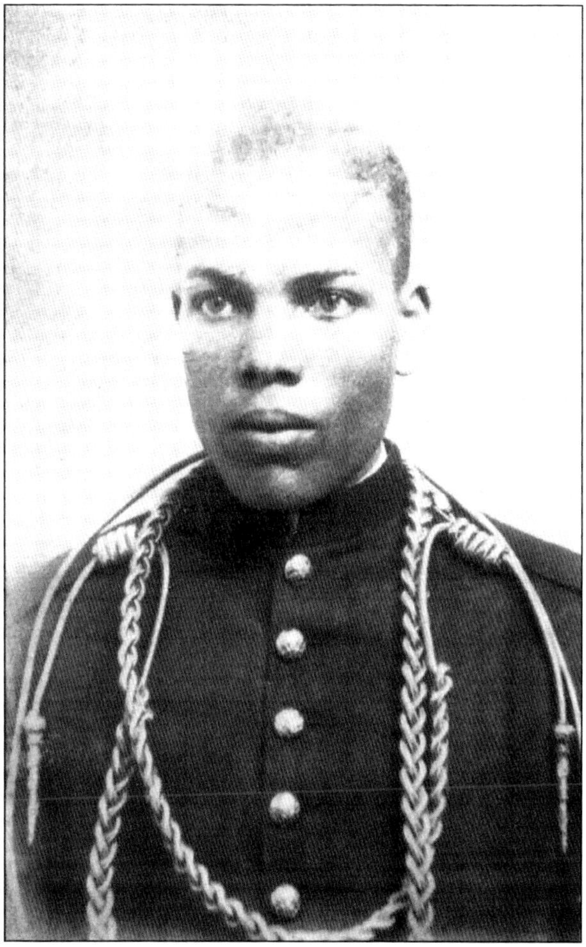

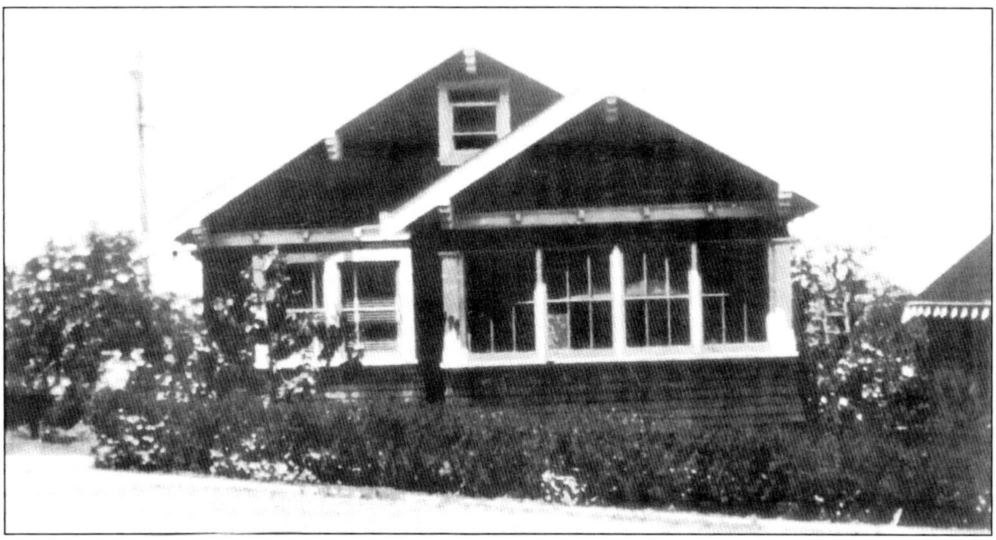

James Owens, thought to be one of the earliest African American building contractors in Vallejo, built his home on Denio Street in 1918.

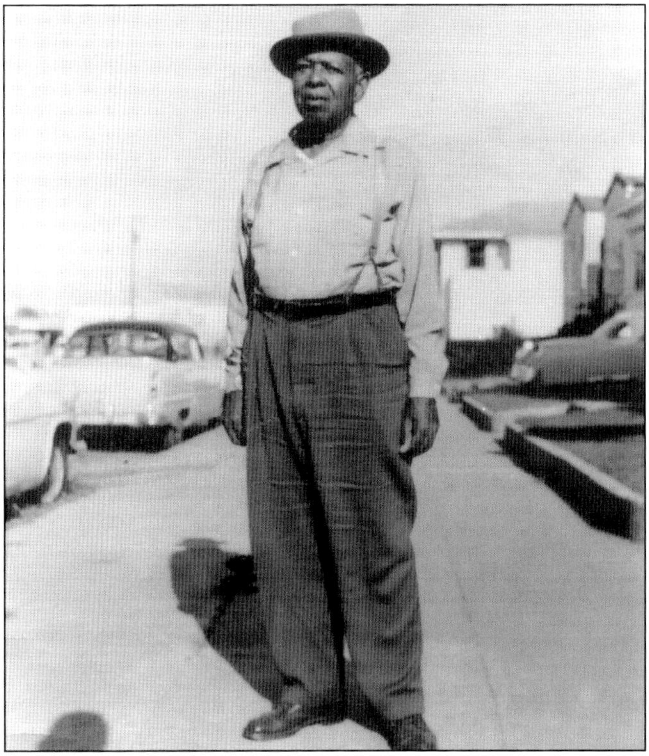

Alonzo Gholikely came to Vallejo in 1902 from Georgia following the Spanish-American War, in which he served in the Army. He was one of many Buffalo Soldiers who settled in Vallejo following the war. Gholikely worked in the Mare Island Navy Yard Dry Docks for more than 40 years. He worked his way up to become a superintendent, the first African American at the Navy yard to achieve that position. For many years, the Gholikely family lived next door to Prince Hall Masons, Firma Lodge No. 27 on 1209 Georgia Street. (Courtesy of Richard Whitesides.)

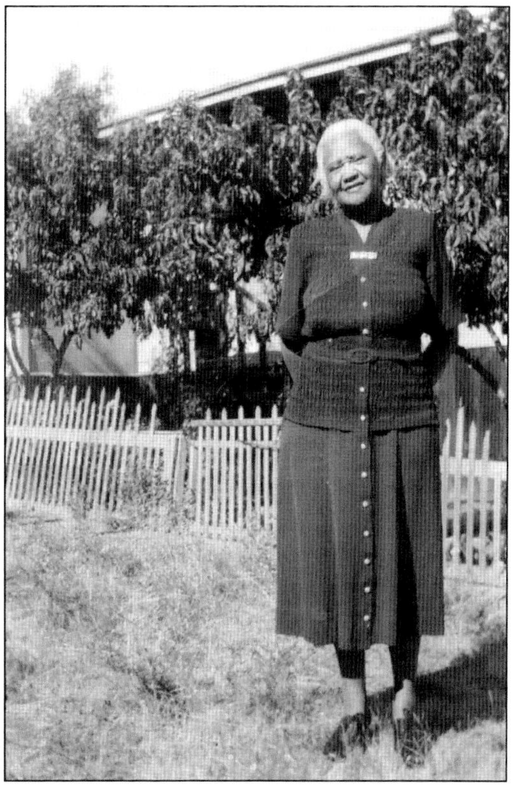

Marstella Gholikely, sister of Alonzo, followed her brother to Vallejo. (Courtesy of Richard Whitesides.)

The Brown brothers, Sam, Burl, Green, and Sidney, came to Vallejo around 1918 from Georgia. They were the sons of Samuel Brown Sr., who had served in the Union army during the Civil War. The brothers were active in Second Baptist Church, fraternal orders, the Vallejo branch of the National Association for the Advancement of Colored People, and countless other organizations. (Courtesy of the late Mary Johnson.)

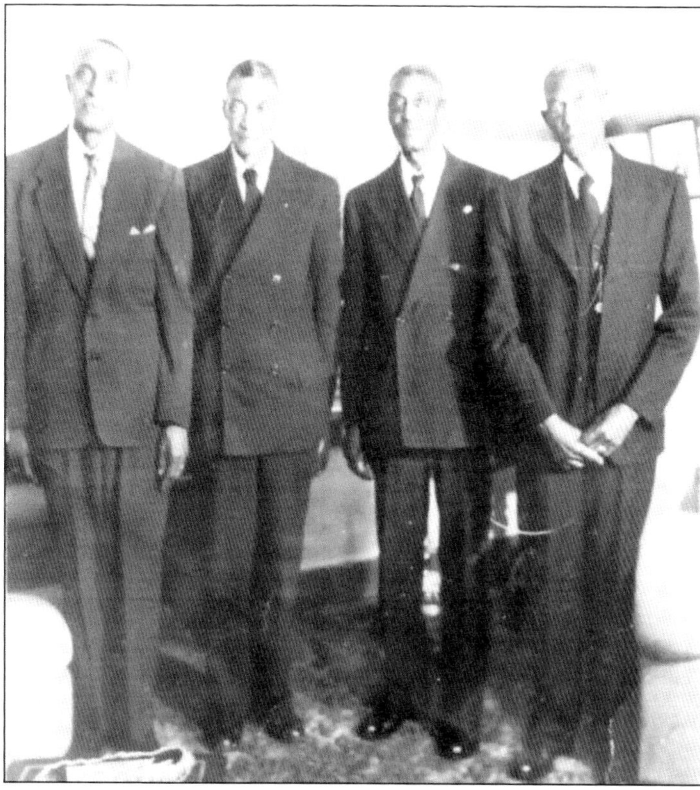

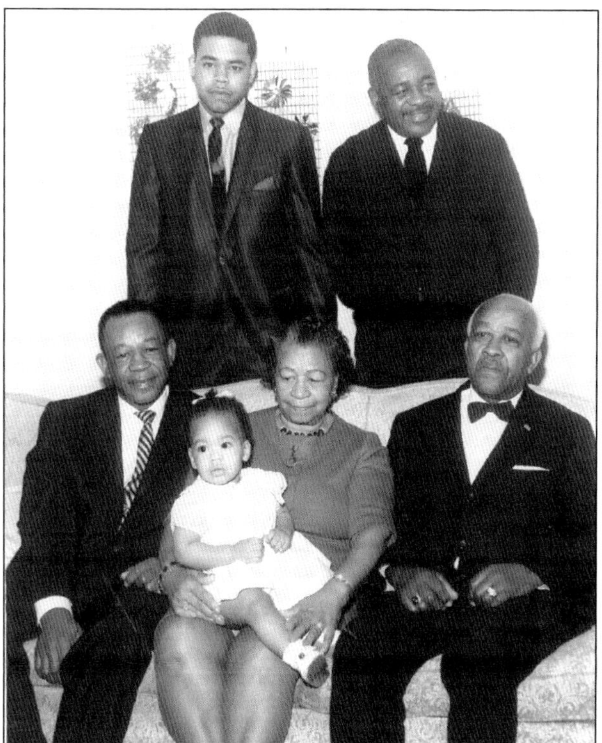

The Toney family was one of the families found here in the early 1900s. The family patriarch, Charles H. Toney, came to Vallejo from Texas in 1907. Charles started the Vallejo Industrial and Normal School around 1911. The school was for African American children and was modeled on Booker T. Washington's Tuskegee Institute. In this 1967 photograph are Charles's offspring, including (sitting) Cornelius Toney, Emma (holding a grandchild), and Charles's son Marion Toney (far right) on the occasion of his 71st birthday; (standing) Cornelius Toney II and Harvet Toney. (Courtesy of the Vallejo Naval and historical Museum.)

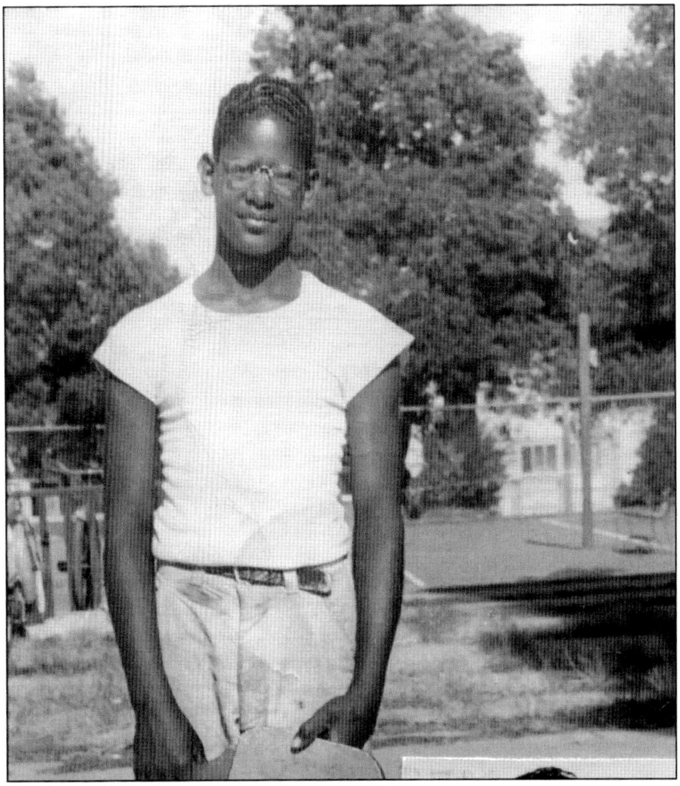

A lifelong California resident, the late James Williams was born in Vallejo. His father, Peter Williams, was an active member of Prince Hall Masons, Firma Lodge No. 27 and an early member of the Vallejo branch of the NAACP. In the 1950s, James Williams had the distinction of being one of the first African Americans to work for a white-owned company in downtown Vallejo when he took a job at Meyer's Jewelry Store on Georgia Street. (Courtesy of James and Ursula Williams.)

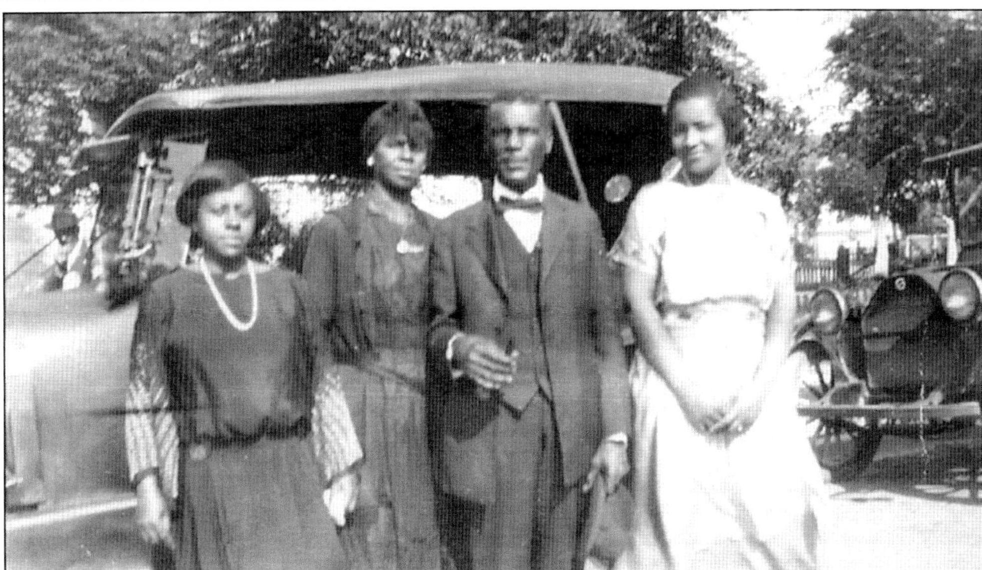

Clarke McGee, second from right, was born in Alabama and came to Vallejo in the late 1800s following service in the Spanish-American War. This former Buffalo Soldier, who served at the Presidio in San Francisco, worked for many years at Mare Island Navy Yard as a gardener. He owned property near Firma Lodge No. 27 and in East Vallejo, off of Springs Road. He was an early member of Prince Hall Free and Accepted Masons, Firma Lodge No. 27 and a founding member of the Vallejo branch of the NAACP. (Courtesy of the Boyden collection.)

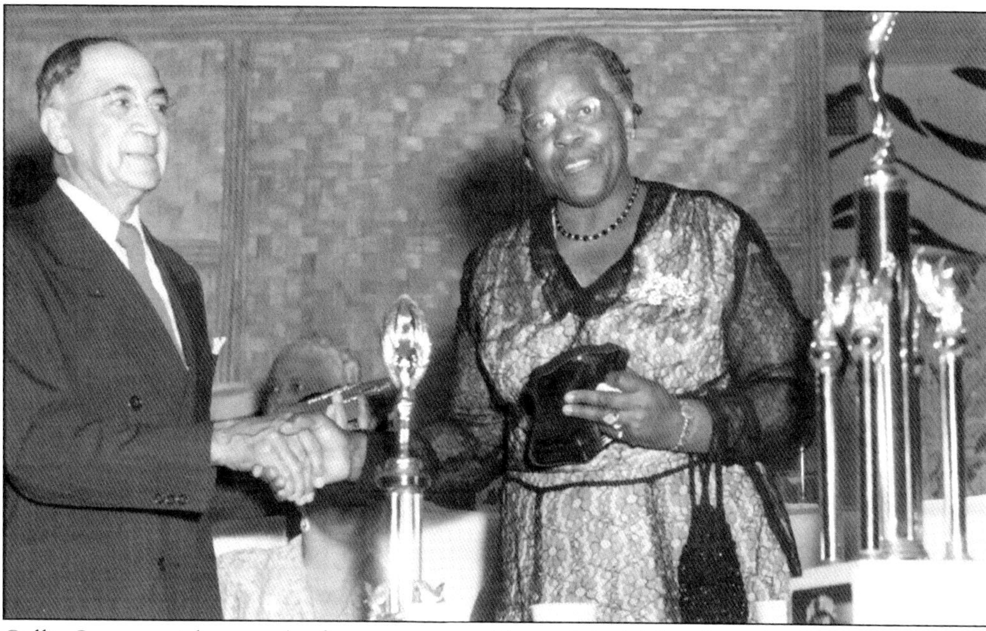

Collia Scruggs, right, was the first woman president of the Vallejo branch of the NAACP. She held that office from 1951 to 1953. Born in South Carolina around 1890, she came to Vallejo in the early 1900s. In the photograph, she is receiving an award for the local chapter from Dr. Claude Hudson during the 1952 NAACP's convention in Oklahoma. In the 1940s and 1950s, she edited the monthly newsletter of the Vallejo branch of the NAACP. (Courtesy of the Vallejo Naval and Historical Museum.)

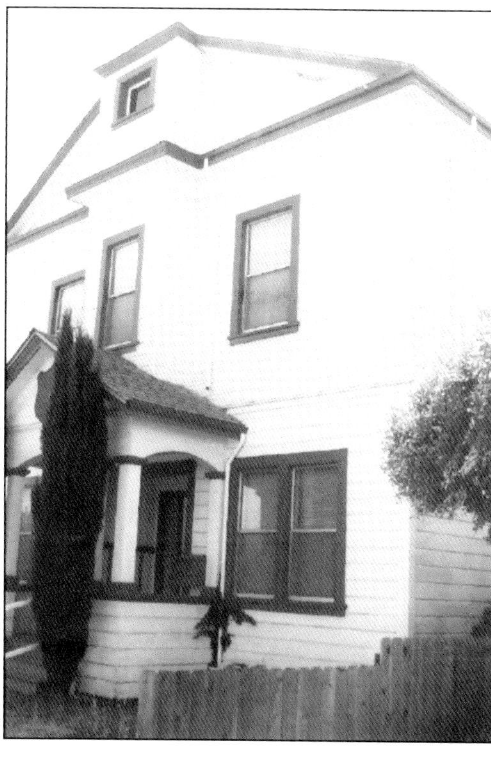

The Prince Hall, Firma Lodge No. 27 building, located at 1209 Georgia Street, was built between 1914 and 1916 for African American veterans of the Spanish-American War. The two-story building was one of the main meeting places for early Vallejo African Americans. Weddings, club meetings, funerals, teas, dinners, and classes were held in the building. During the war years of the 1940s, the building became the United Service Organization (USO) for African Americans. Under the direction of Grace Logan, the building became the gathering place for dances and other functions for black military personnel and the Vallejo community. In the early 1950s, Golden State Mutual Insurance opened its first office in the building. Over its nearly 100-year history, the building has been the temporary meeting place for the churches of Second Baptist, Kyles AME Temple, and Friendship Missionary Baptist. In the 1960s, the Continentals of Omega Boys Club met in the lodge hall. (Courtesy of the author.)

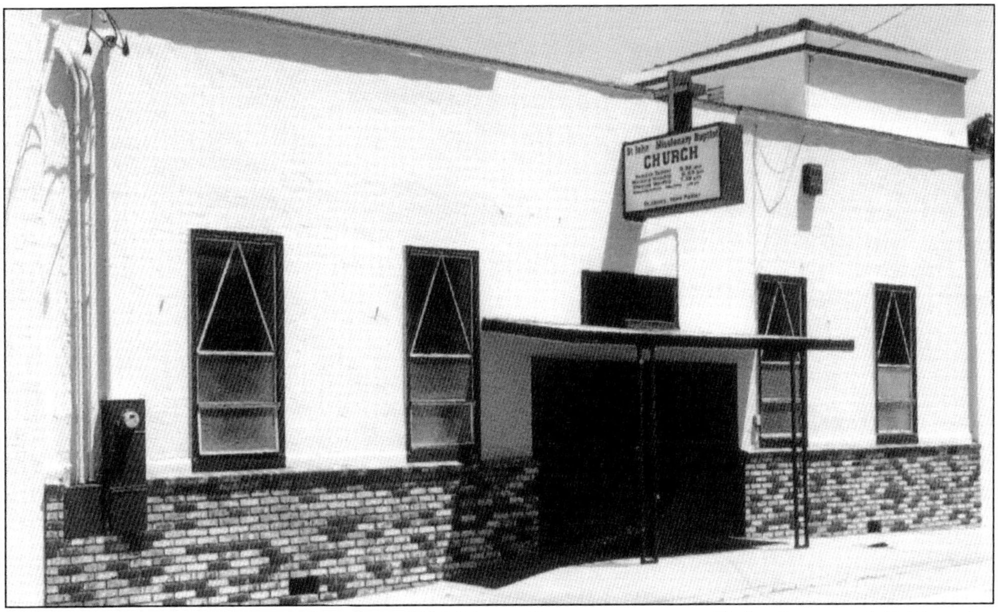

St. John Missionary Baptist Church at 2010 Marin Street was originally built around 1916 as the Vallejo Industrial and Normal School. African American students, primarily girls, were trained to perform domestic tasks, like cooking. The Reverend C.H. Toney, a former Texas schoolteacher, operated the school. Controversial from its start, the Vallejo branch of the NAACP filed suit against Toney and the school, claiming the school inadequately educated students. After more than a 20-year battle, the school was finally ordered to close in the early 1930s. By the late 1930s, the school had become St. John Baptist Church. (Courtesy of Clarence Payne.)

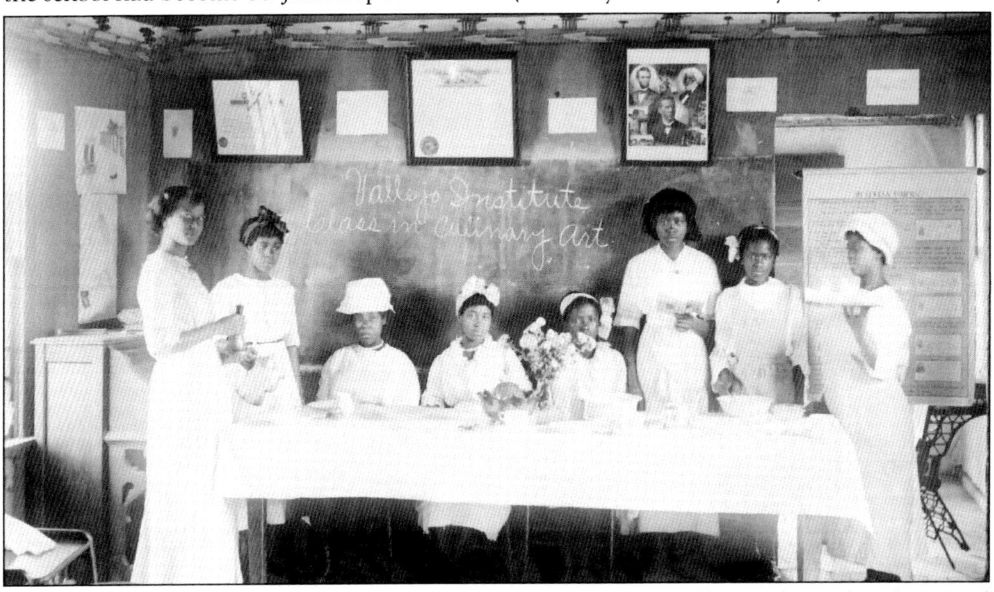

Many young women, like those pictured, were students of the Vallejo Industrial and Normal School at 2010 Marin Street in the early 1900s. Trained primarily to become domestics, the students received both classroom and practical training. The school was modeled on Booker T. Washington's Tuskegee Institute, founded in the late 1800s, in Alabama. (Courtesy of the Vallejo Naval and Historical Museum.)

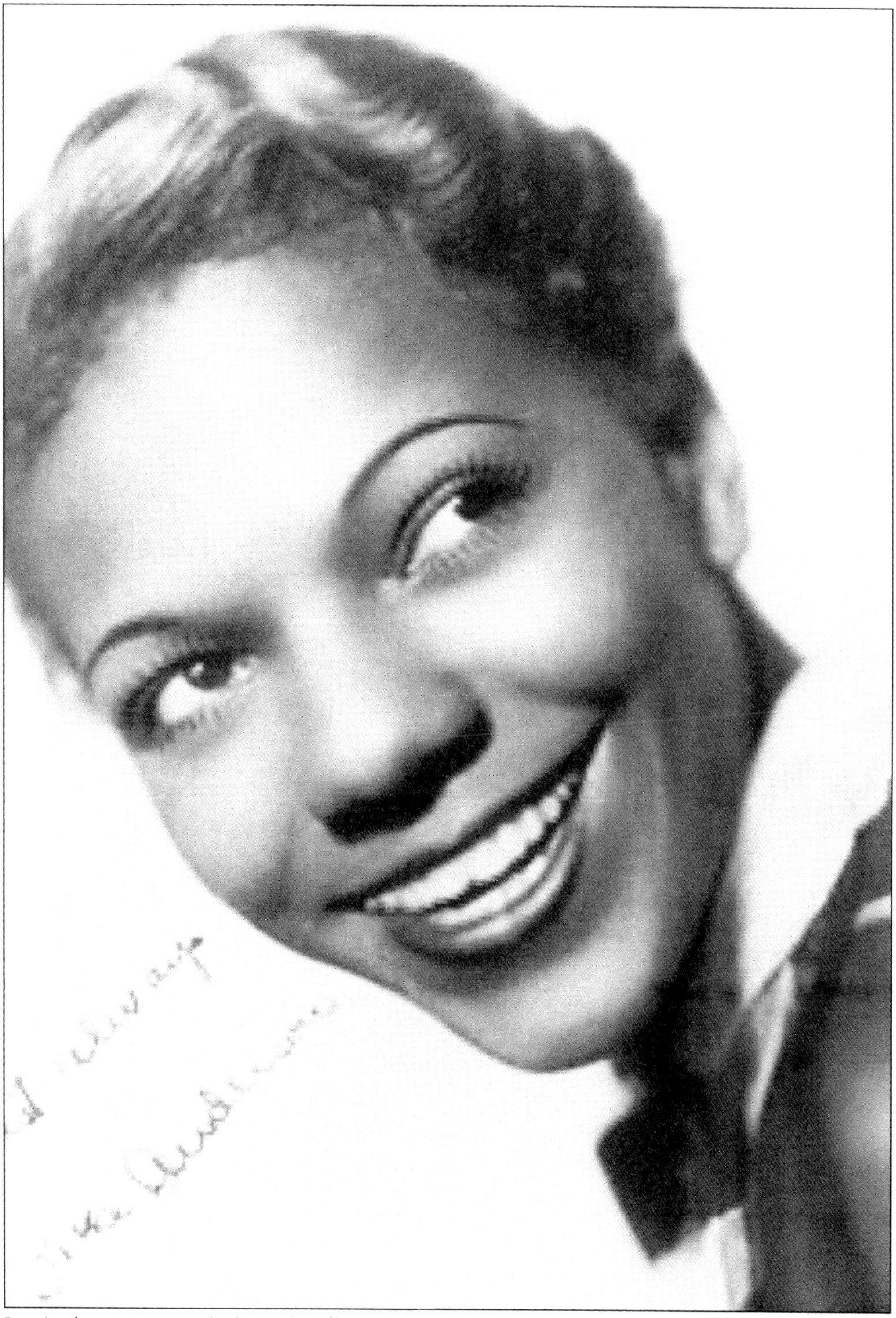

Ivy Anderson sang with the Duke Ellington Band in the 1930s and early 1940s but lived in Vallejo before her big band debut. According to the 1920 federal census, she lived with her uncle and aunt, Lewis and Bennie Jones, at 133 Denio Street. (Courtesy of the author.)

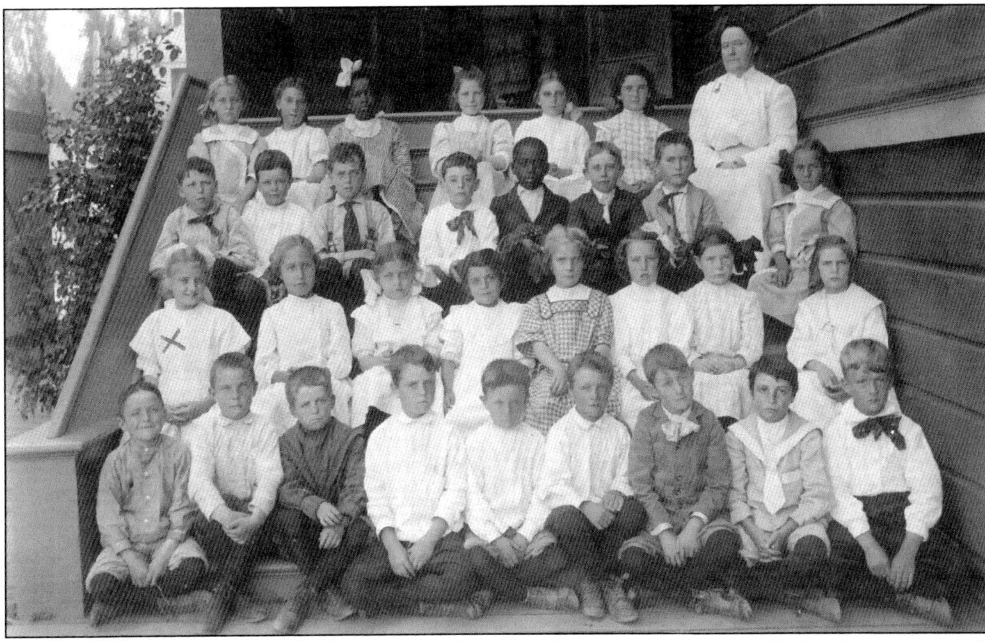

The two African American children in the third and fourth rows were enrolled at Farragut Grade School at the foot of Tennessee Street. The boy, A. Wayne Amerson, came to Vallejo in the early 1900s from Texas. (Courtesy of the Vallejo Naval and Historical Museum.)

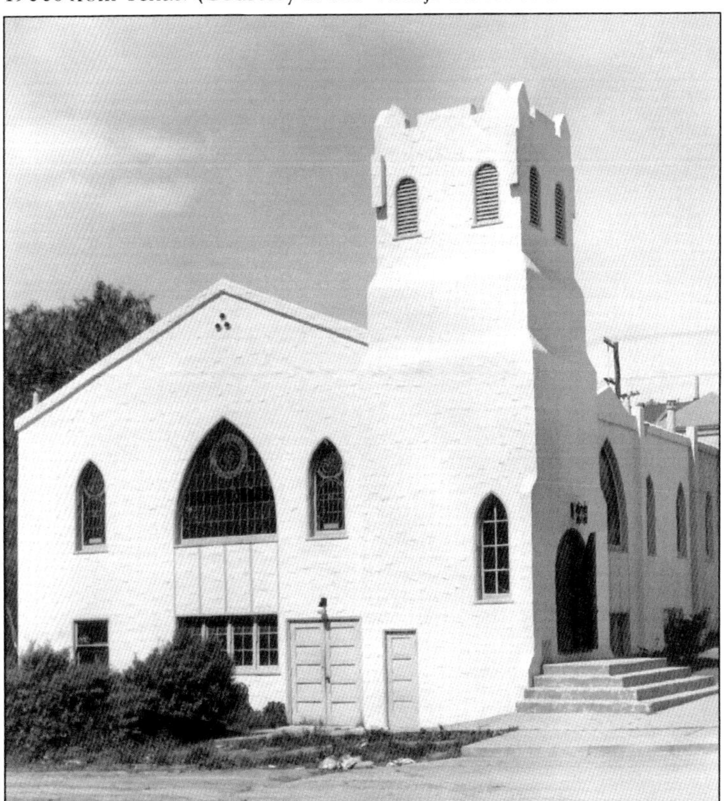

Second Baptist Church is Vallejo's oldest formally organized African American church. In 1907, a group met in the Carolina Street home of J.L. and Sophia Malone to organize Second Baptist. For several years prior to building the first sanctuary at Capitol and Branciforte Streets, members met in various meeting halls, including Firma Lodge No. 27 at 1209 Georgia Street. (Courtesy of the Vallejo Naval and Historical Museum.)

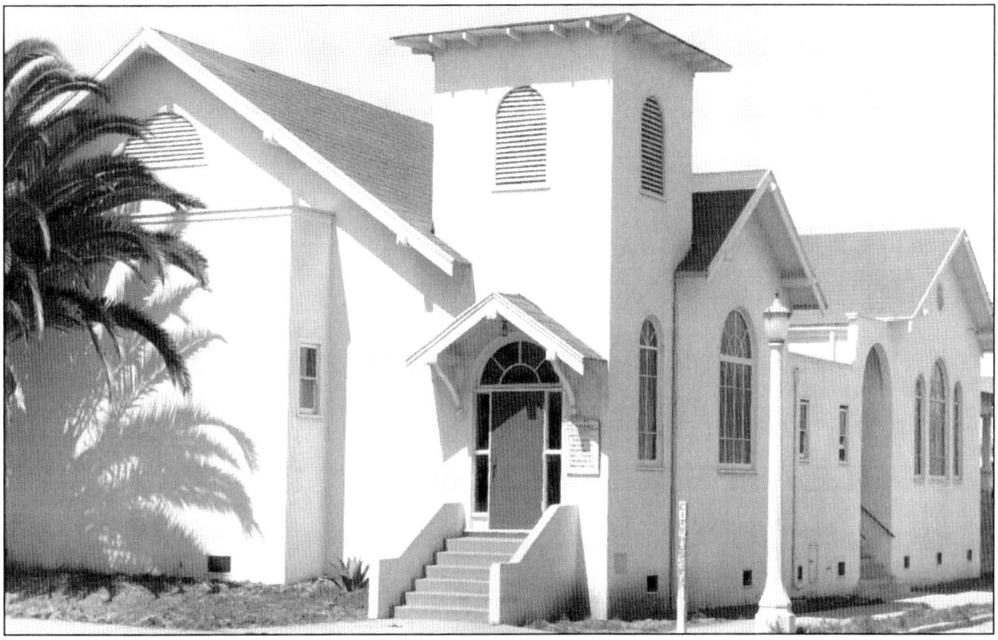

Kyles Temple African Methodist Episcopal Zion Church was founded in 1910. Kyles Temple was Vallejo's second formally organized black church. Among its earliest members were men and women who moved to Vallejo in the 1800s. In 1919, Kyles Temple Church members purchased the old white-owned Methodist church building and moved the historic building to property near Illinois Street and Sonoma Boulevard. In November 1919, an arsonist, angered by the purchase, burned the structure down. By 1921, church members built a new structure that served the community until the late 1990s. Today, the church is located at 912 Florida Street. (Courtesy of the Vallejo Naval and Historical Museum.)

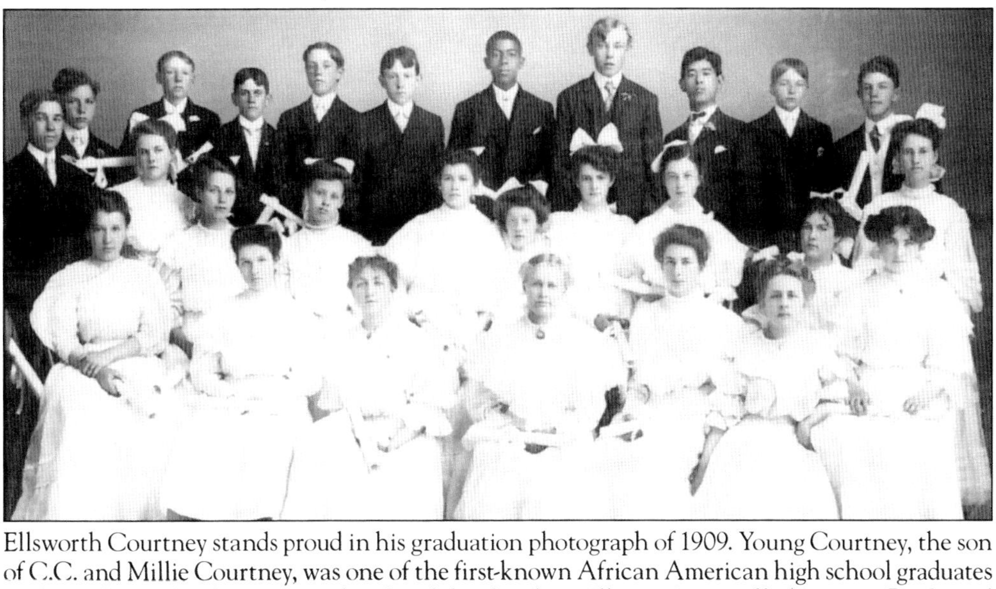

Ellsworth Courtney stands proud in his graduation photograph of 1909. Young Courtney, the son of C.C. and Millie Courtney, was one of the first-known African American high school graduates in the Vallejo school system. He lived with his family on Illinois Street off of Sonoma Boulevard in the early 1900s. That neighborhood was an early enclave for African American families at the turn of the 20th century. (Courtesy of the Vallejo Naval and Historical Museum.)

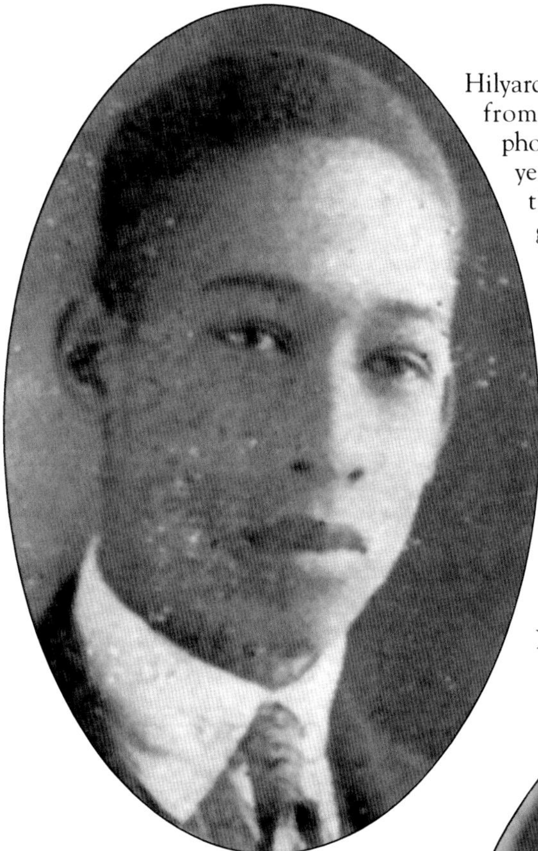

Hilyard Moore and Roosevelt Williams graduated from Vallejo High School in 1920; these photographs are from the Vallejo High School yearbook of that same year. They were among the early African American high school graduates, following Ellsworth Courtney who graduated in 1909. Young Moore and Courtney lived on Illinois Street near the old Kyles Temple AME Zion Church. Black children were long a part of the Vallejo school system, dating back to the 1860s, when they attended a segregated school at Maine and Marin Streets in a downtown Vallejo hotel on the waterfront. Vallejo's school system officially desegregated in 1874, although African American children were still taught in separate sections of the school building, which was then located on Carolina Street. (Courtesy of the Vallejo Naval and Historical Museum.)

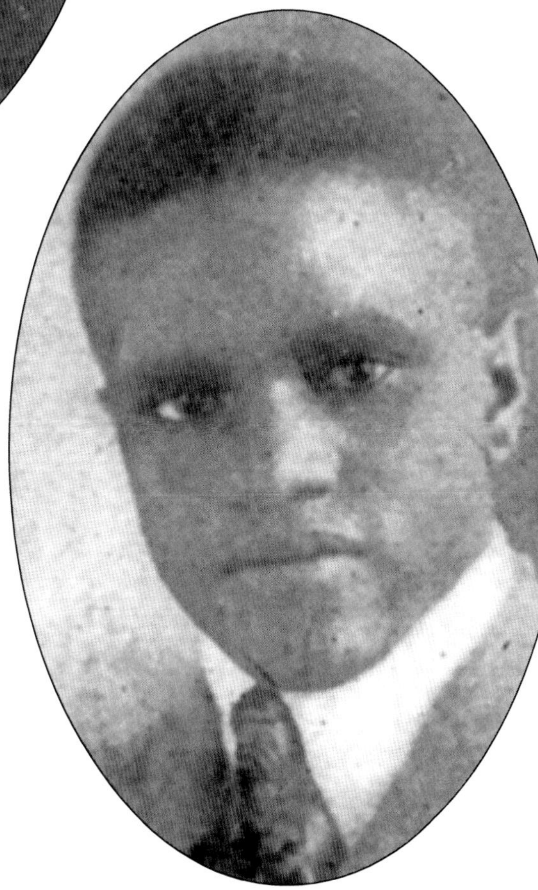

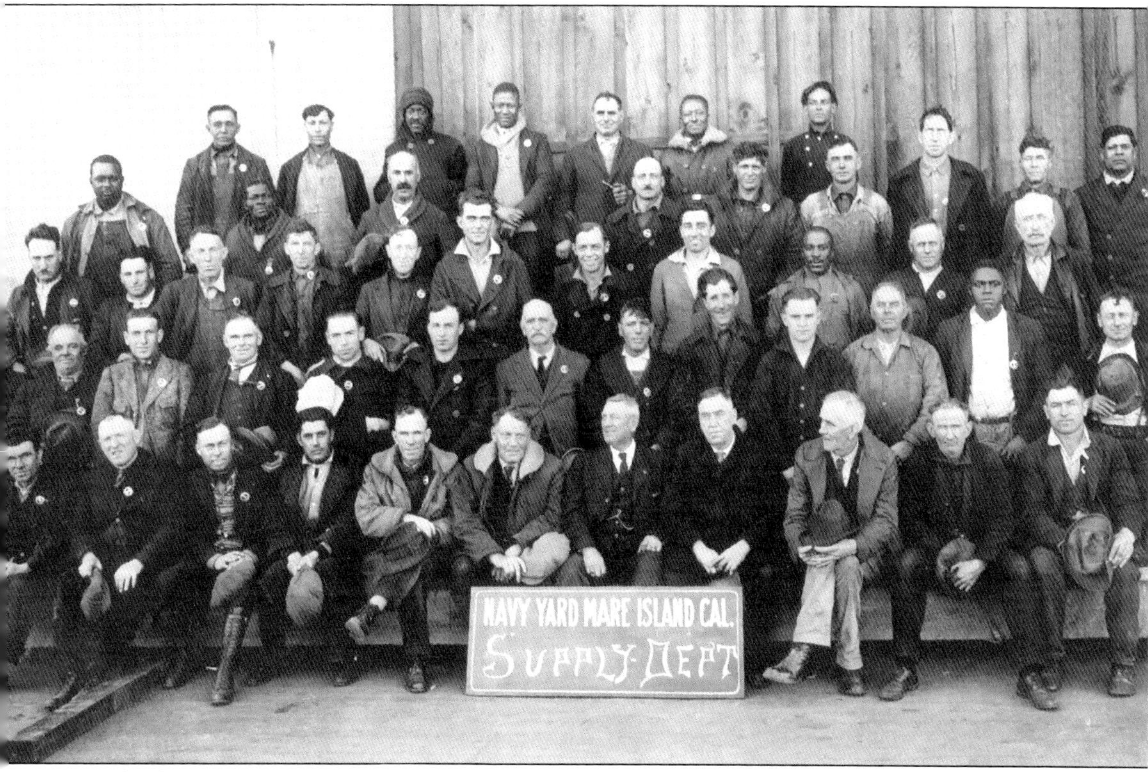

Several African Americans were among the Mare Island Supply Department employees who posed for this photograph on January 16, 1926. Mare Island Naval Shipyard was a major reason so many African Americans moved to Vallejo during the early part of the 20th century. While there had been earlier migrations of African Americans to Vallejo during the late 1800s, the number of blacks moving to Vallejo exploded in the war years of the 1940s. As early as 1870, a Bay Area African American newspaper encouraged black people to apply for jobs at the Vallejo shipyard. (Courtesy of the Vallejo Naval and Historical Museum.)

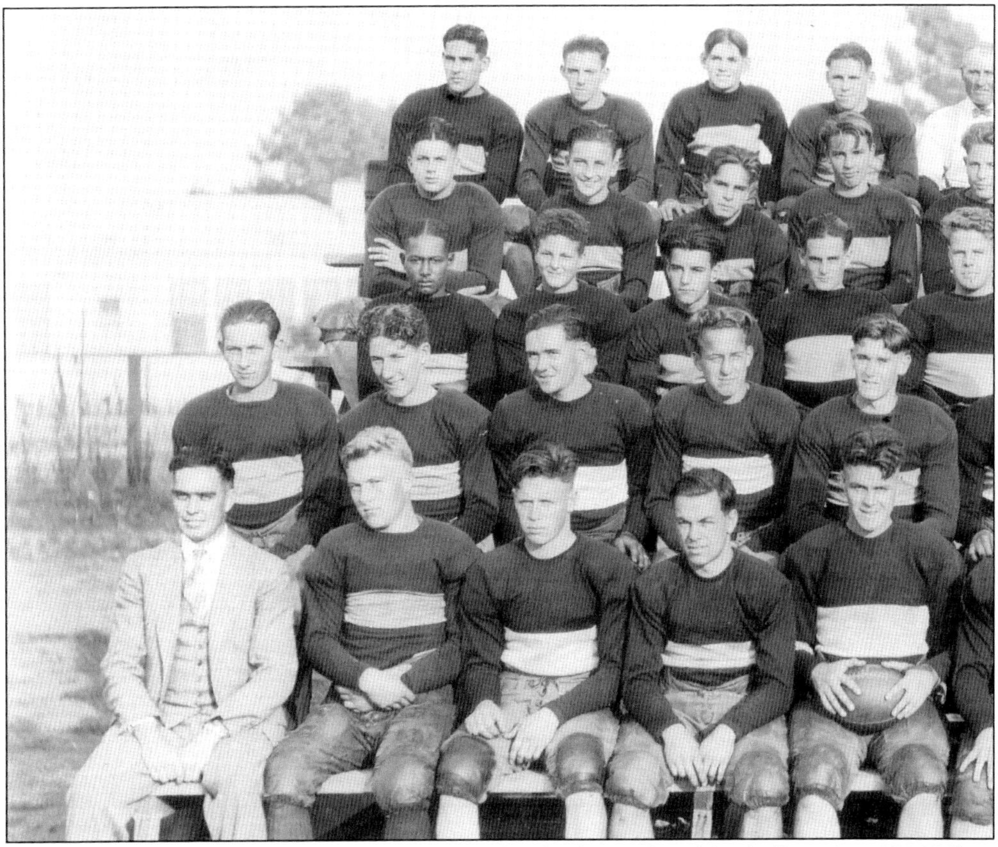

The young African American on the far left in the third row played football on the 1920 Vallejo High School Apache football team. (Courtesy of the Vallejo Naval and Historical Museum.)

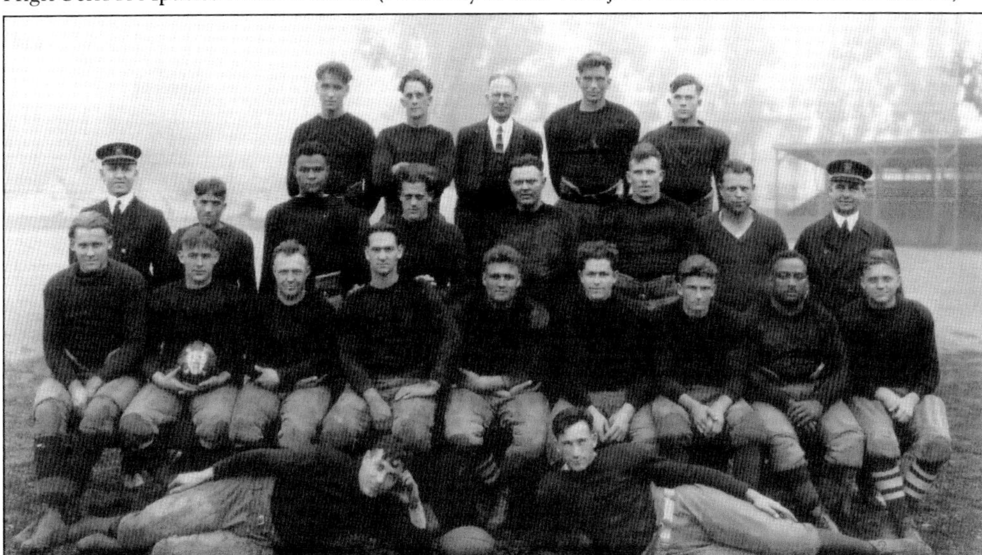

A young African American sailor was a member of the 1924 USN Submarine Division football team at Mare Island. (Courtesy of the National Archives.)

Two

VALLEJO AND THE GREAT MIGRATION AT ITS PEAK

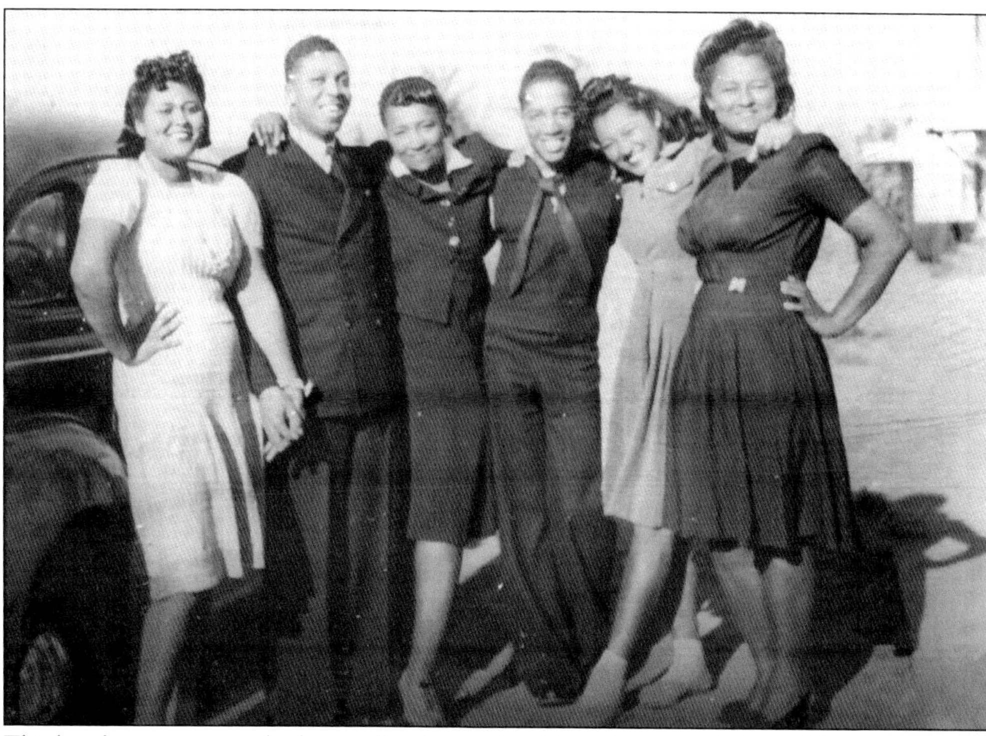

This handsome group, with Florence Boyden on the right, epitomizes the hope African Americans must have felt upon arrival to their new West Coast home in the 1940s. Thousands of young African American civilians and military men and women converged on the city with dreams of forging new lives for themselves and their families. (Courtesy of the Boyden collection.)

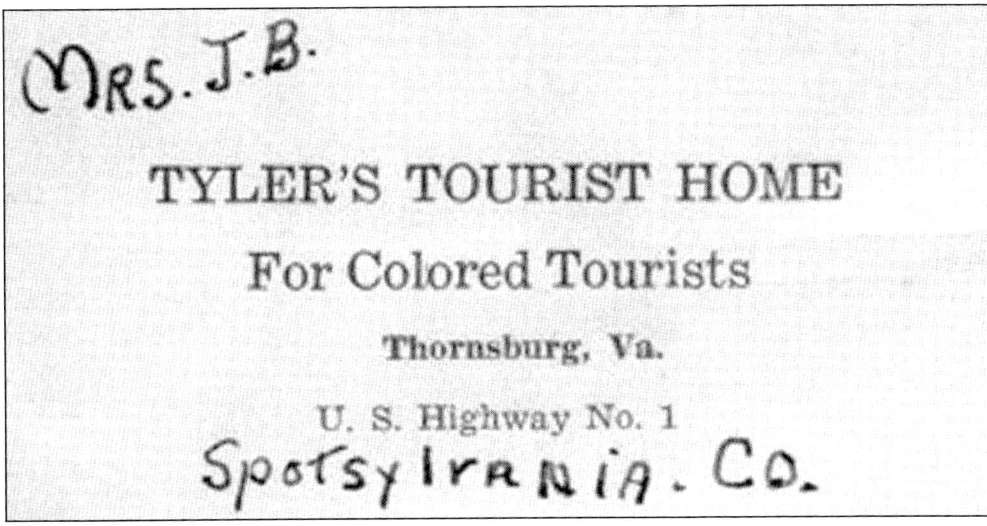

This business card advertising Tyler's Tourist Home for Colored Tourists in Thornburg, Virginia, was no doubt used by a family connected to Vallejo. During the height of the Great Migration, the 1940s through 1960s, knowledge of accommodations for African Americans was vital for those families leaving the South. The *Negro Motorist Green Book*, which advertised these businesses from 1936 to 1961, helped guide many African Americans to their destinations. The reference guide contained addresses of hotels, motels, and "tourist homes," which were privately owned residences, open to black people. (Courtesy of the Boyden collection.)

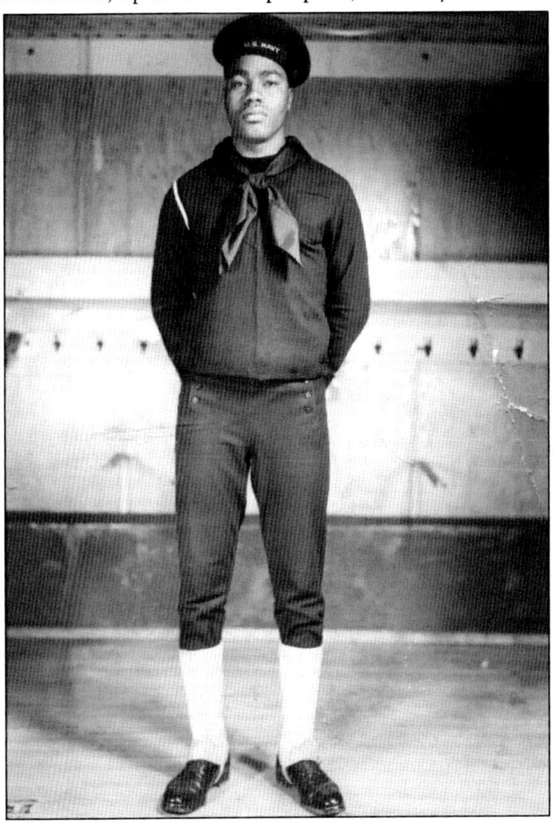

Young African Americans like Haskell Forte answered the call of military service during the early days of World War II. About 18 when he signed up, the young Oklahoma native enlisted in Portland, Oregon. Shown here in the uniform of an apprentice seaman, young Forte was in boot camp at Camp Moffett, Great Lakes Naval Training Center, in Illinois. In the early months of the war, the Navy Department designated the Great Lakes as the site for training African Americans in boot camp, as well as Navy specialties. Following boot camp, Forte was stationed at Alameda Naval Air Station in 1942. (Courtesy of Haskell Forte.)

Haskell Forte, left, is with a friend at the Alameda Naval Air Station. Following the war, Forte worked as a barber in Vallejo for many years. (Courtesy of Haskell Forte.)

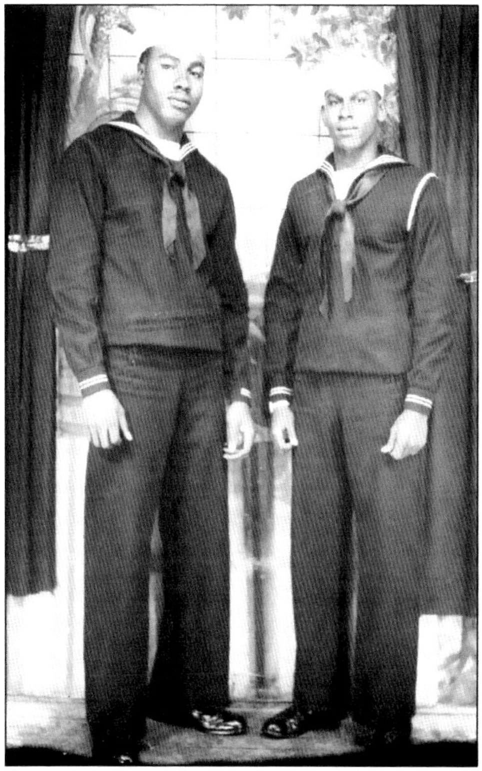

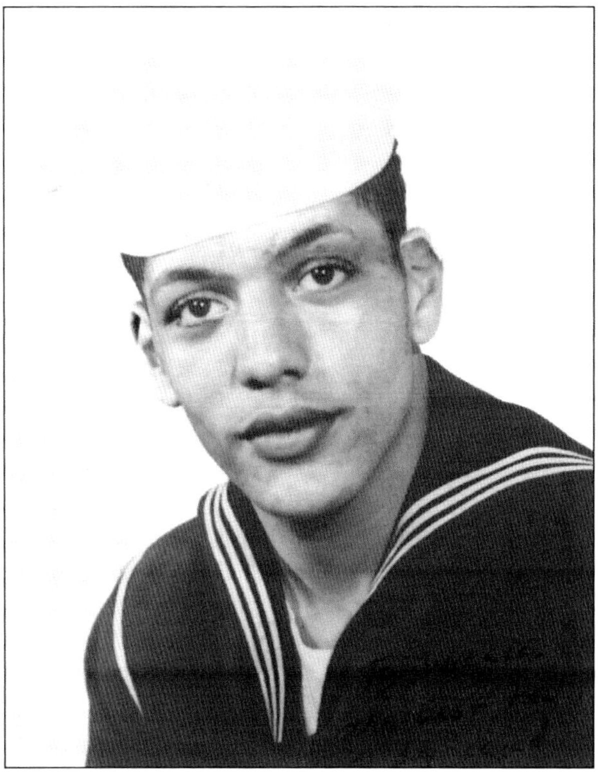

Sixteen-year-old Don Owens, who was born and raised in Vallejo, told naval personnel he was 18 in order to enlist in the Navy. (Courtesy of Robbie Henderson.)

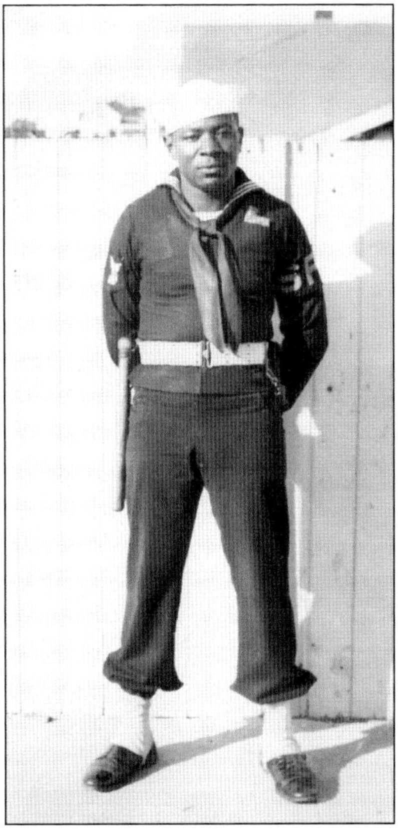

Richard Nixon, shore patrol, was among the thousands of African American sailors who came through Mare Island Naval Shipyard during World War II. Prior to World War II, African American sailors mostly served as stewards or mess attendants. Wartime pressures and African American patriotism targeted political pressure from outside organizations, like the NAACP, and created change in the Navy. Though the Navy remained racially segregated in training and in most service units, the enlisted rates in 1942 were opened to all qualified personnel. In 1944, the Navy commissioned its first-ever African American officer. (Courtesy of the Boyden collection.)

Within a year of this photograph, Bernice McGriff, right, along with her husband Marshall, were on their way West to settle permanently in Vallejo. This photograph, taken in 1950 in Lake Wales, Florida, shows Bernice McGriff with her aunt Essie Mae McGee Noakes, sitting with four McGriff children. Sitting on Noakes's lap is the author, Sharon McGriff-Payne, while siblings Michael, Melody, and Marshall McGriff sit nearby. (Courtesy of the author.)

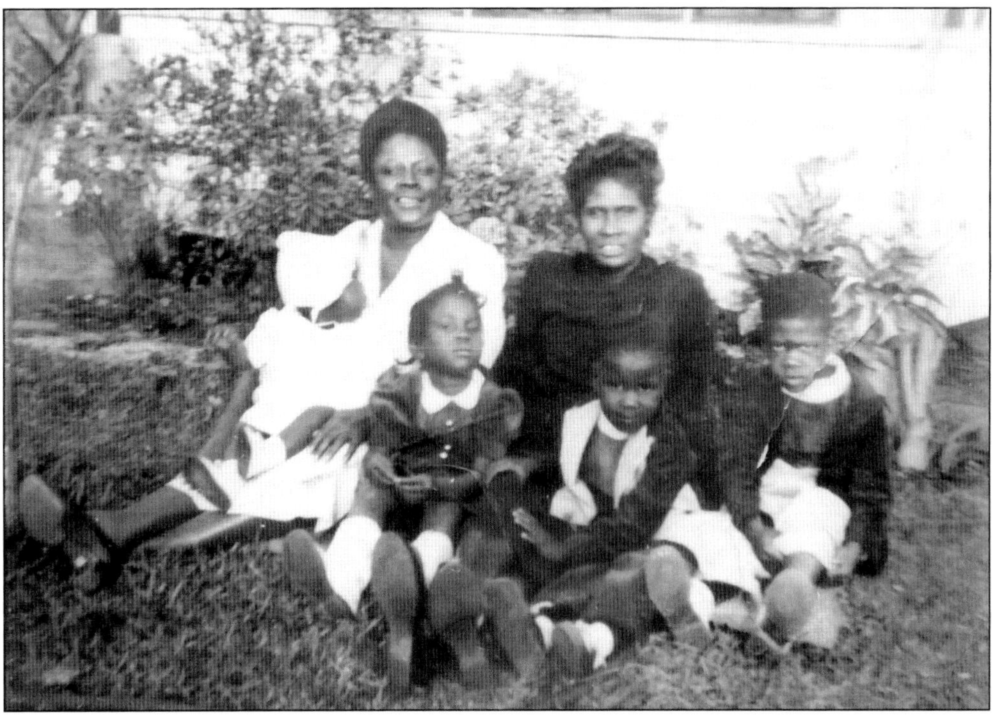

Around the spring of 1951, the McGriff family headed to California in a black 1949 Oldsmobile, with a small trailer in tow. As they drove through Slidell, Louisiana, the family stopped in the African American section of the city and asked an elderly woman if they could park in front of her house for the evening. Not only did the woman agree, but she also fed the family that evening. Within a week of the McGriffs' arrival in California, Alice Carter, Bernice McGriff's mother, called and said that she had received a letter from the woman in Slidell, reporting that she had seen the McGriff family and that they were fine. Bernice McGriff is pictured with her son Marshall, who was born at Mare Island Hospital in May 1945. (Courtesy of the author.)

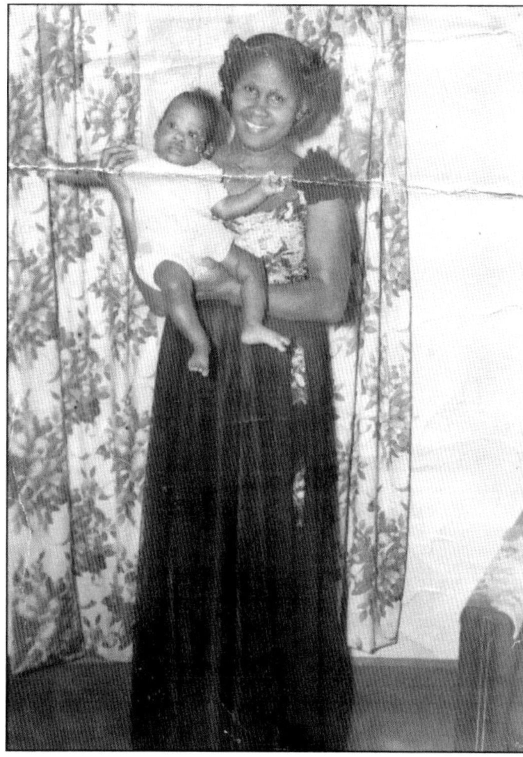

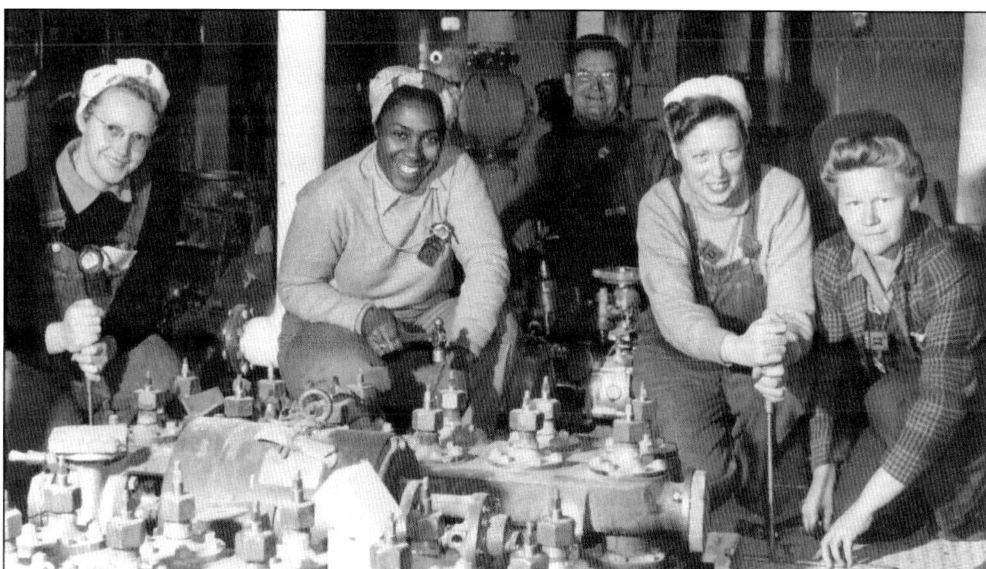

Large numbers of African American women, including Lola Thomas (center), worked at Mare Island Naval Shipyard during World War II. Because of the huge demand for workers, a result of the war effort, these women worked jobs that were traditionally held by men who were overseas fighting for America. These women, whom historians would later refer to as Rosie the Riveters, worked as ship and pipe fitters, riveters, forklift operators, electricians, and truck drivers. Pictured with Thomas are, from left to right, Betty Pierce Margaret Houston, Thelma Mort, and Katie Stanfill. (Courtesy of the Vallejo Naval and Historical Museum.)

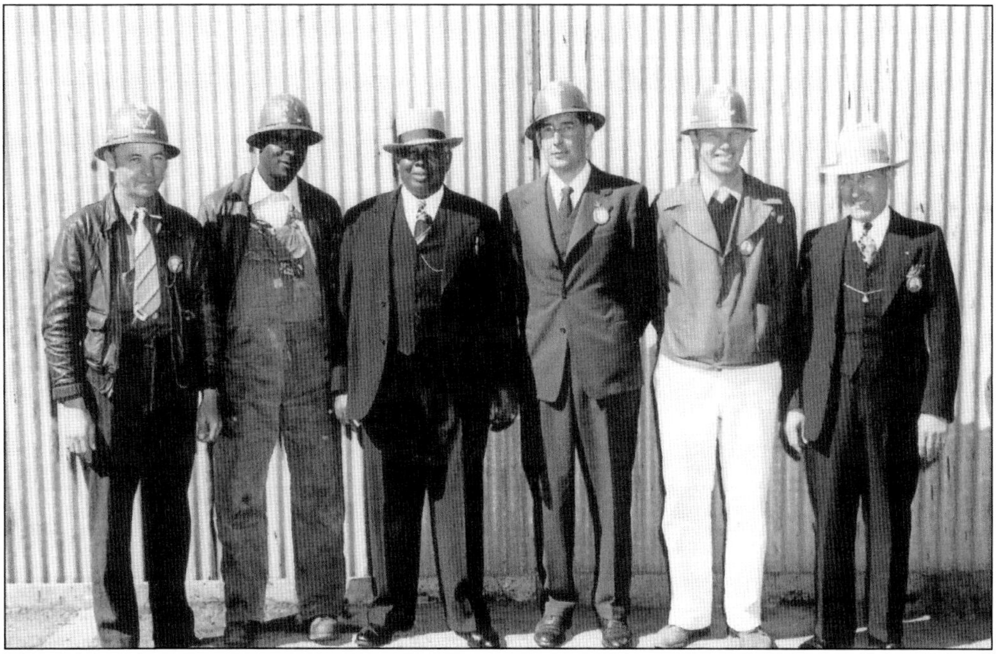

Mare Island was the lure for thousands of African Americans coming to Vallejo in the 1940s. Alonzo Gholikely, third from the left in this 1944 photograph, had worked at Mare Island since the turn of the 20th century. Gholikely, who worked in the shipyard's dry dock, was one of its first African American superintendents. (Courtesy of the National Archives.)

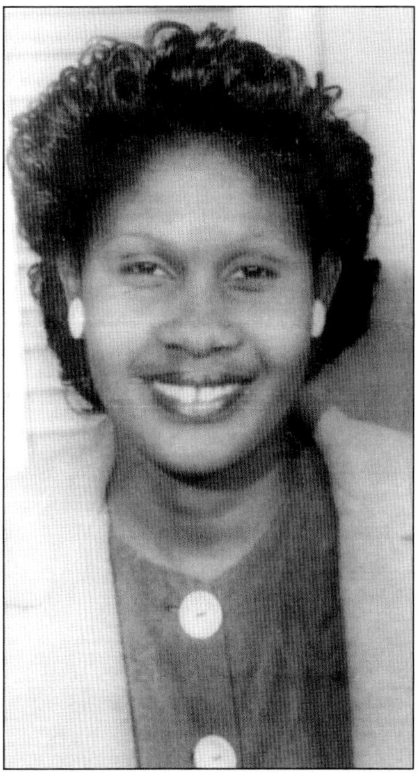

The author's mother, Bernice McGriff, is pictured around the time she worked at Mare Island in the early 1940s. A forklift driver on the Navy yard, McGriff said that she applied for a job on the Navy yard and was hired on the spot, which was the day after she arrived in Vallejo in 1941. (Courtesy of the author.)

Ora Stacy came to Vallejo in 1944 from Heidelberg, Mississippi. She was hired at Mare Island shortly after her arrival. Stacy, who was 19, hoped her work at the Navy yard would hasten the return of American men, including her boyfriend, from the war overseas. Stacy said Bernice McGriff taught her how to drive a forklift. (Courtesy of Ora Stacy.)

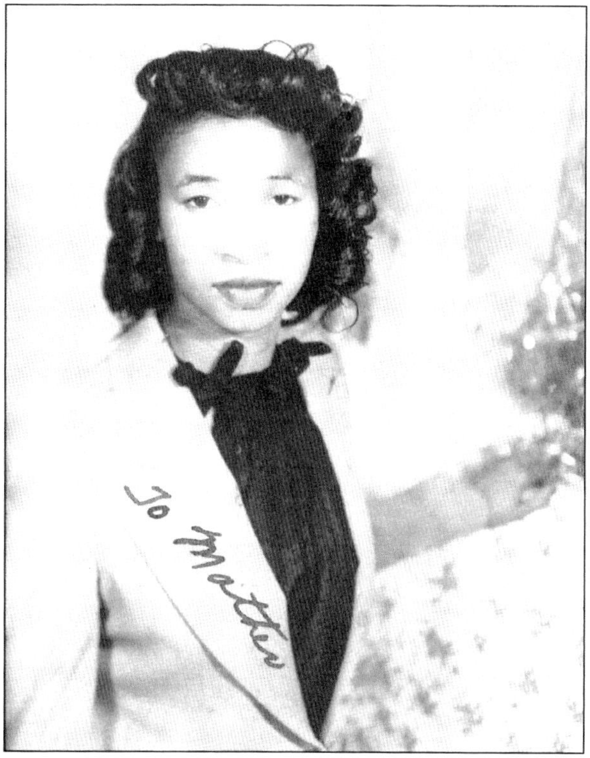

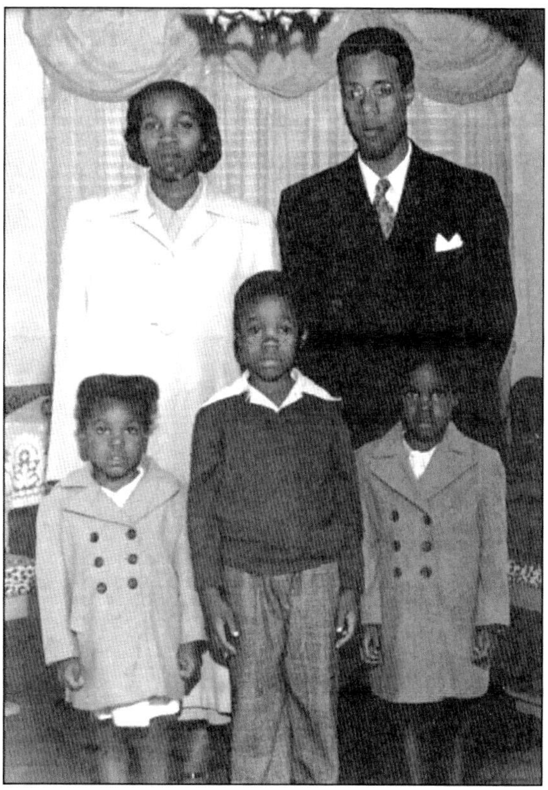

Walter Freeman (standing on the right) poses with his wife, Lloydicia, and their three children, from left to right, Marcia, Leslie, and Elaine in their Chabot Terrace apartment around 1949. A native of Stockton, Walter believed Vallejo was a wonderful opportunity to forge a better life for his family. He worked at Mare Island Navy Yard and Travis Air Force Base for a number of years before becoming an insurance agent for Golden State Mutual Insurance Company. (Courtesy of Elaine Freeman.)

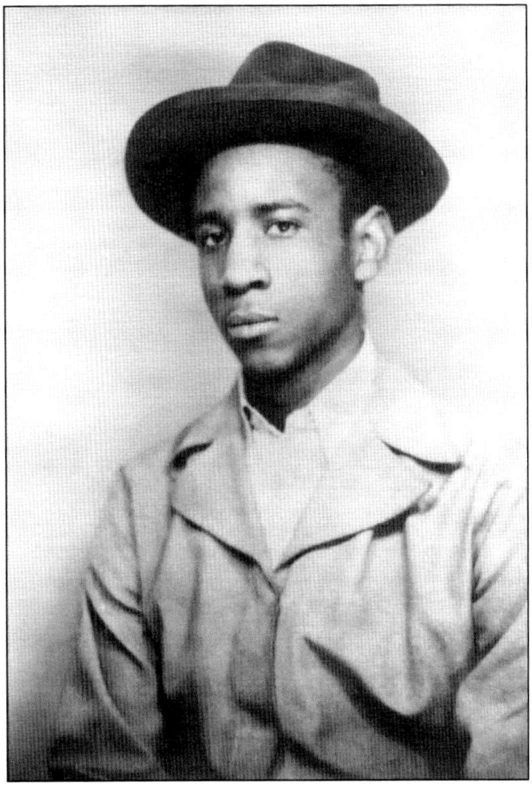

For decades, the late Sargent Johnson was a fixture in downtown Vallejo. Owner of De Luxe Shoe Service, he was known as the shoe repairman of Vallejo. Born in Oakvale, Mississippi, he was raised in nearby Laurel, where he learned the trade of shoe repair from his shoemaker father, Corinth Johnson. Before moving to Vallejo in 1945, the Johnson family spent time in Memphis, Tennessee, and the Washington State. After working for another shoemaker, he eventually opened his own shop on the lower end of Georgia Street in 1951. (Courtesy of Bettye Johnson.)

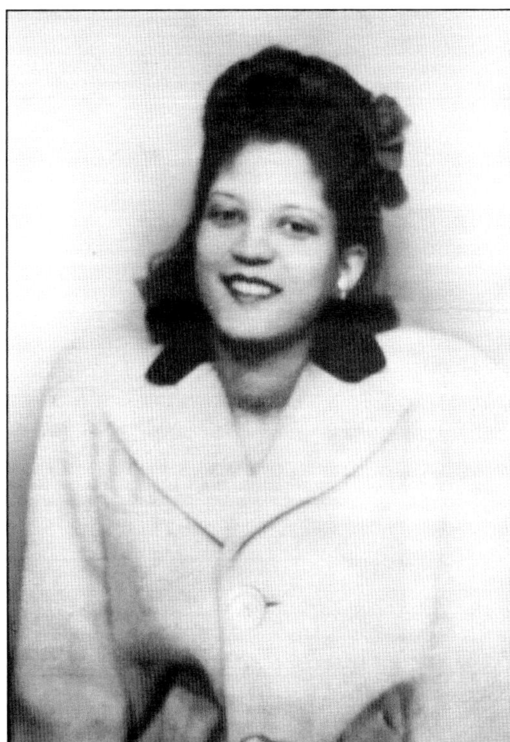

Christine Carpenter married her childhood sweetheart, Sargent Johnson, in June 1940. (Courtesy of Bettye Johnson.)

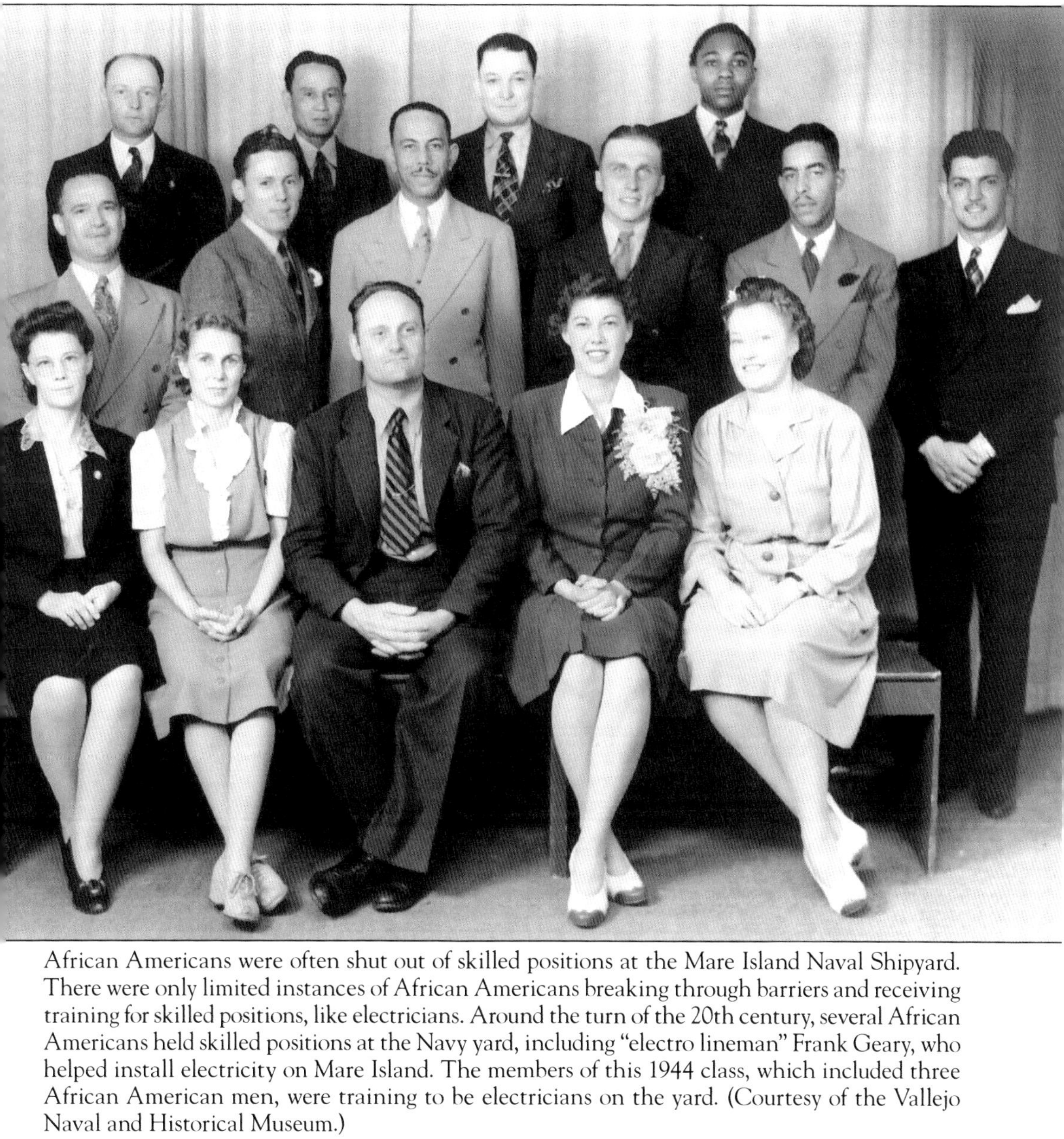

African Americans were often shut out of skilled positions at the Mare Island Naval Shipyard. There were only limited instances of African Americans breaking through barriers and receiving training for skilled positions, like electricians. Around the turn of the 20th century, several African Americans held skilled positions at the Navy yard, including "electro lineman" Frank Geary, who helped install electricity on Mare Island. The members of this 1944 class, which included three African American men, were training to be electricians on the yard. (Courtesy of the Vallejo Naval and Historical Museum.)

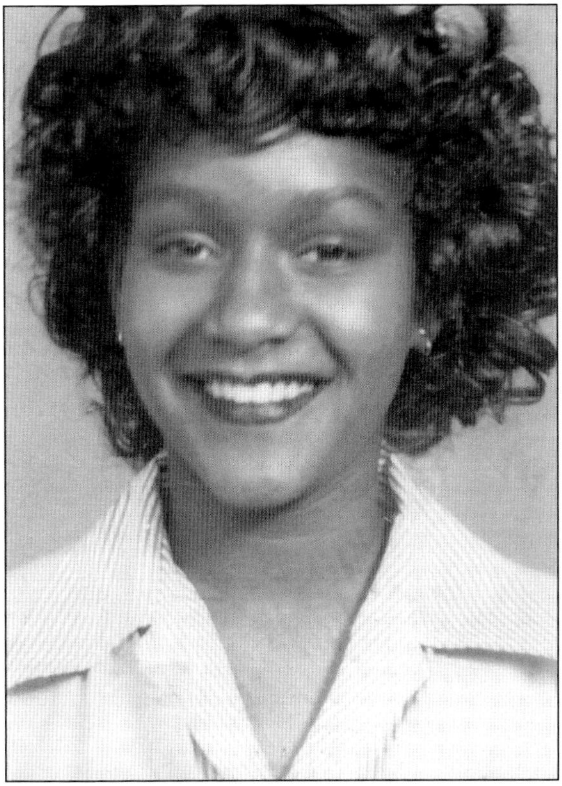

Ursula Williams came to Vallejo in the early 1940s with her three sisters, Mabel Hayes, Margaret Wilson, and Anna Mae Bell. Ursula, who attended local schools, lived in the Victory Apartments, Chabot Terrace, and later moved to Floyd Terrace. Following graduation from Vallejo High School, Ursula attended court-reporting school in San Francisco and became a court stenographer. In 1949, she and her high school sweetheart, James Williams, were married. He was born in Vallejo and was a member of a longtime pioneer family. (Courtesy of James and Ursula Williams.)

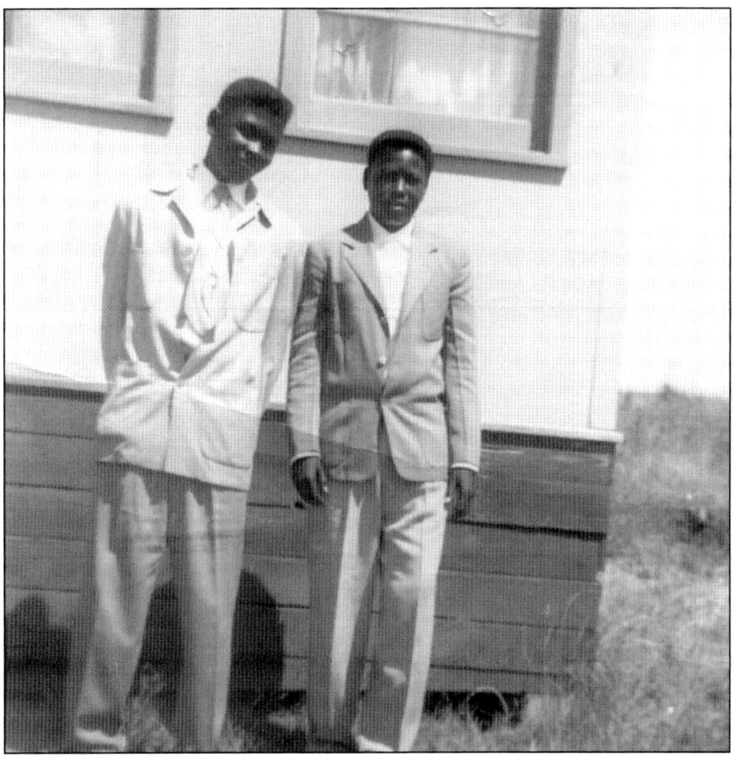

Willie Jackson and Norman Lissier pose in front of Jackson's Chabot Terrace home in the late 1940s. Jackson, who would later become Solano County's first African American probation officer, hailed from Edwards, Mississippi, via Memphis, Tennessee. Jackson described growing up in Chabot Terrace as "nearly idyllic." (Courtesy of Essie Jackson.)

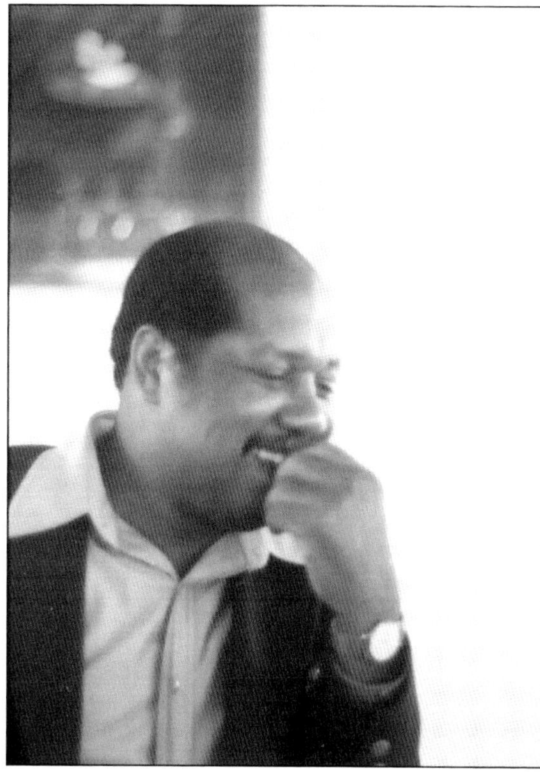

Renowned author Ernest Gaines migrated to Vallejo with his mother and stepfather, Adrienne and Raphael Colar Sr., from Oscar, Louisiana, in 1948. Gaines, who was called "Ernie" by classmates and friends, was 15 at the time of the move to Vallejo. He found sanctuary in the Vallejo Public Library, where he devoured the writings of famous authors and started to hone his writing skills. Gaines would later go on to write the acclaimed *The Autobiography of Miss Jane Pittman* and *A Gathering of Old Men*. (Courtesy of John F. Kennedy Public Library.)

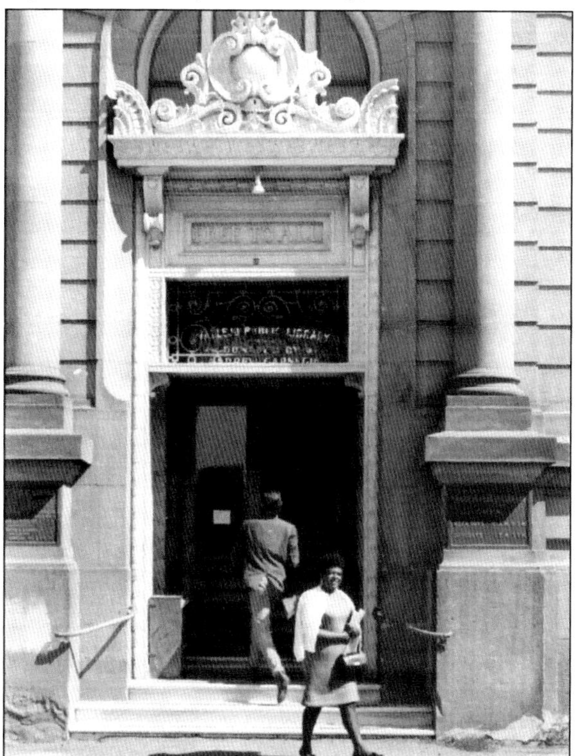

In the 1950s, Ernest Gaines spent countless hours in the old Vallejo Public Library in downtown Vallejo. (Courtesy of John F. Kennedy Public Library.)

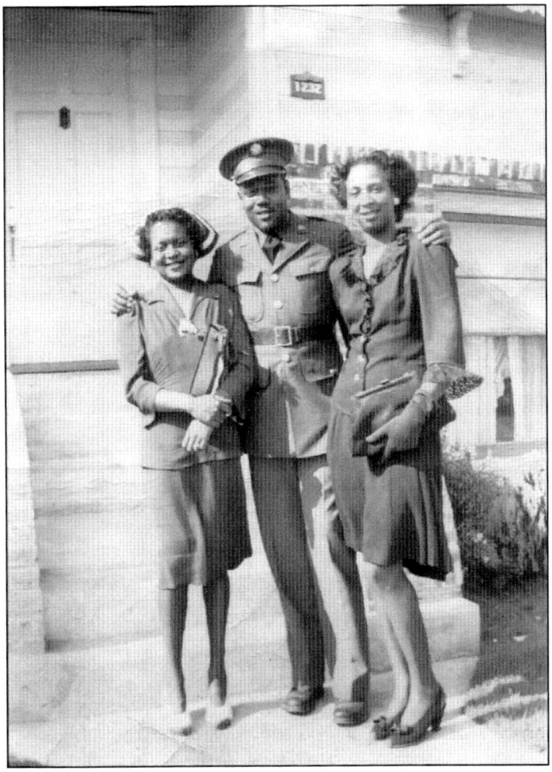

This well-dressed trio is prepared to go out on the town in mid-1940s Vallejo. While Vallejo was a Navy town during the war years of the 1940s, many African American members of the Army and Air Force came to Vallejo to take part in the busy social scene of that era. (Courtesy of the Boyden collection.)

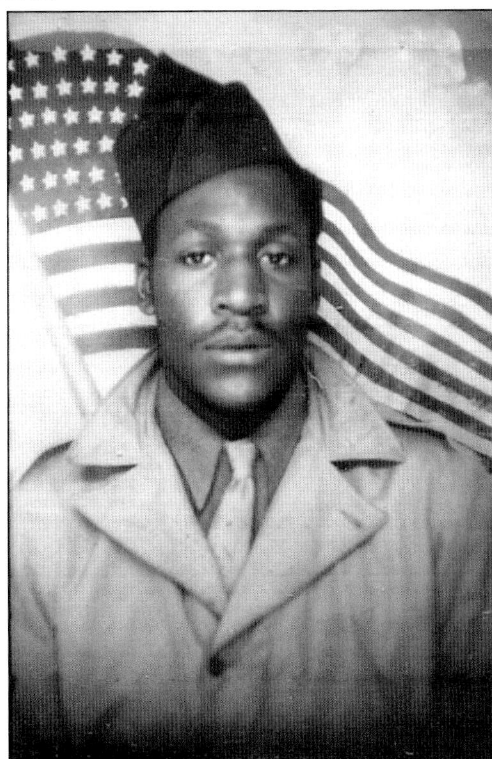

Billy Thomas, pictured in his Air Force uniform in the 1940s, was raised in Vallejo. (Courtesy of the Boyden collection.)

Like so many young African American couples, Johnny and Ruth Love came to Vallejo via the Navy during the 1940s. They were natives of Palmetto, Florida, and Ruth came to Vallejo in 1944 to join her husband, Johnny, who arrived at Mare Island two years earlier. (Courtesy of Ruth Love.)

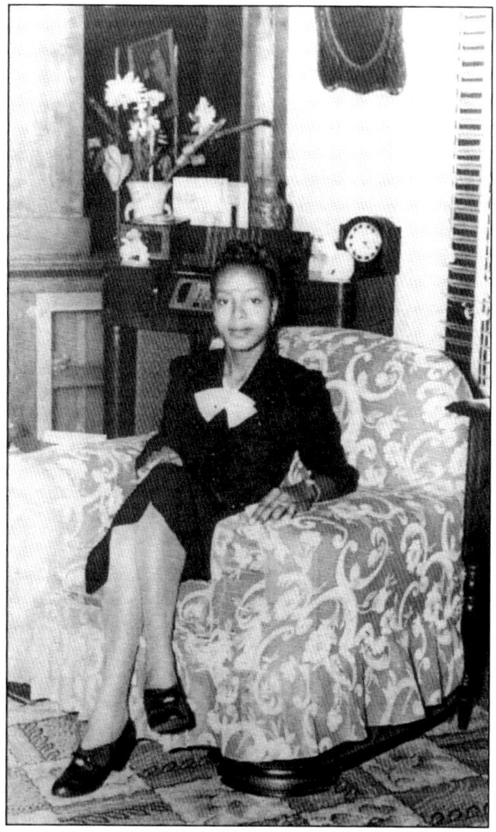

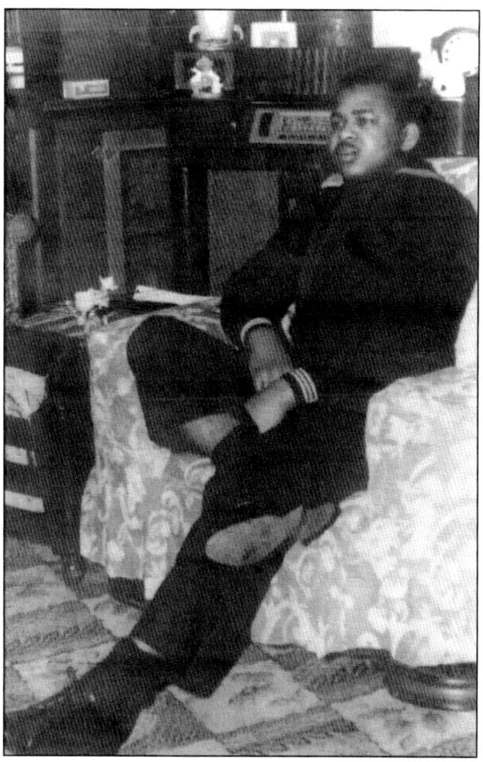

Before being joined by his wife, Johnny Love lived in the segregated barracks at the foot of Sonoma Boulevard at Ryder Street. Ruth Love's first job after arrival to Vallejo was in housekeeping at the Hillside Dormitories. (Courtesy of Ruth Love.)

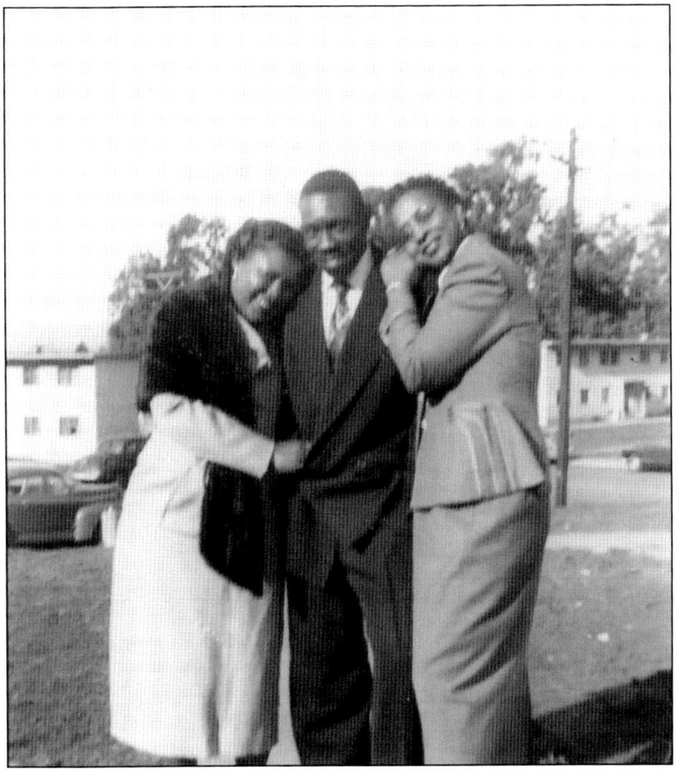

Charles Smith, center, came to Vallejo in the mid-1940s from Muscogee, Oklahoma. Geneva Turner, pictured left, hailed from Alexandria, Louisiana, and migrated to Vallejo after a friend, already working at Mare Island, encouraged her to come. Shortly after Geneva arrived, a smitten Charles told friends he was going to marry her. After courtship and marriage, the young couple moved to the newly built Harry Floyd Terrace housing project on Vallejo's north side. Charles Smith later worked for Benicia Arsenal and, following its closure in 1964, he returned to Mare Island, where he worked as a mechanic until he retired in 1979. (Courtesy of Ann Grant.)

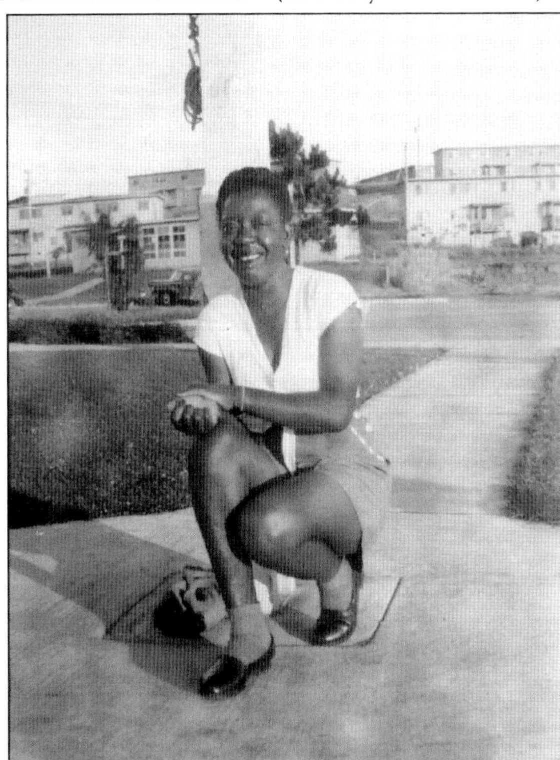

Emma Lee Turner, sister of Geneva Smith, came to Vallejo at the request of Geneva. (Courtesy of Ann Grant.)

Young couples like Jesse and Ora Stacy, pictured here with daughter Sandra, started raising families as soon as they moved to Vallejo. (Courtesy of Ora Stacy.)

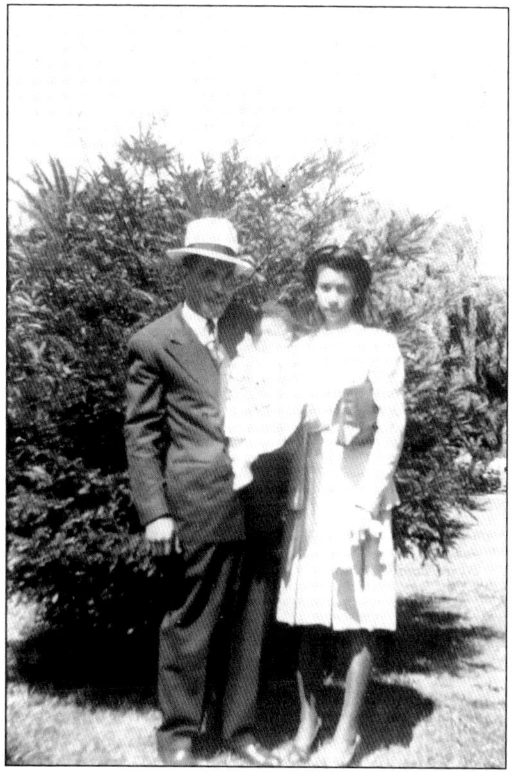

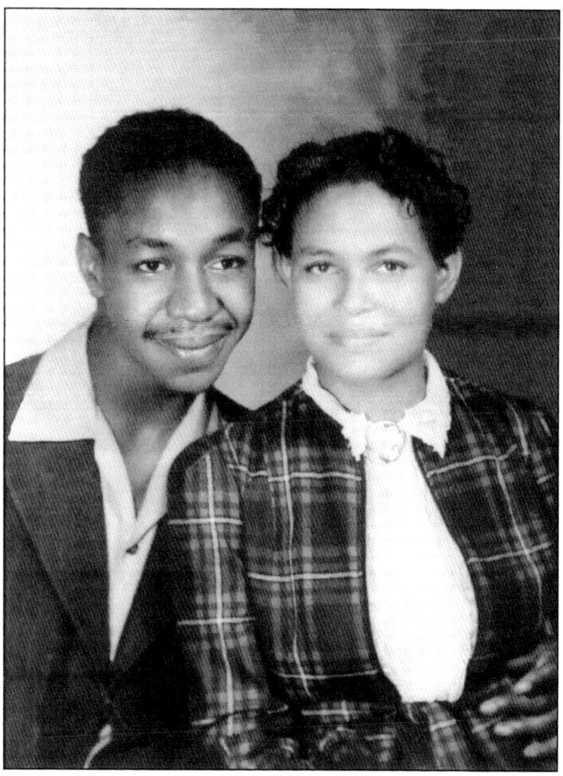

Clyde Folds and Mary Gullette met at Paul Lawrence Dunbar High School in Little Rock, Arkansas. They fell in love and were married on September 2, 1941. Determined to make the best living possible for their family, the young couple headed West, leaving their daughter Greta with Mary's mother. Clyde Folds worked construction and eventually found a job at Mare Island, where he worked for the next 34 years until he retired in 1982. While at Mare Island, Folds was promoted to boilermaker instructor, the first African American to hold that position at Mare Island. (Courtesy of LaJuana Williams.)

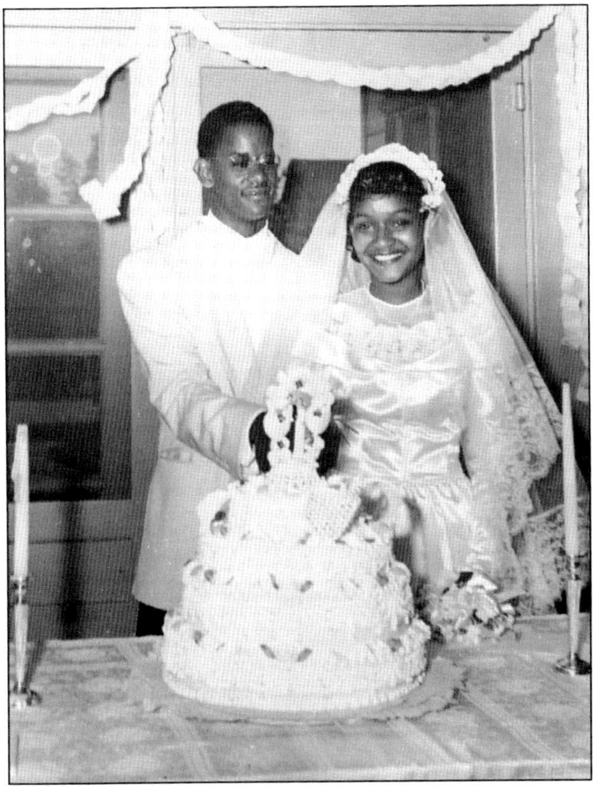

In 1949, James Williams, who came from one of Vallejo's older African American families, married his high school sweetheart, Ursula. (Courtesy of James and Ursula Williams.)

Michelle, Mark, and Kathy Williams, the children of James and Ursula Williams, pose in this 1950s photograph. (Courtesy of James and Ursula Williams.)

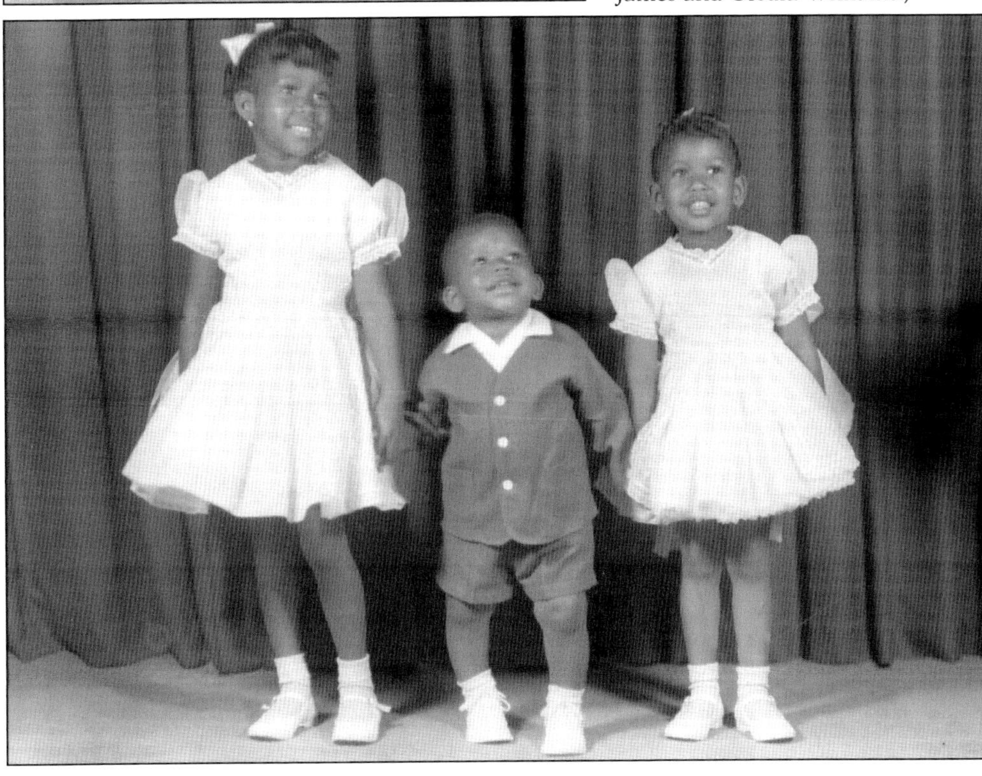

James and Ruby Hicks moved to Vallejo during the height of the Great Migration. (Courtesy of Ruby Hicks.)

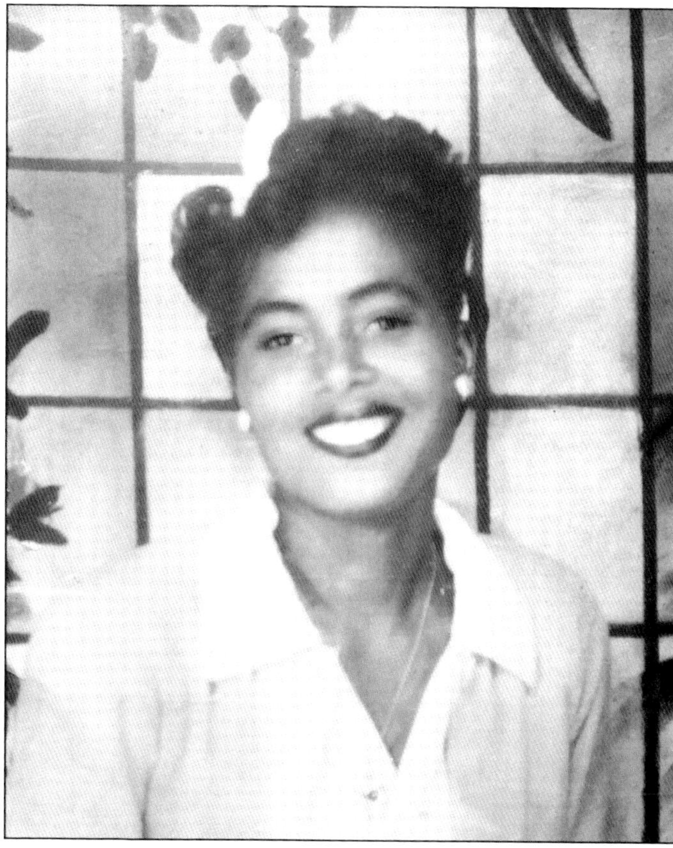

Ora Stacy is seen sitting outside her Chabot Terrace home in 1946 with daughter Sandra. (Courtesy of Ora Stacy.)

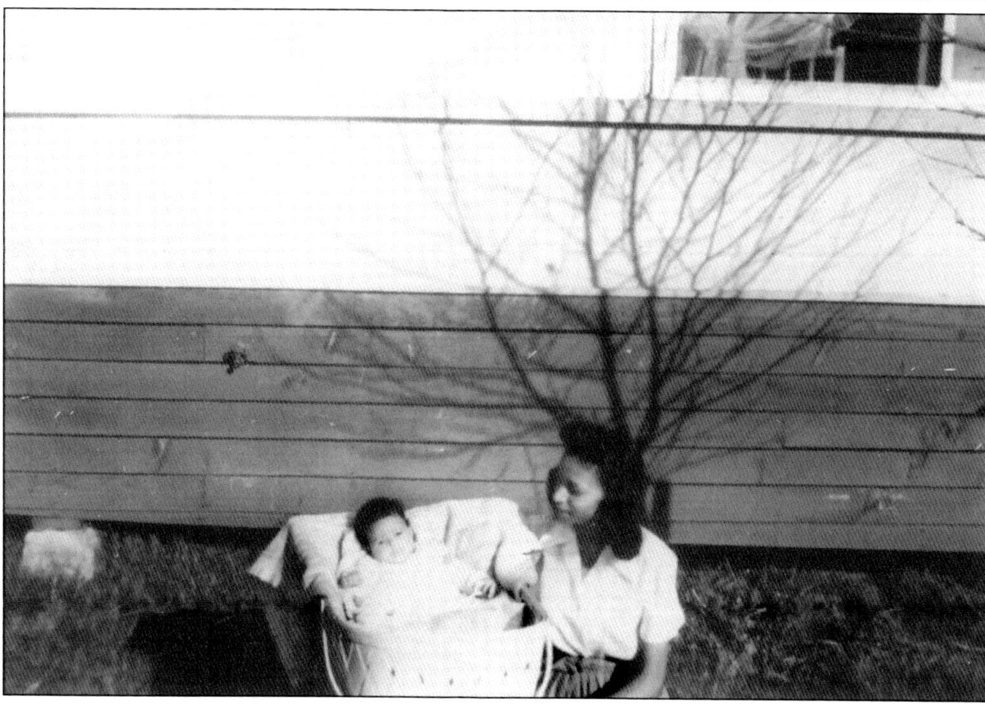

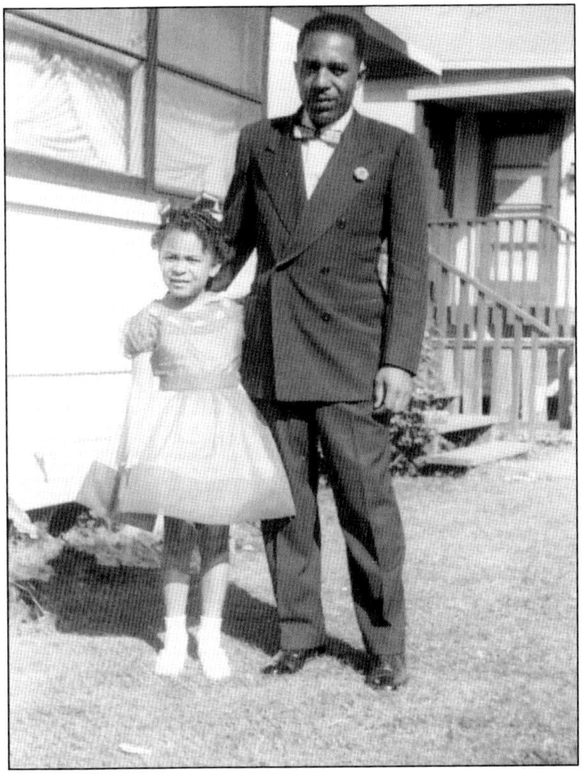

Albert Morrow and his daughter Jennifer are pictured outside his Catskill Street home in Chabot Terrace in the early 1950s. Albert Morrow hailed from Coweta, Oklahoma. His wife, Jeannette, was raised in Reserve, Louisiana. The pair met while working at the Oakland Army Depot, shortly after Morrow left the Navy. They married in 1945 and moved to Vallejo at the end of 1950, Shortly after arrival in Vallejo, Morrow was hired at Mare Island. (Courtesy of Jennifer Hendrix.)

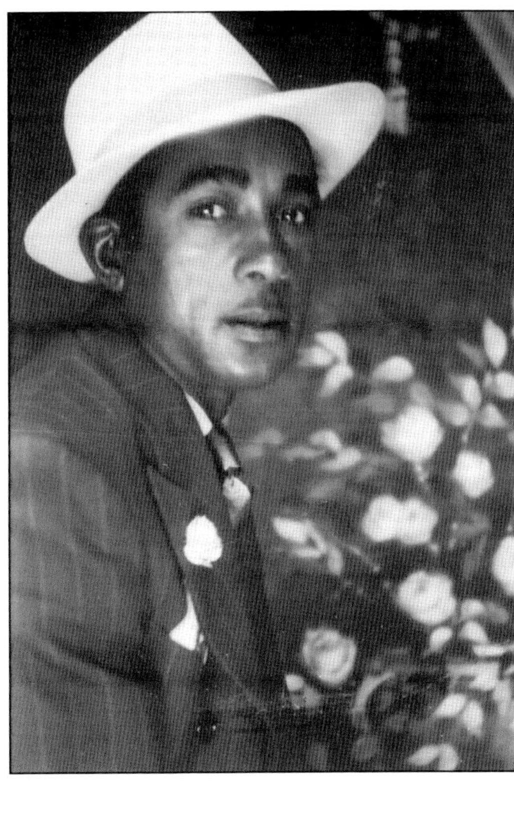

Leaving his wife, Willida, and his two daughters behind in Texas in 1942, Horace Calhoun hopped freight trains with two friends to get to Vallejo. They had heard about Mare Island and the jobs being offered there. Calhoun sent for his family shortly after he arrived in Vallejo and landed a job. (Courtesy of Brenda Calhoun.)

When Willida Calhoun arrived in Vallejo to join her husband, Horace, in 1942, they moved into a garage that belonged to Katie Brown. Crowded living conditions, created by newly arrived job-seekers during the war years of the 1940s, resulted in many families living in garages, trailers, and single rooms. The Calhoun family eventually moved to Chabot Terrace. (Courtesy of Brenda Calhoun.)

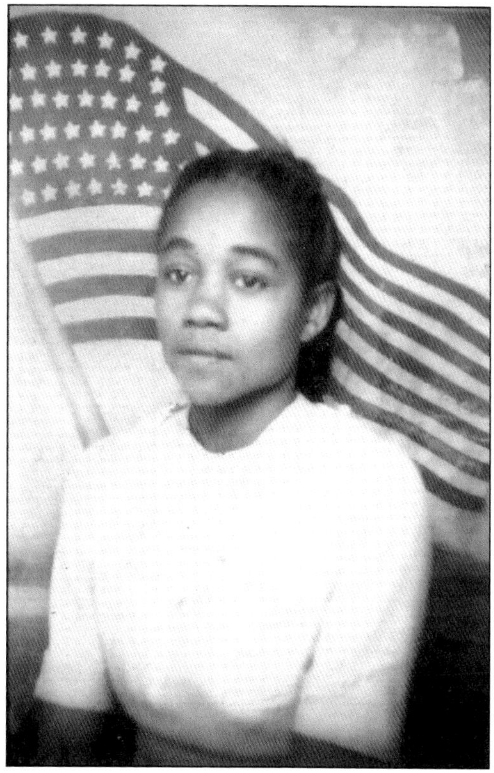

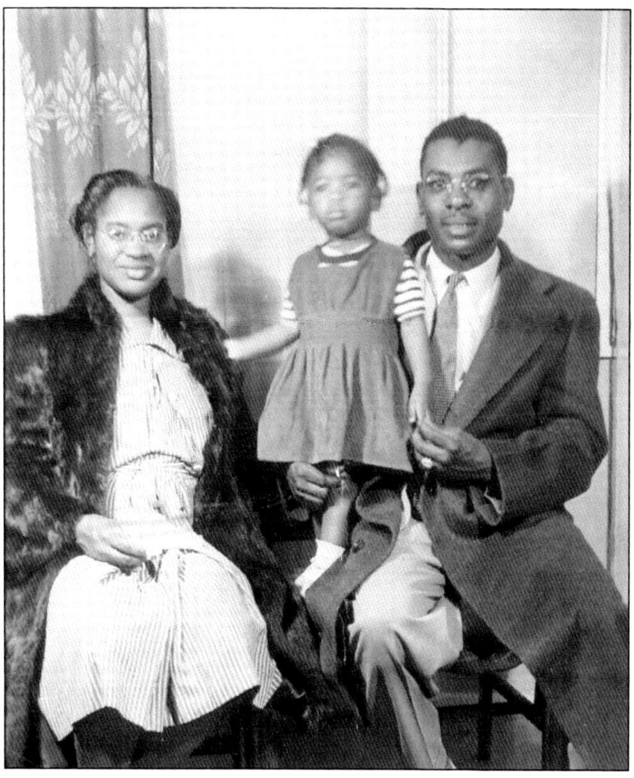

Bertram Perry, pictured in 1944 with his wife, Emma, and their daughter Patricia, also hopped a freight train to get to California, traveling on the Los Angeles–bound train with friend R.A. Smith. Perry would later tell family members it was a hard trip. Raised in Franklin, Louisiana, Perry had heard of the jobs from friends who had made their way west. Once in Vallejo, he was hired at Mare Island within a week. He sent for Emma shortly after. Perry worked at the Navy yard as a pipefitter for five years. By the late 1940s, he was hired at Travis Air Force Base, where he painted planes for more than 30 years, retiring from that position as a supervisor. (Courtesy of Emma Perry.)

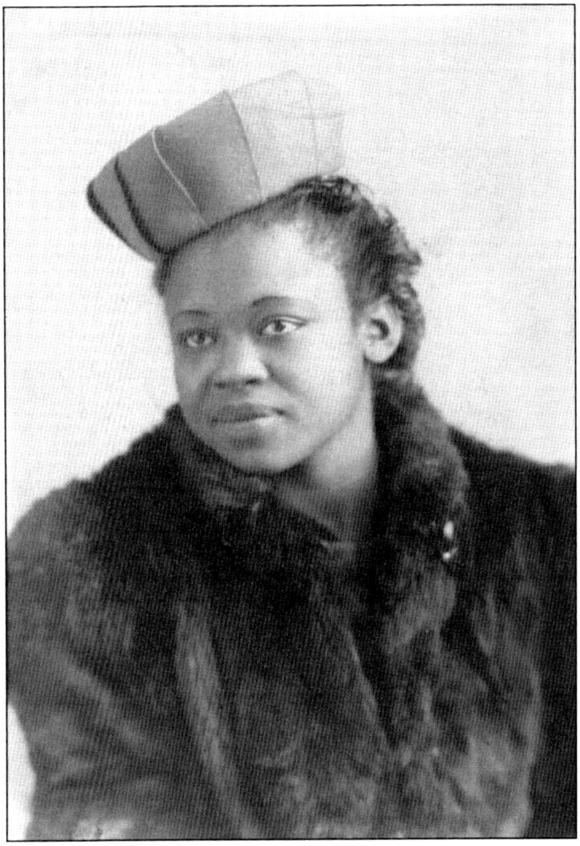

Juanita Nelson came to Vallejo around 1944 from Golden Valley, Oklahoma. She had heard of the jobs at Mare Island from relatives who encouraged her to relocate. Nelson was the descendant of Oklahoma pioneers, who, in the late 1800s, left their Georgia home and moved westward as part of the land rush of the 1800s. Shortly after leaving her Mare Island job following the end of the war, Nelson went to work as a domestic in San Rafael, where she worked for many years. (Courtesy of Cherubim "Jake" Speaks.)

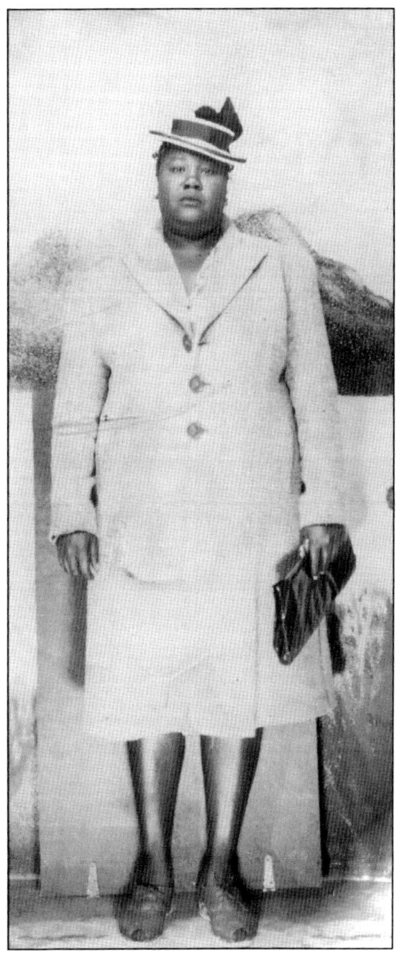

Willie Butler hailed from Tallulah, Louisiana. Around 1940, she made her way West. She first worked in an onion factory in Stockton. She then moved to Vallejo and worked as a domestic in nearby San Rafael for years. (Courtesy of Barbara Nash McKinley.)

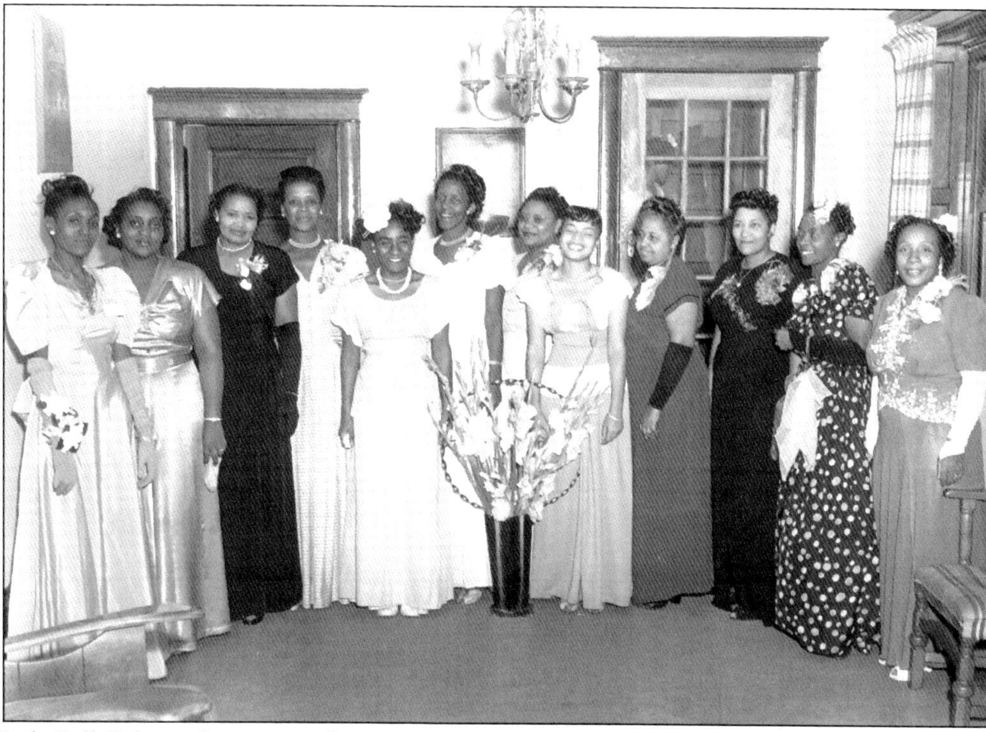

Lulu Bell Calip, right, poses with friends during a formal affair in the early 1950s. (Courtesy of Roy Calip.)

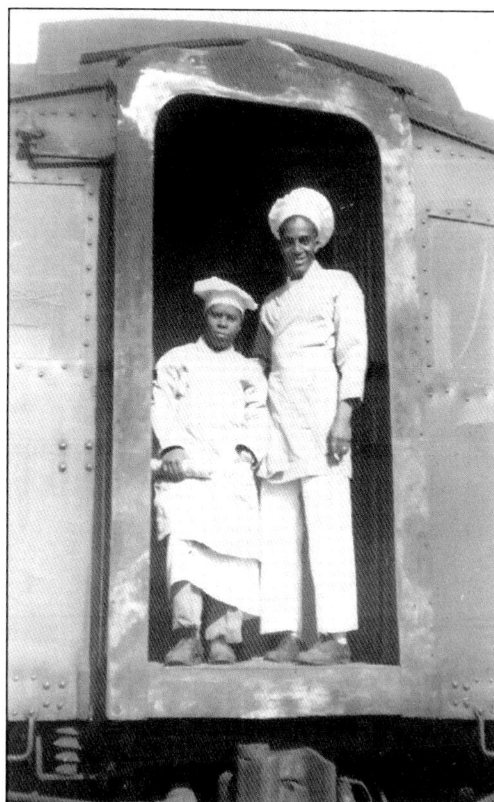

One of the first jobs Curtis Wiggins landed when he arrived in the Bay Area in the 1940s was as a railroad cook out of West Oakland. By the 1940s, he was working at Mare Island as a welder. (Courtesy of Curtis Thomas.)

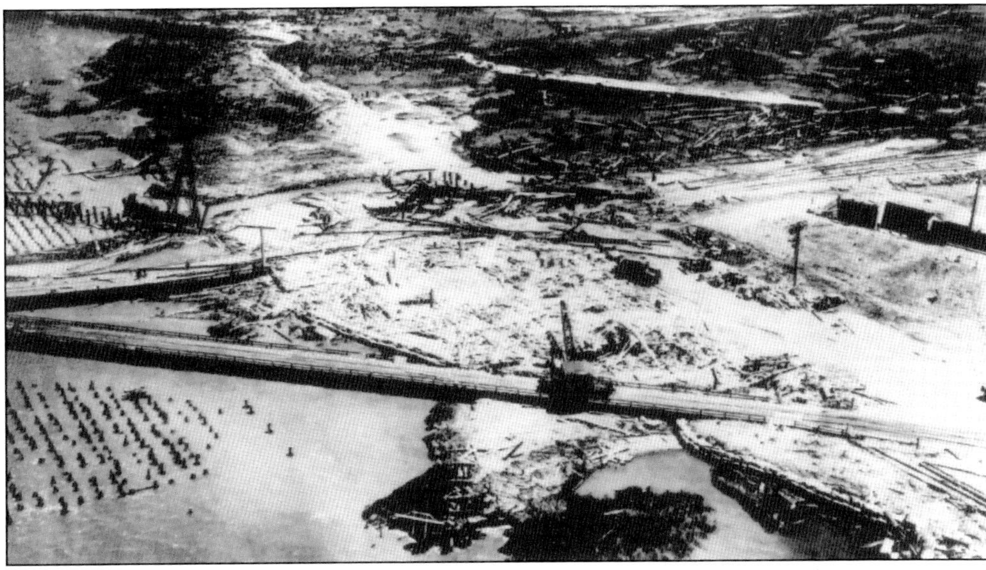

The Port Chicago disaster of July 1944 that killed 320 men, 202 of whom were African Americans, had a huge impact on the Vallejo black community. Friends and family members of the dead and injured lived in Vallejo. Marshall McGriff, the author's father, served with many of the Port Chicago victims while in basic training at the Great Lakes Naval Training Center in Illinois in the early 1940s. (Courtesy of the National Archives.)

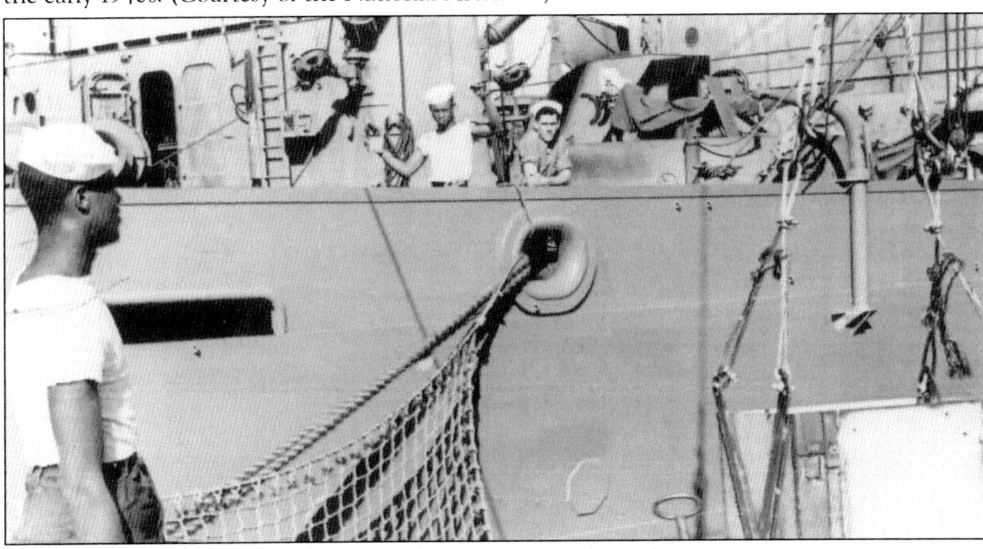

The dangerous job of loading and unloading munitions often fell to African American sailors, as it had at Port Chicago. Here, young sailors load munitions aboard a ship at an unspecified site. A month after the devastating explosion at Port Chicago, 258 African American sailors refused to return to the unsafe conditions of handling munitions at Mare Island. The decision to stop work took place in the segregated barrages on Ryder Street in South Vallejo. After refusing to return to work, the sailors were forced to stay on a barge on the water near Ryder Street in the sweltering summer heat. A Navy admiral threatened the sailors with court martial and death at the hands of a firing squad if they refused to return to work. Ultimately, 50 of the 258 sailors were tried with mutiny and sentenced to long terms in prison, an unprecedented act in US military history. (Courtesy of the National Archives.)

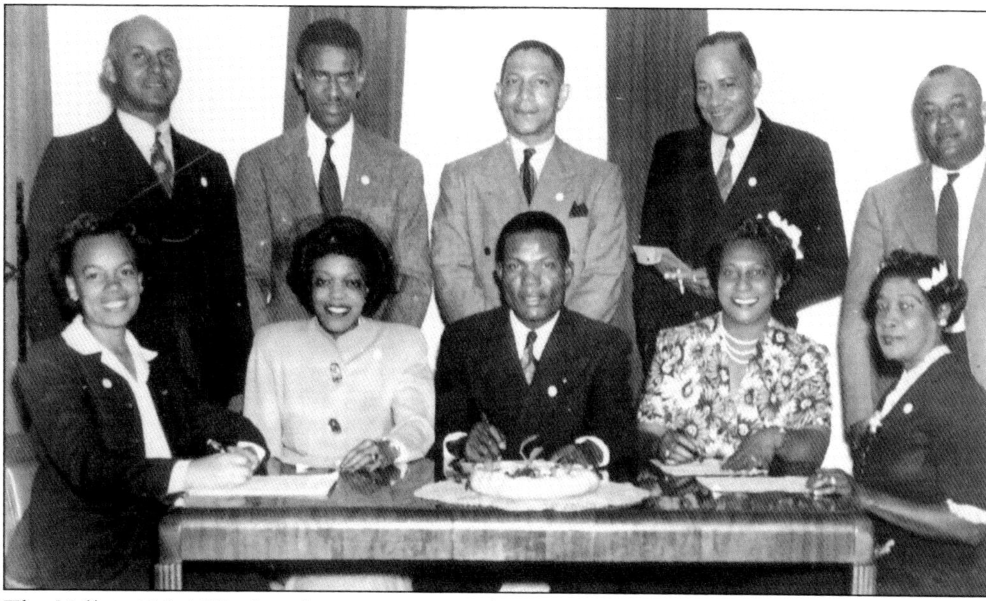

The Vallejo NAACP played an important role in getting the word out about the 1944 Port Chicago disaster and the subsequent trial of 50 African American sailors who refused to return to unsafe working conditions loading ammunition. Thurgood Marshall, who was then a young attorney working for the NAACP Legal Defense Fund, was sent to the Bay Area to support the sailors during their trial. The Vallejo NAACP, led by Frank Shipp (center, sitting) and Arthur Scott (standing, second from left), kept the case in the public eye by continually dispatching articles to popular African American publications, such as the *Chicago Defender* and a Pittsburg newspaper. (Courtesy of the Library of Congress.)

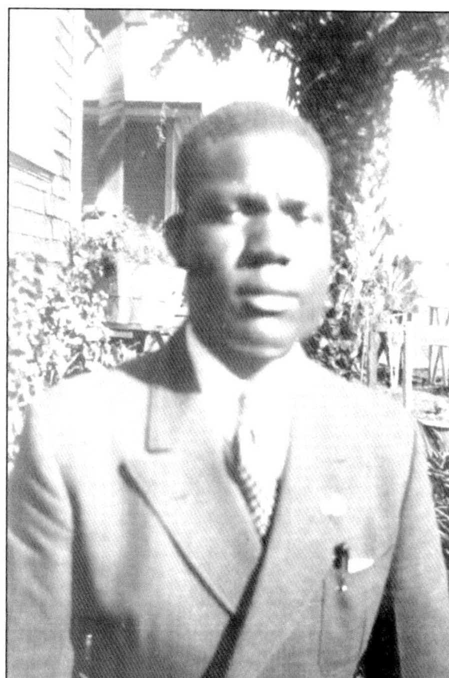

Born in Greensboro, North Carolina, Frank S. Shipp held the presidency of the Vallejo branch of the NAACP at one of its most crucial times. During the early 1940s, while Shipp headed the organization, thousands of African Americans were pouring into Vallejo. As third president of the organization, Shipp launched steps to assist blacks in obtaining better positions at Mare Island, where he worked. In the 1930s, he joined 1930s he joined the Navy and served for a period at Mare Island Navy Yard. On Palm Sunday in 1937, he married Mary E. Owens, a member of an early Vallejo family. (Courtesy of David Shipp.)

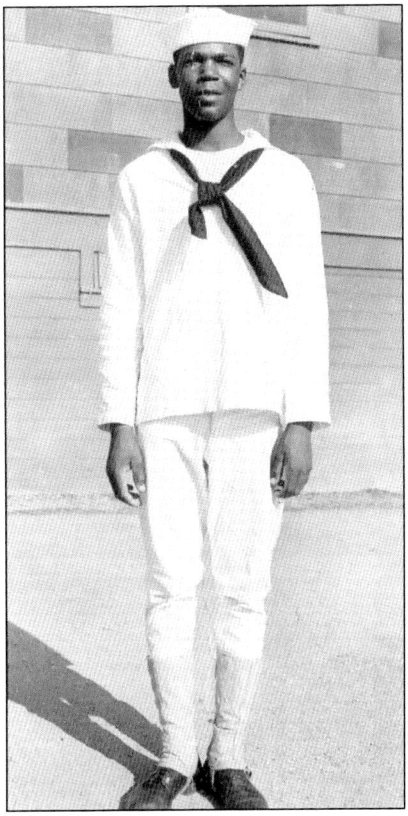

Jake Speaks Sr. was barely out of his teens when he enlisted in the Navy. By the early 1940s, young Speaks was a munitions worker at Port Chicago. On the evening of the explosion, Speaks was asleep in his Port Chicago barracks. The force of the explosion catapulted Speaks out of his bunk and onto the floor. Following the war, Speaks, a native of Columbia, South Carolina, married Edna "Beauty" Nelson. The couple moved to Walnut Street in North Vallejo in 1951, making them one of the earliest African Americans families in the rural neighborhood. (Courtesy of Cherubim "Jake" Speaks.)

Willie V. McKnight was a noted musician who played with Cab Calloway before moving to Vallejo in 1943. A native of Memphis, Tennessee, McKnight was part owner of the 126 Club on Georgia Street in downtown Vallejo during the 1940s. For many years, McKnight served as a music teacher in the Vallejo Unified School District. At the time of his death in 2006, he was serving his fourth term as trustee for the Solano Community College Governing Board. In 1990, he became the first African American from his district in Vallejo to win that position. (Courtesy of the Vallejo Naval and Historical Museum.)

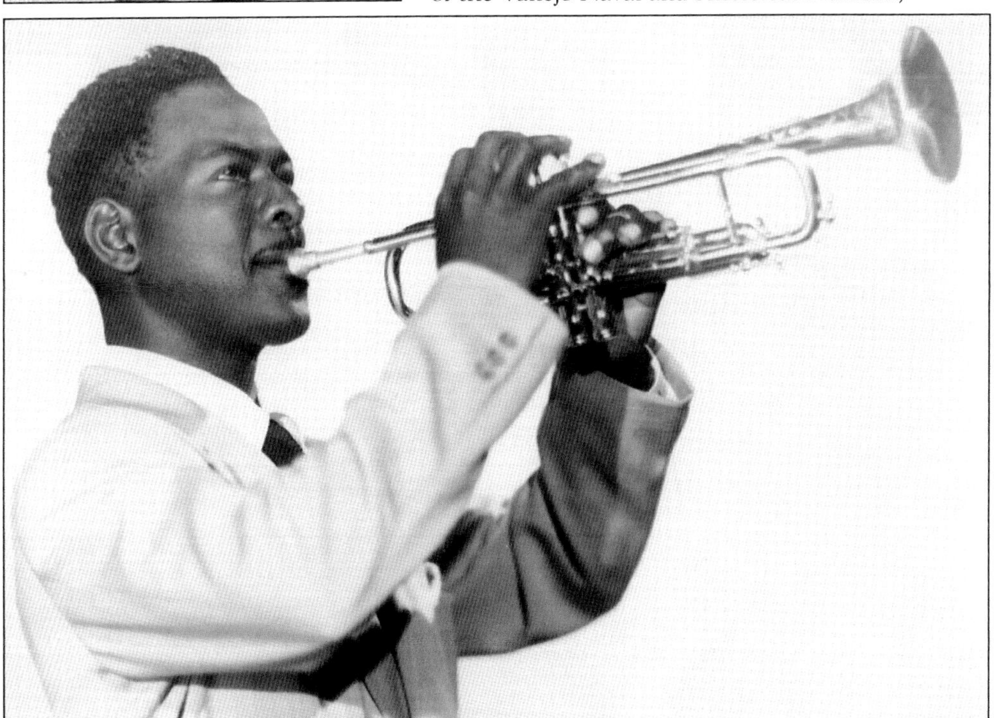

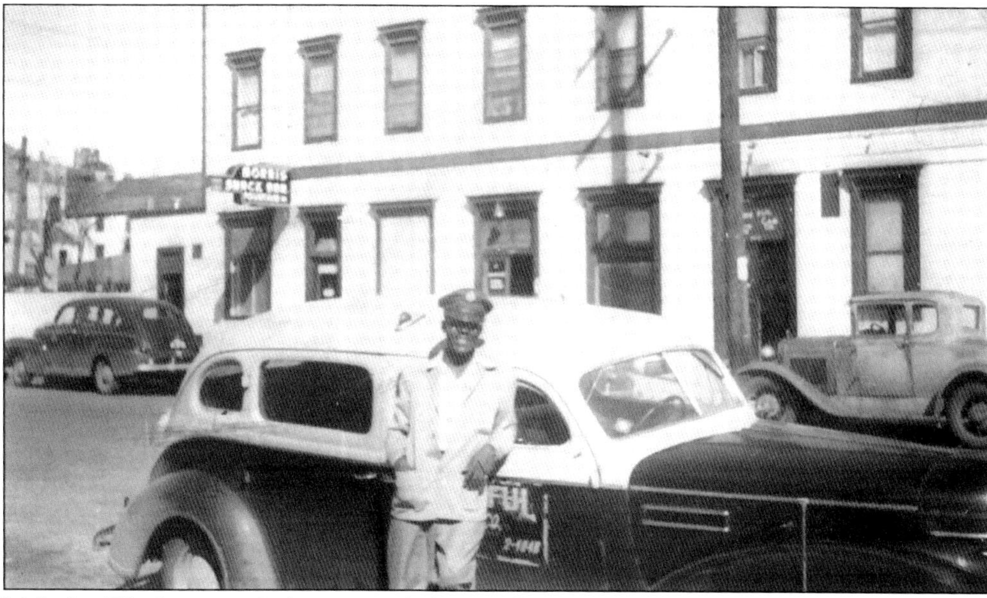

Malcolm Whaley waits for his next cab fare on the Branciforte Street side of Hotel Georgia in the late 1940s. Whaley worked for Black and White Cab, an African American–owned company formed in 1946 when Dan Wroten and Harry Taylor joined their separate cab companies. C.C. Courtney owned a taxi service on Georgia Street around 1910. (Courtesy of the Vallejo Naval and Historical Museum.)

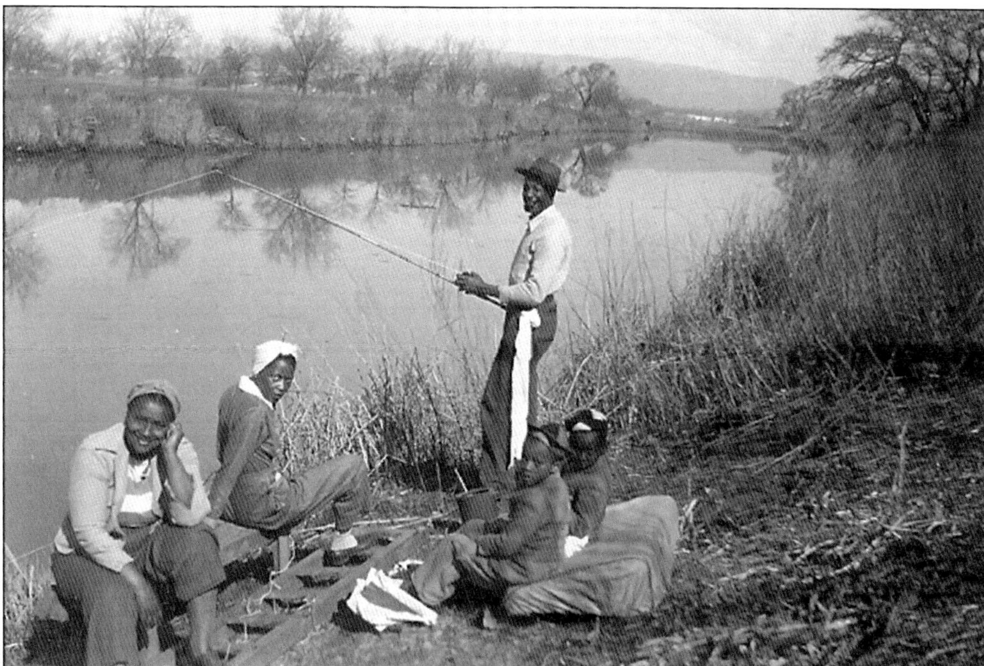

Families found time to relax and enjoy themselves in a variety of ways. Here, Thomas (standing) and Florence Boyden (sitting on the far left) enjoy fishing in Rio Vista. Looking on are the Boydens' grandchildren James "Jimmy" and John Boyden. The other woman is unidentified. (Courtesy of the Boyden collection.)

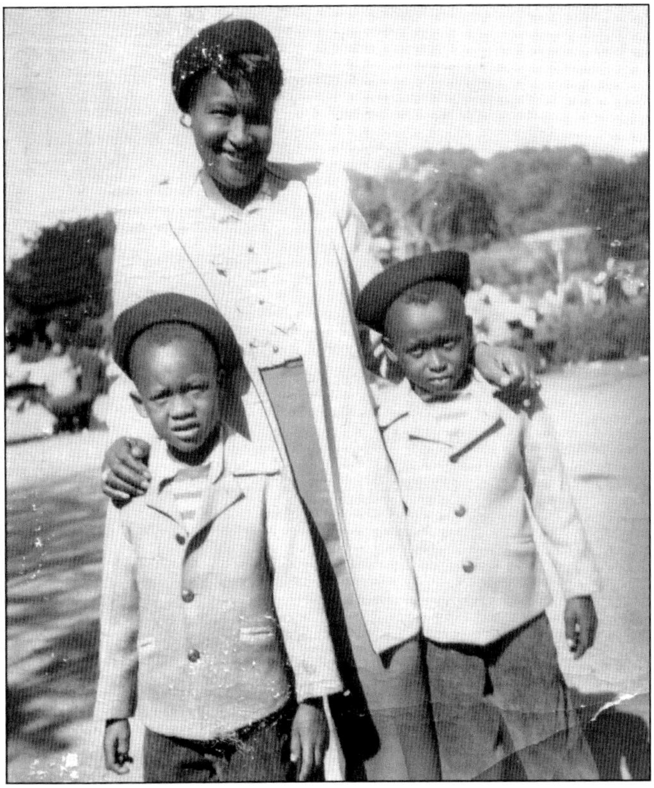

With their beanie caps on, James "Jimmy" and John Boyden enjoy an afternoon out with grandmother Florence Boyden in the late 1940s. Jimmy was born in the Prince Hall Masonic Hall at 1209 Georgia Street. A year after World War II began, housing was so scarce that people were forced to find it wherever they could. For a brief period, a portion of the Masonic hall was converted into a rooming house. (Courtesy of the Boyden collection.)

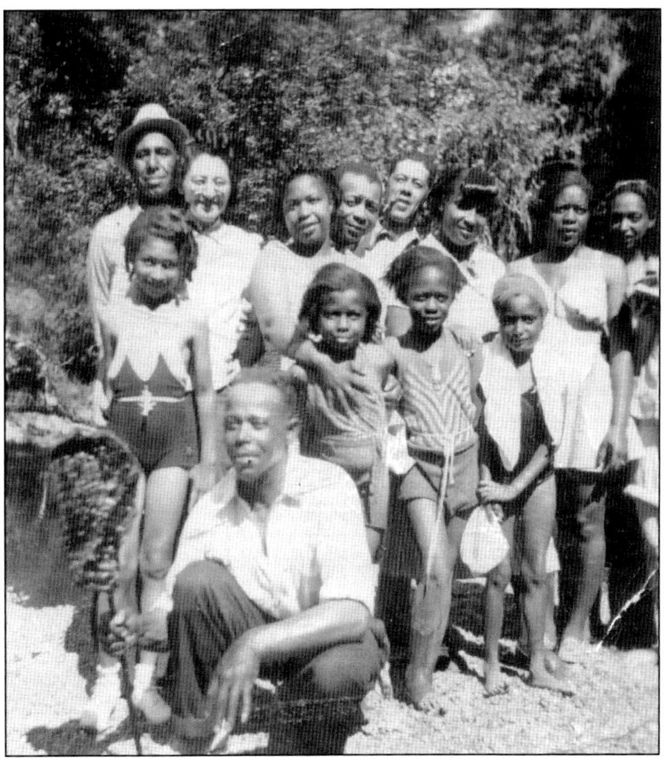

This happy group of children enjoyed a fun-filled afternoon of swimming at a Vallejo park in the 1940s. (Courtesy of the Boyden collection.)

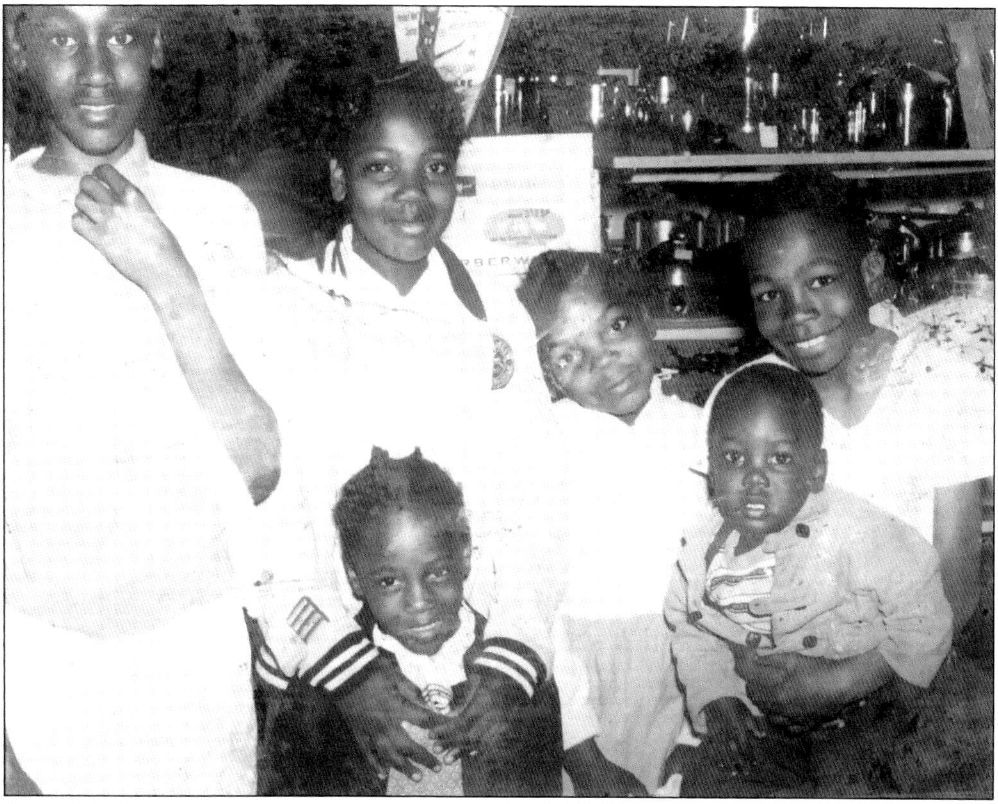

Annie Nash was trying out a new camera in the AGE Department Store in the early 1960s when she snapped this photograph of her children and their friends. In this photograph are Betty and Barbara Nash, Sylvia Moore, Robert Nash, and Richard Edwards. (Courtesy of Barbara Nash McKinley.)

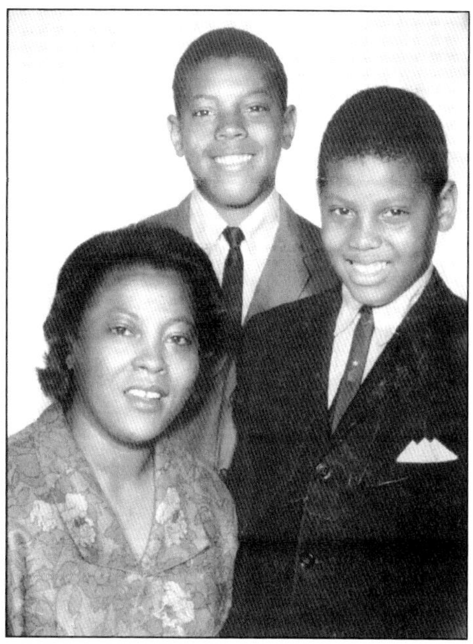

It was 1956 when Mildred Thomas Quinn and her two young sons, Michael and Mitchell, migrated to California from Clinton, Kentucky. After first settling in Richmond for about a year, Quinn and her family moved to Vallejo. For many years, Quinn—who later had two more children: Cortez and Corinne—worked as a housekeeper in Marin County. She also worked for the Solano County Health and Human Services Department. (Courtesy of Corinne Quinn.)

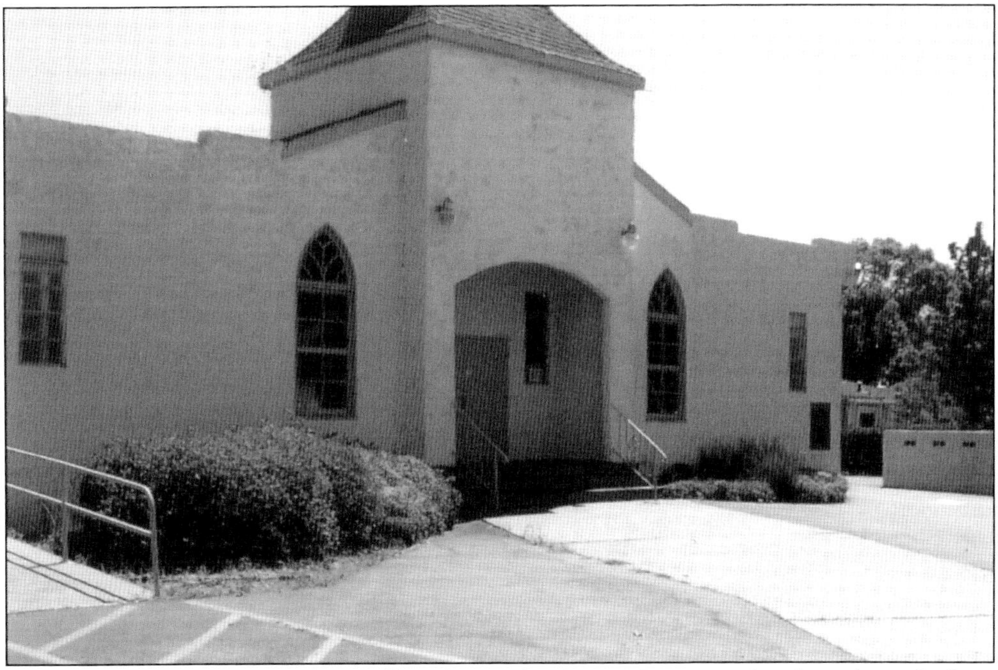

As African Americans moved to Vallejo during the Great Migration, they brought with them their strong faith. With that faith, new places of worship were formed. Many of the transplants found new homes in the churches that were already here, like Second Baptist and Kyles Temple AME Zion Churches. In September 1943, Rev. A.R. Walsh and about a dozen people gathered in the Chabot Terrace home of Lee and Willie Jolly, and Union Missionary Baptist Church was born. In the late 1950s, a new sanctuary was built. That building was replaced with a new, larger structure (pictured) in the 1990s. (Courtesy of the author.)

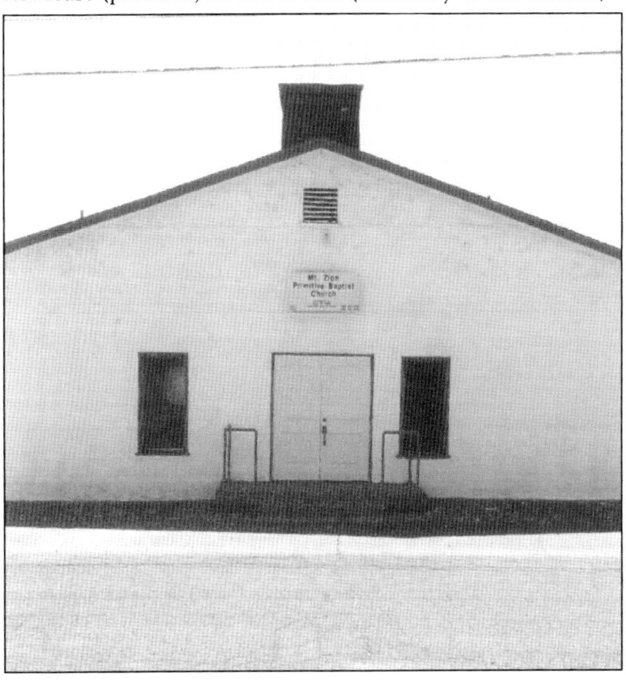

In 1944, Johnny and Ruth Love moved into a house in the unincorporated part of Vallejo. Because housing was at a premium in wartime Vallejo, the Loves shared space with other young couples needing a place to stay. Clarke McGee, a longtime Vallejo resident and former Buffalo Soldier who moved to Vallejo around 1900, owned the house. That original house on Tregaskis Street was later converted into a church, and it is St. Simons Primitive Baptist Church today. (Courtesy of Charles E. Oliver.)

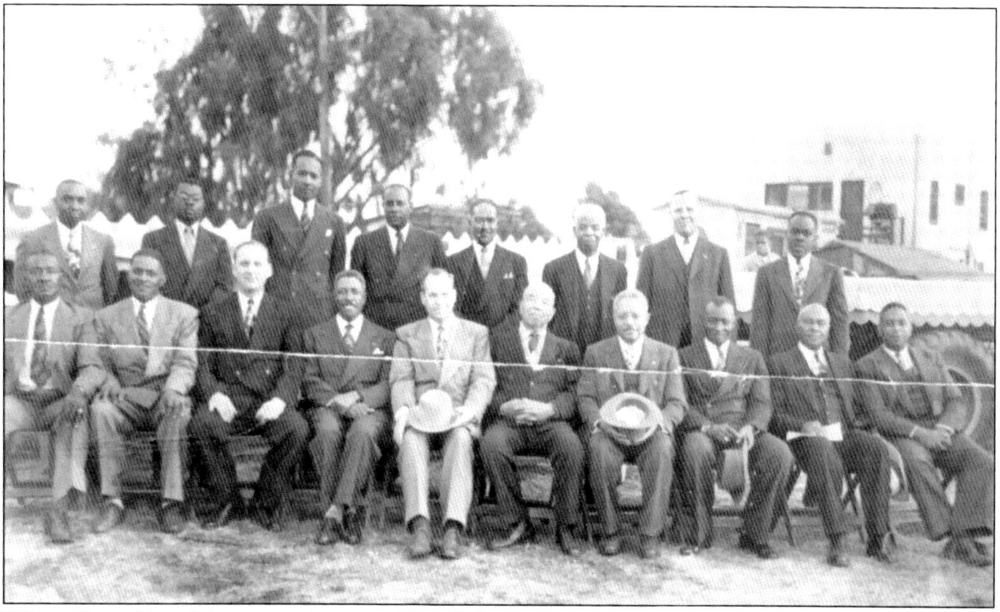

When Friendship Missionary Baptist Church broke ground in the late 1940s, at least two people present could tell the precise history of Vallejo's earliest African American churches because they were there at the beginning of those institutions. L.J. Williams, sitting sixth from the left, and D.G. Corbin, standing sixth from the left, were prominent Vallejo black leaders dating back to the turn of the 20th century. Elected in 1918, Corbin was Vallejo's first president of the local branch of the NAACP. He was president for nearly 20 years and was known throughout Vallejo as "owning large chunks of the city." L.J. Williams was a bookkeeper and clerk at Mare Island as early as 1905. He was a founding member of Second Baptist Church in 1907 and Prince Hall Masons, Firma Lodge No. 27. Williams was also a member of the Vallejo NAACP. (Courtesy of Emma Perry.)

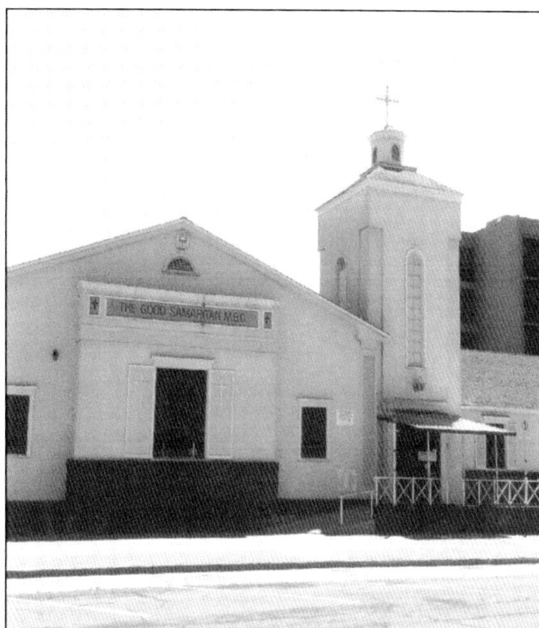

Good Samaritan Missionary Baptist Church was organized in 1958 with 18 charter members. The Reverend Haley H. James was the first pastor, and their first sanctuary was the old Farragut Grade School on Tennessee Street. On November 15, 1966, the congregation moved to their present-day church on Capitol Street. (Courtesy of Charles E. Oliver.)

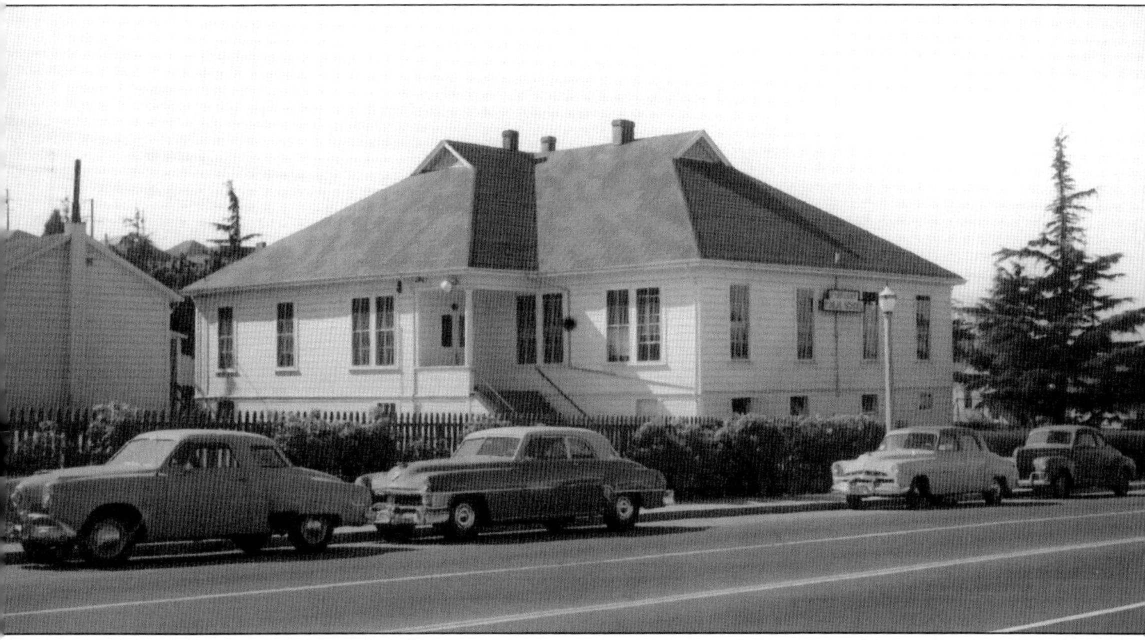

When Farragut Grade School at 111 Tennessee Street, one of the city's oldest schools, closed its doors in the late 1950s, it took on new life as Good Samaritan Missionary Church. (Courtesy of the Vallejo Naval and Historical Museum.)

Lulu Bell Calip was active in a number of organizations in the 1940s and 1950s. In the 1950s, she organized a Vallejo gospel group made up of local teenagers. The group sang throughout the Bay Area. (Courtesy of Roy Calip.)

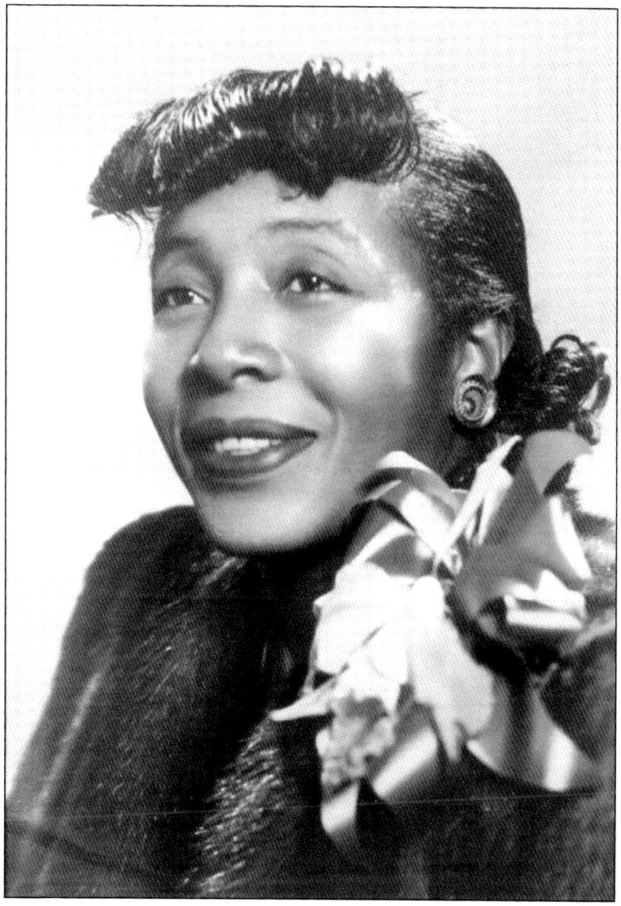

Church played a major role in the lives of the people of the Great Migration. From Sunday school to evening worship, Vallejo's newest residents of the 1940s found solace and down-home familiarity in their new church homes. Lulu Bell Calip, a Topeka, Kansas, transplant, joined Second Baptist Church and was an active member. In this photograph from the late 1940s or early 1950s, Calip is joined by the children of her Sunday school class. (Courtesy of Roy Calip.)

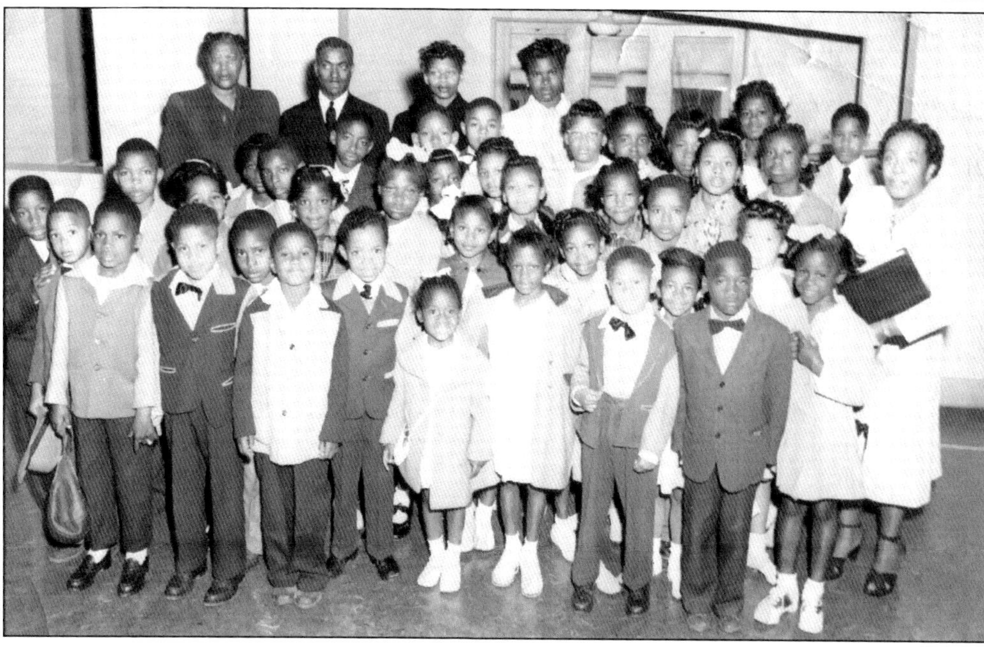

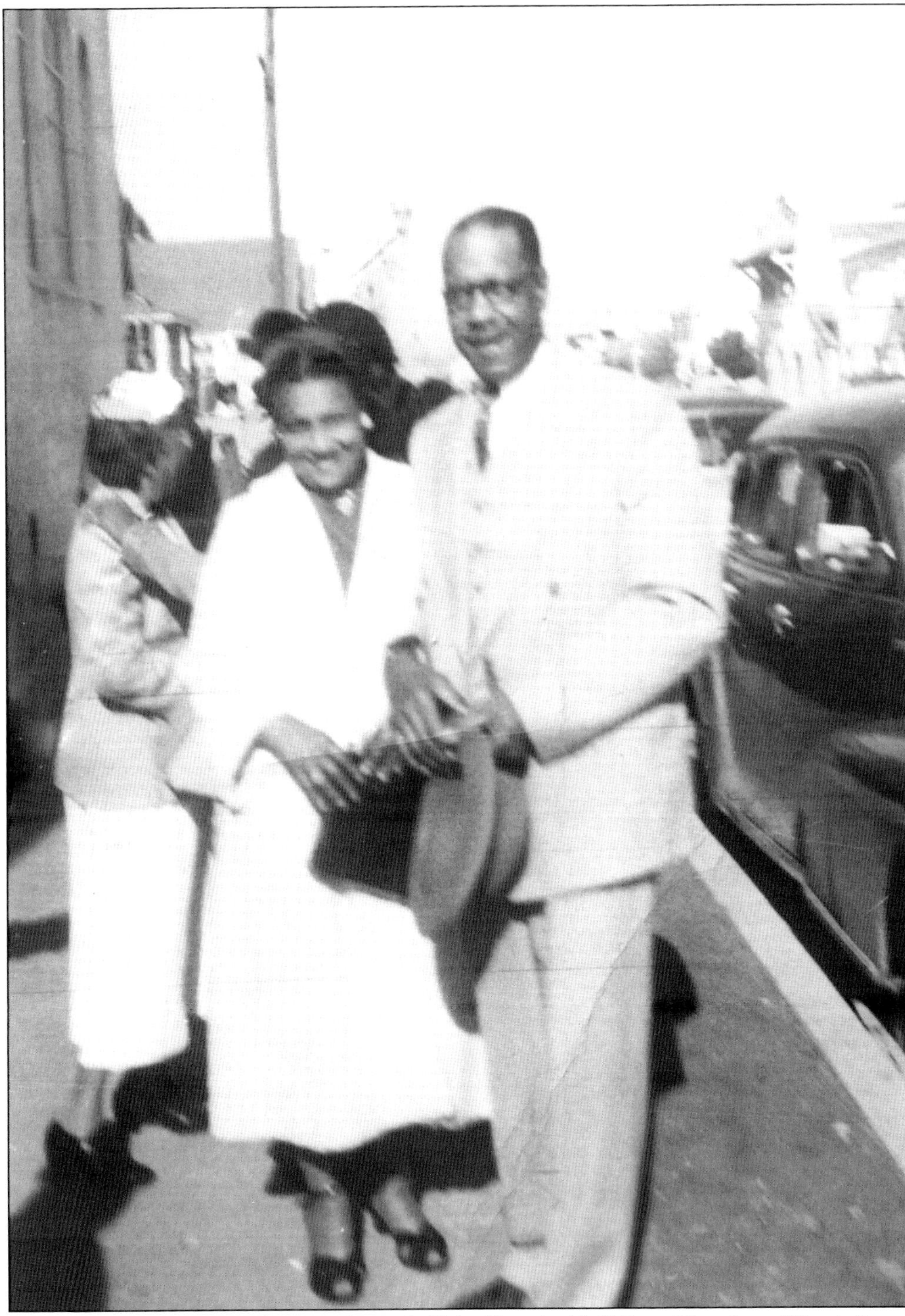

Thomas and Florence Boyden stand outside Kyles Temple AME Zion Church on Illinois Street and Sonoma Boulevard in the 1940s. Following Sunday services, churchgoers would gather at ball fields at Wilson Park and Washington Park to play softball. Thomas served as umpire for many of these games (Courtesy of the Boyden collection.)

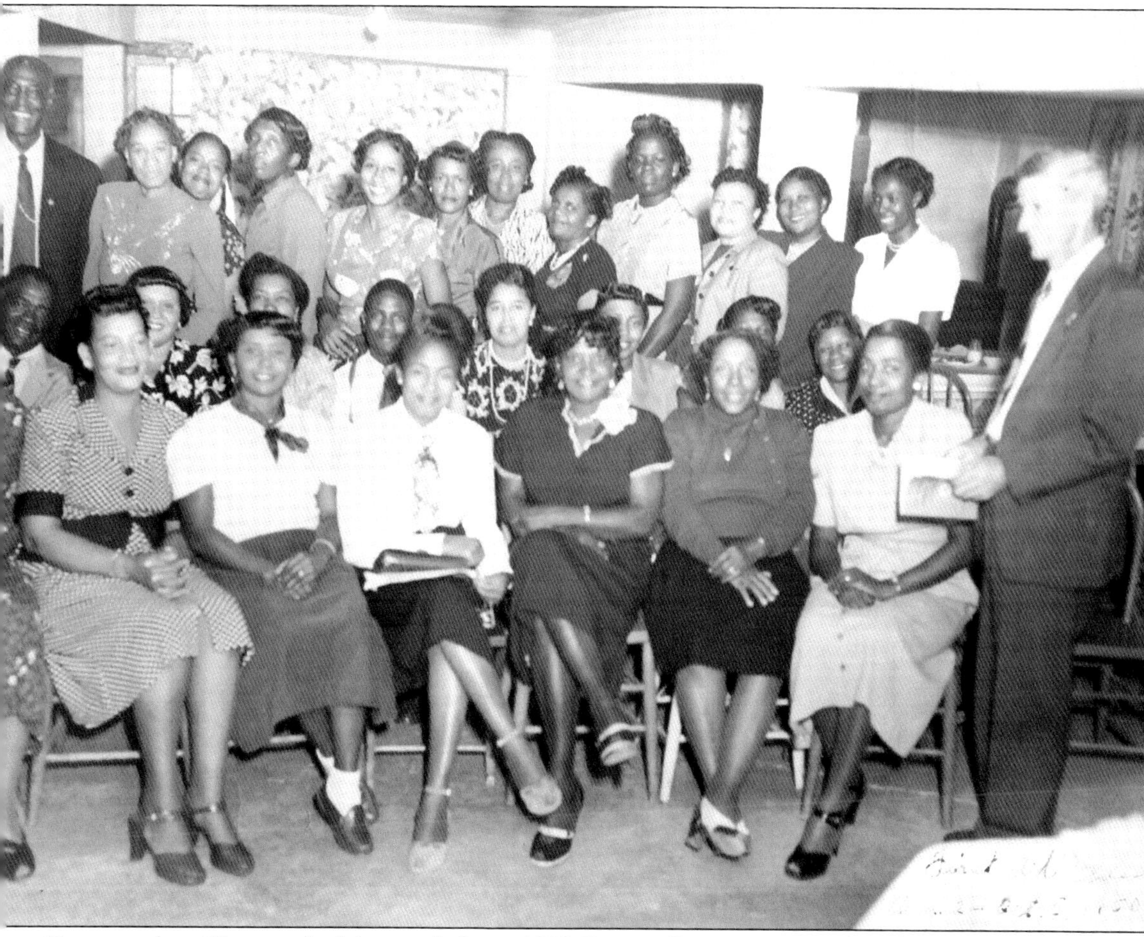

For more than 50 years, the Masonic lodge at 1209 Georgia Street was central to the social lives of Vallejo's African American community. In the 1940s and 1950s, events as varied as dances and classes were held in the historic building. At the height of World War II, people lived in the lodge. In this photograph, a first-aid instructor speaks to a group of eager residents gathered at the lodge. The class, according to a handwritten note on the bottom right-hand corner of the photograph, was held from August through October 1950. Pictured from left to right in this Georgia Brooks photograph are (first row) unidentified, Lucille Mansfield, Jacqueline Moshe, Annie Lewis, Grace Smith, Lulu Calip, and Bertha Braxton; (second row) Lucious Toney, Katherine Jackson, Ala Glover, S. Greene, E. Hansbourgh, Grace Wroten, and Myrtle Binkston; (third row) Green Brown, E. Taylor, Ruth Matthews, Gertrude Smith, A.M. Bass, Evan Thomas, S. Jefferson, Alyene Thompson, Miss Daniel, I. Frazier, S. Esque, and Janice R. McMcCrary. (Courtesy of Roy Calip.)

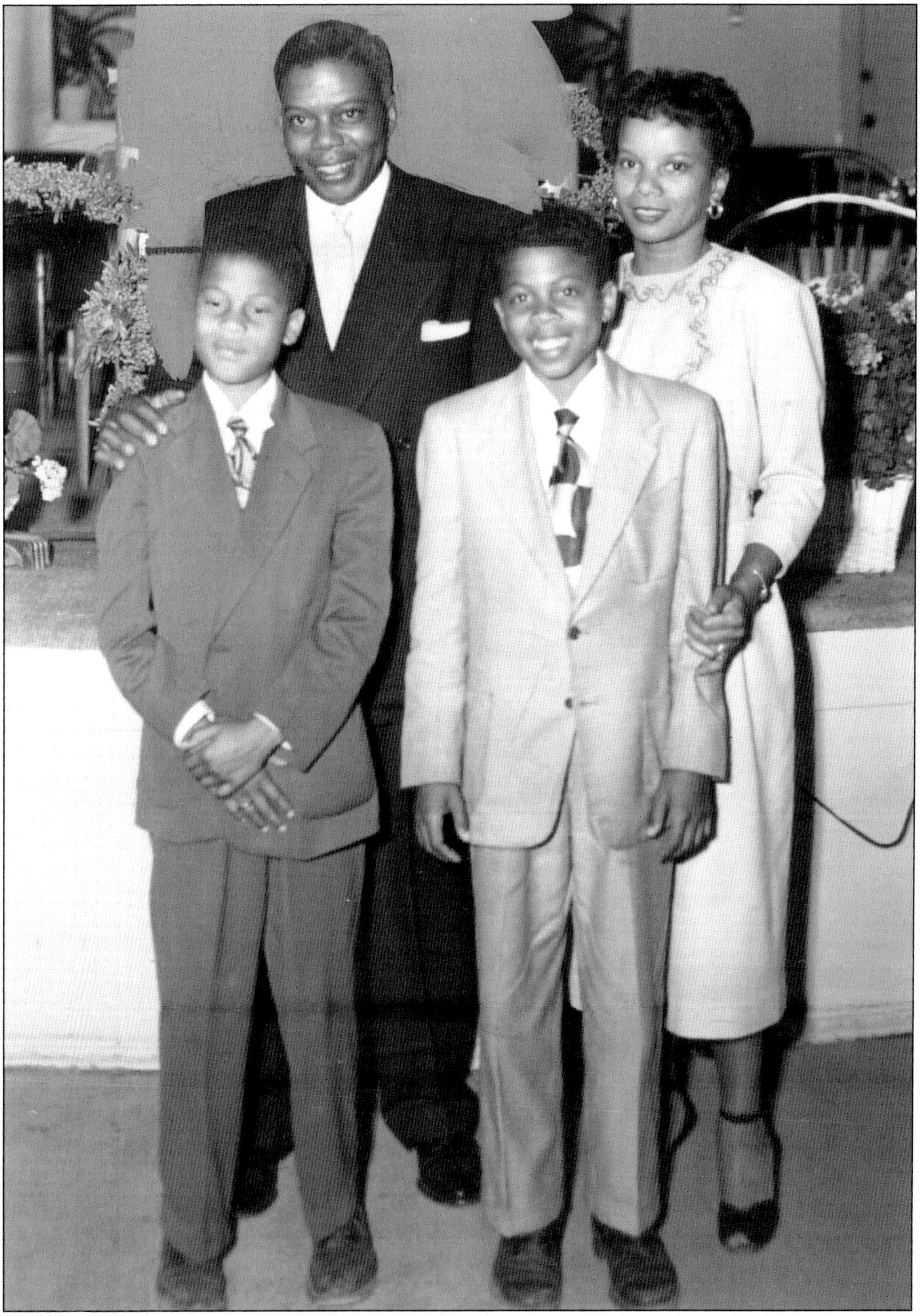

Rev. Haley H. James, seen here with a family his church was assisting in the 1950s, served as minister for Second Baptist Church in the 1940s and later pastored at Good Samaritan Missionary Baptist Church. This image was originally retouched to be used as a headshot. (Courtesy of Vallejo Naval and Historical Museum.)

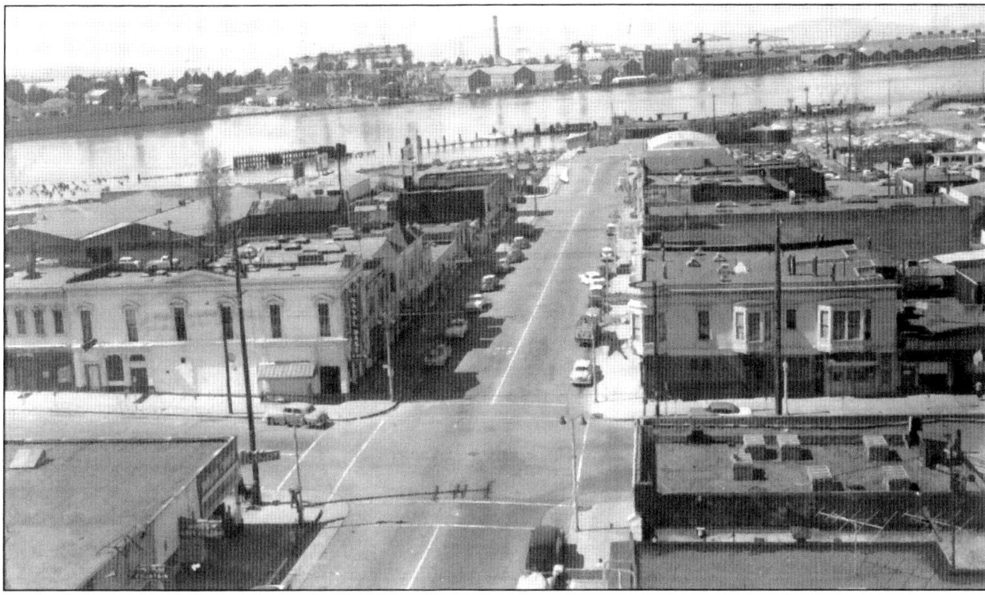

The lower end of Georgia Street and other parts of downtown Vallejo were a Mecca for African American business owners during the 1940s and 1950s. Sailors and civilians looking for entertainment during the height of the Great Migration converged in downtown Vallejo. Popular musical acts, like Lowell Fulsom, who worked at Mare Island and lived in Vallejo during the 1940s, were familiar sights downtown. Other musicians, like Jimmy McCracklin, Bobby "Blue" Bland, Sugar Pie DeSanto, and Etta James, performed at area clubs and dances. The nightspots included the 126 Club, Bud Green's, the Corner Club, Astor House, the Green Lantern, the Tavern, the Knotty Pine, and the Golden Pheasant. (Courtesy of the Boyden collection.)

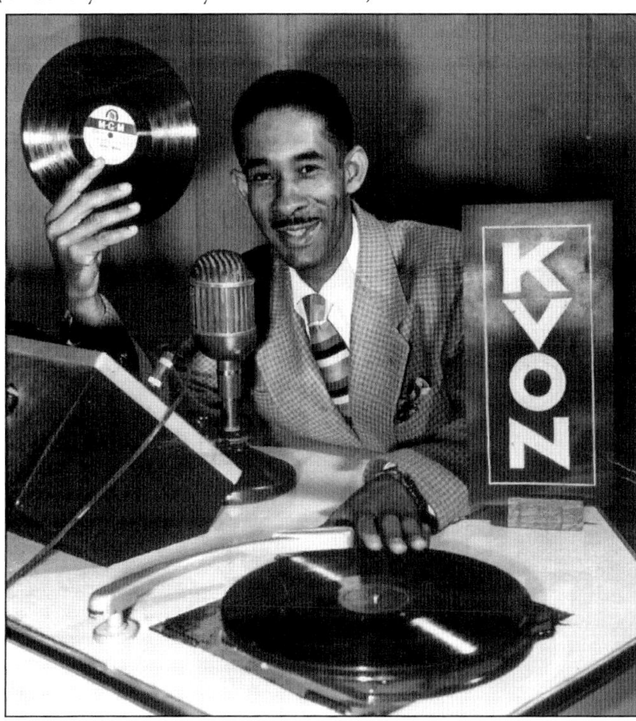

Sy Simon, KVON's first black disc jockey, catered to a variety of musical tastes in the 1940s and early 1950s. From gospel to rock and roll, Simon's weekly show was popular among Vallejo residents. (Courtesy of Haskell Forte.)

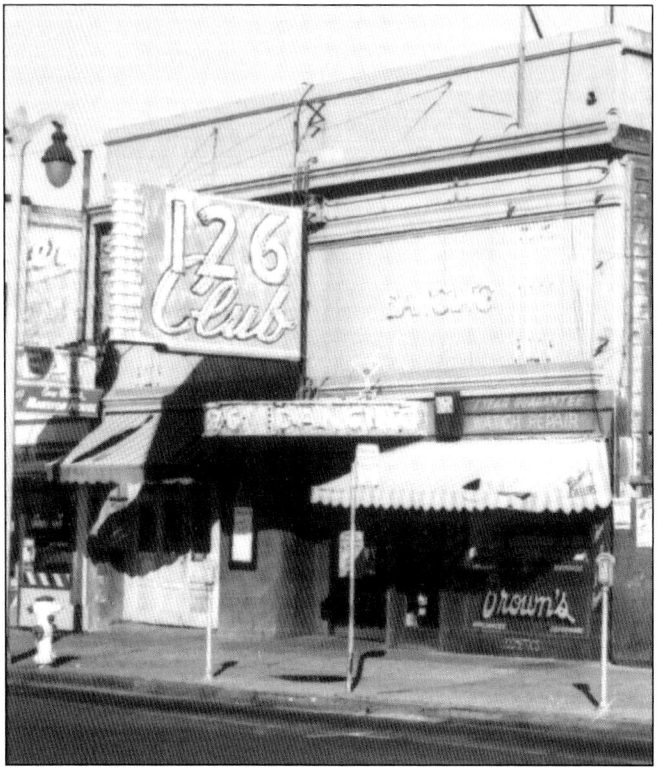

The 126 Club, located at the lower end of Georgia Street, was by far one of the most popular nightspots for Vallejo African Americans in the 1940s and 1950s. This photograph shows the club shortly before it was razed to make way for redevelopment. African Americans owned a number of businesses in downtown Vallejo during the 1940s through 1950s, including restaurants, bars, pool halls, a funeral parlor, beauty salons, and barbershops. (Courtesy of the Vallejo Naval and Historical Museum.)

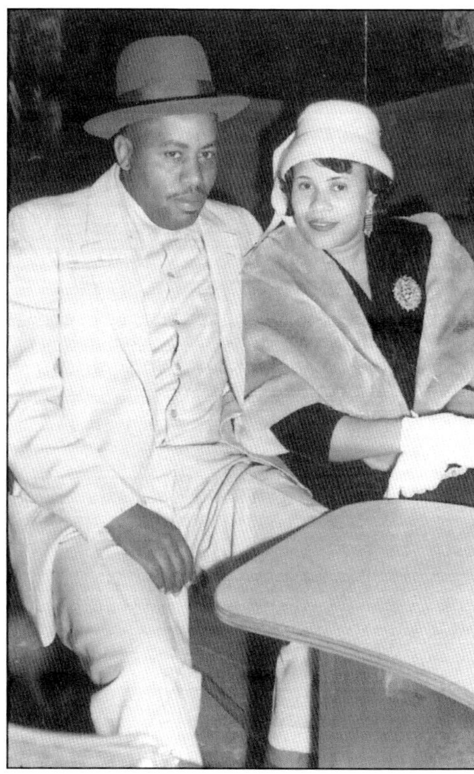

Ninus and Mary Francis "Sweetie" Harris enjoy a night out at the 126 Club in downtown Vallejo. People dressed in their finery to dance the night away in clubs. The Harris family came to Vallejo in the mid-1940s. (Courtesy of Linnie Joiner and Yvonne Johnson.)

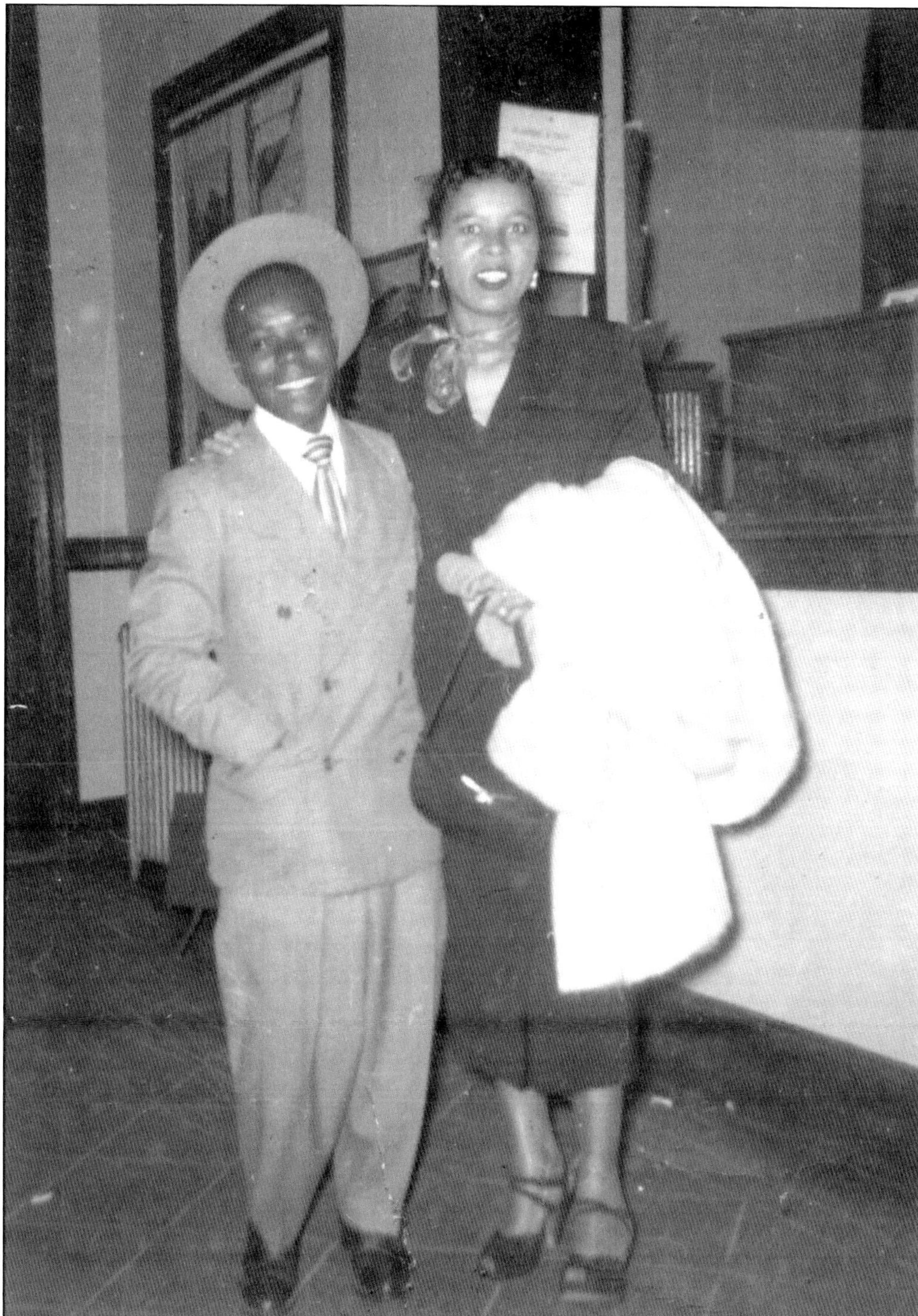

Curtis Wiggins and his date are enjoying a night out in Vallejo during the 1940s. African Americans attended dances at a number of venues throughout Vallejo and surrounding areas, including the Dream Bowl on old Napa Road, where they would hear big bands like the Jimmy Lunceford Orchestra.

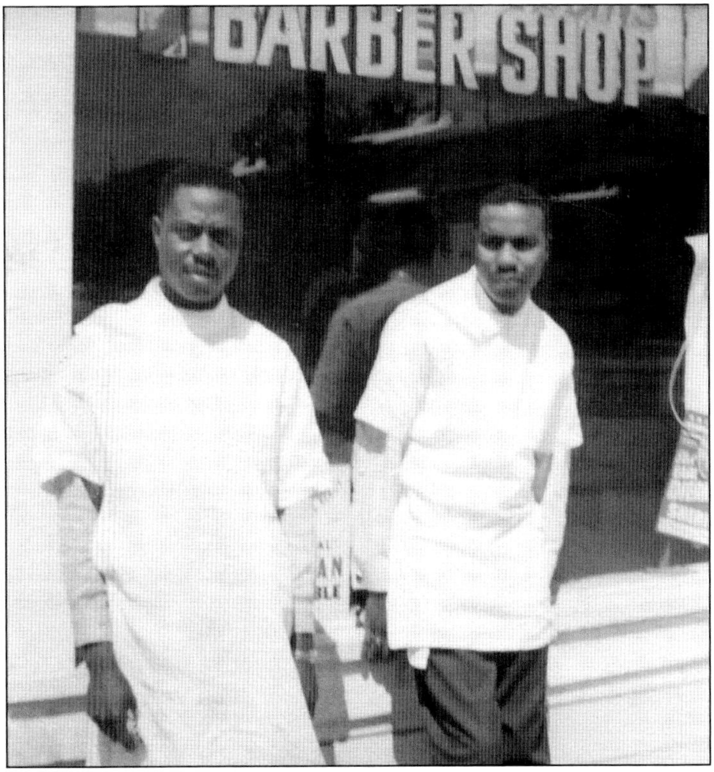

Dan Wroten and Haskell Forte stand outside Wroten's Barber Shop, located in the Hotel Georgia in downtown Vallejo in the late 1940s. After leaving the Navy following the end of World War II, Forte started his barber career in Vallejo, apprenticing under Wroten. African American barbers had long been a part of the business community in downtown Vallejo. In the 1800s, at least five black barbers, including J.R. Landeway and Simon P. Clark, owned barbershops and bathing saloons in downtown Vallejo. (Courtesy of Haskell Forte.)

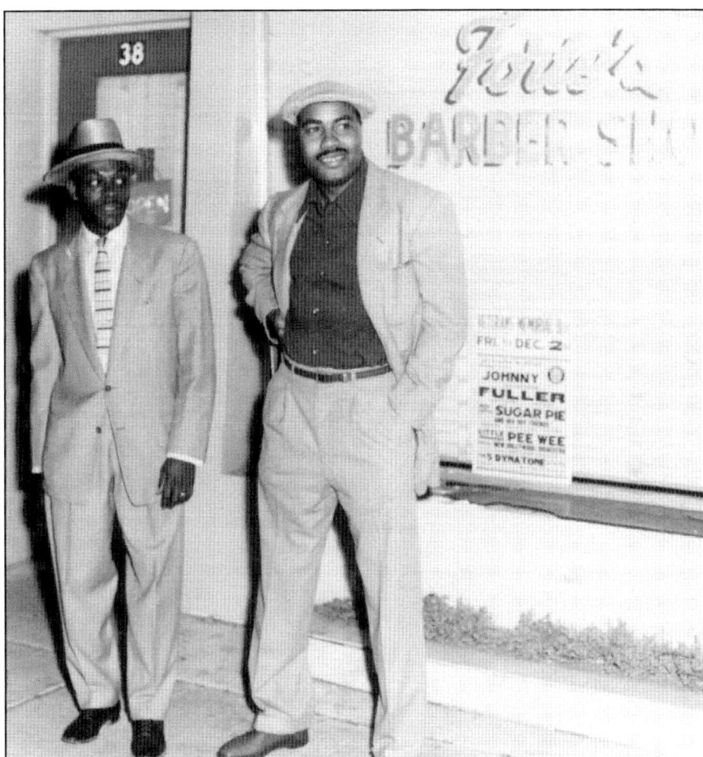

A few years later, Haskell Forte, pictured on the right with an unidentified friend, owned his own barbershop at 35 Georgia Street—at the end of the street. (Courtesy of Haskell Forte.)

During the 1940s, Prince Hall Masons, Firma Lodge No. 27, grew their membership substantially as a result of a burgeoning African American population. In 1946, lodge members purchased the hall from African American Spanish-American War veterans association that built and owned it since 1916. In this 1949 photograph are Firma Lodge No. 27 members, from left to right, (first row) Alvin Logan, Joe Watson, and Walter Freeman; (second row) unidentified, John Edmondson, and Samuel Atwood. (Courtesy of Catherine Fulcher.)

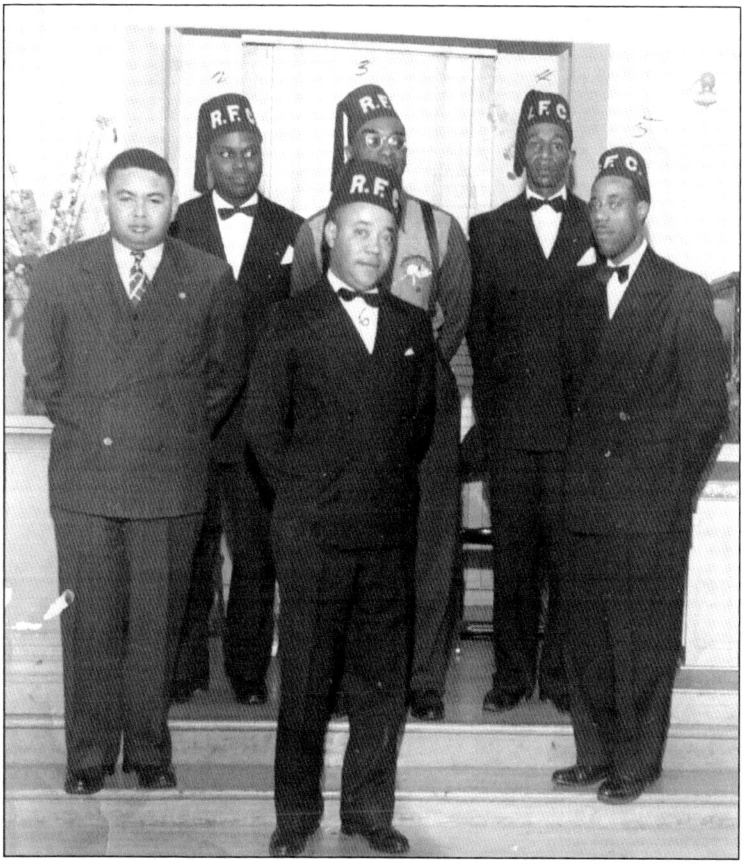

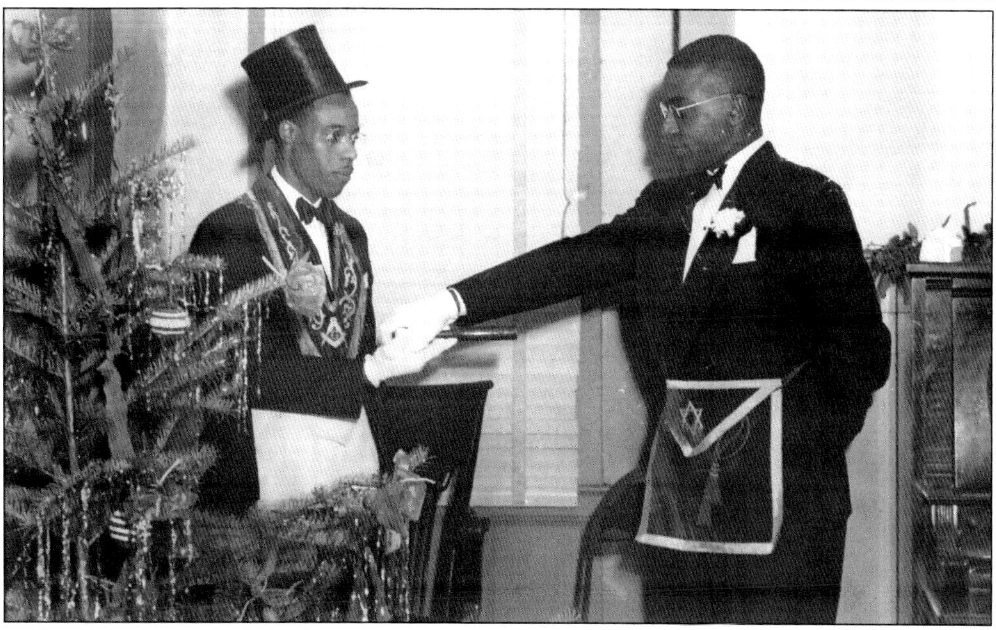

Walter Freeman and John Edmondson install new officers in 1949 during a Masonic ceremony. (Courtesy of Catherine Fulcher.)

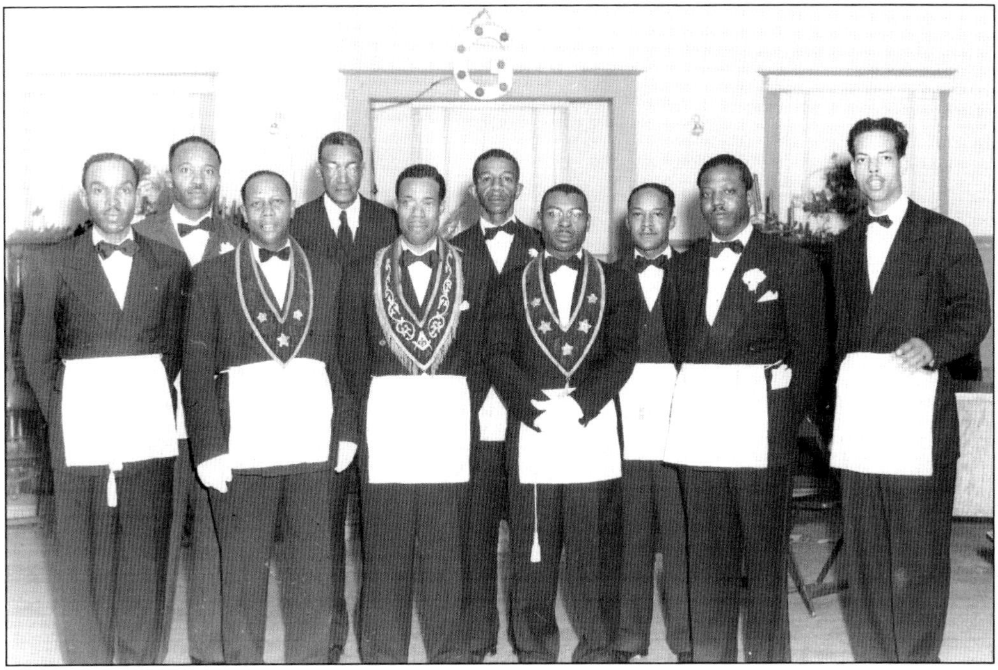

This late-1940s photograph of Firma Lodge No. 27 includes Burrell Brown, Bertram Perry, and Walter Freeman. Out of Firma Lodge No. 27, other lodges and chapters formed, including Fidelus Chapter, Order of Eastern Star in 1923; Amicus Lodge No. 48 and Harmony Court, both organized in 1944; George W. Posey Lodge No. 77 in 1953; and Oriental Chapter in 1953. The George W. Posey Lodge was named after an early member of Firma Lodge No. 27. Posey, a former Buffalo Soldier, moved to Vallejo around 1905. (Courtesy of Emma and Ruth Etta Perry.)

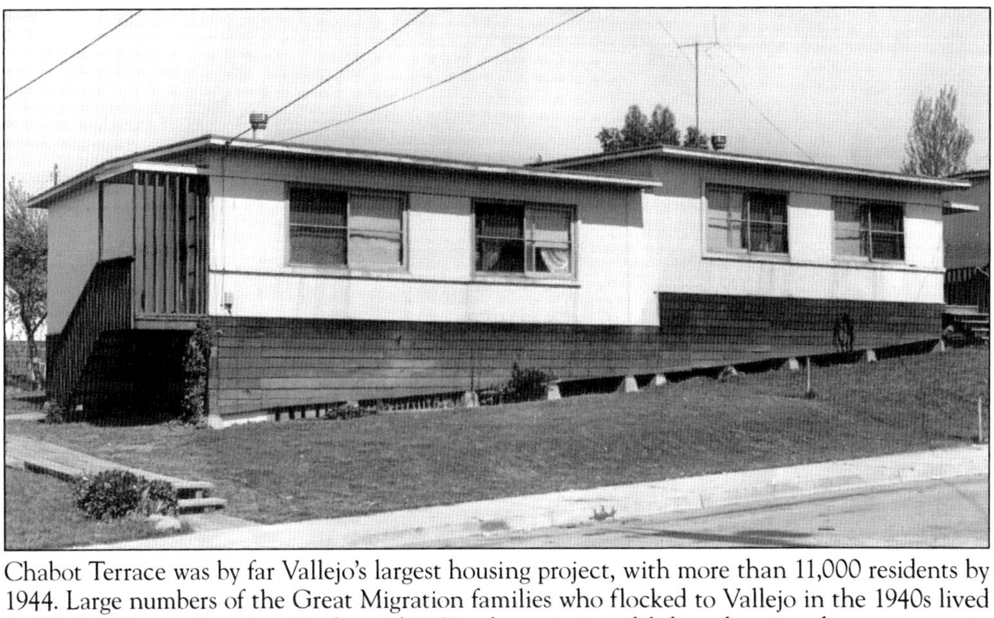

Chabot Terrace was by far Vallejo's largest housing project, with more than 11,000 residents by 1944. Large numbers of the Great Migration families who flocked to Vallejo in the 1940s lived in Chabot Terrace housing. By the mid-1950s, the majority of defense housing that sprang up in Vallejo in the 1940s was gone. Floyd Terrace remained open until 1967. (Courtesy of the Vallejo Naval and Historical Museum.)

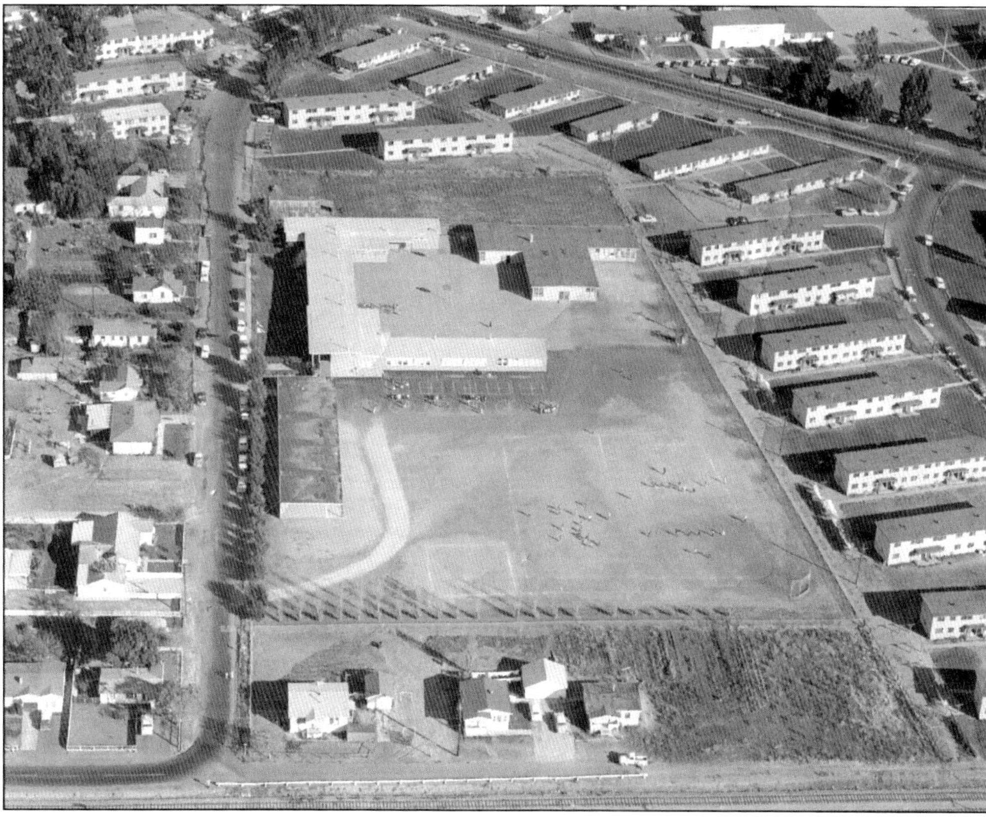

Here is a c. 1962 bird's-eye view of Floyd Terrace and Flosden Elementary School. A Floyd Terrace housing project handbook of the time said that Flosden Elementary School "is within walking distance of all parts of the projects." As for older students, the handbook said, "School buses will be provided for Harry Floyd Terrace children attending junior and senior high school, starting in September 1944. (Courtesy of the author.)

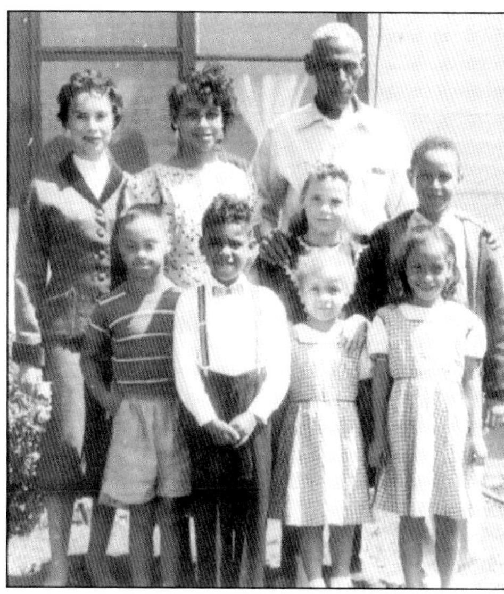

Peter Tholmer; his wife, Dora; their children; and his brother and sister, Frank Henry Tholmer and Emelda Pellabon; moved to California in 1943 from New Orleans. After living in Rodeo for a short time, the family moved to Vallejo and was among the early residents of the Floyd Terrace housing project. Peter Tholmer and his brother Frank were able to find work almost immediately once they moved to Vallejo. During the war, Peter Tholmer worked as a rigger. Following the war, he stayed on at the Navy yard, working as a maintenance man. The Tholmer family included, from left to right, (first row) nephews Paul and Willie Manning, niece Gaynelle Owens, and Regina Tholmer; (second row) Kathleen Autry and Joseph Tholmer; (third row) Theresa, Linda, and Peter Tholmer. (Courtesy of Linda Anderson.)

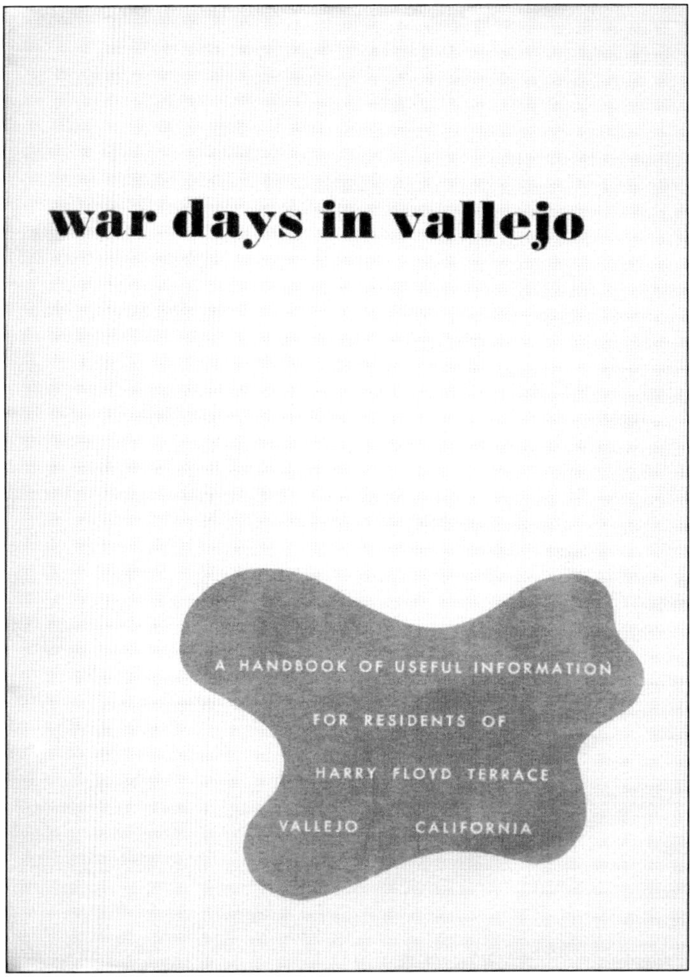

This handbook was given to all new residents of Harry Floyd Terrace housing project when it was built in 1944. Floyd Terrace was named for Harry Floyd, who was a business representative of the Plumbing and Steamfitters Local No. 343 of the American Federation of Labor. He died in July 1942. (Courtesy of Vallejo Naval and Historical Museum.)

Children from the surrounding North Vallejo neighborhoods of Floyd Terrace and Flosden Acres attended Flosden Elementary School on Hobbs Avenue. Built in the 1940s, the school was later turned into People's High School, an alternative high school.

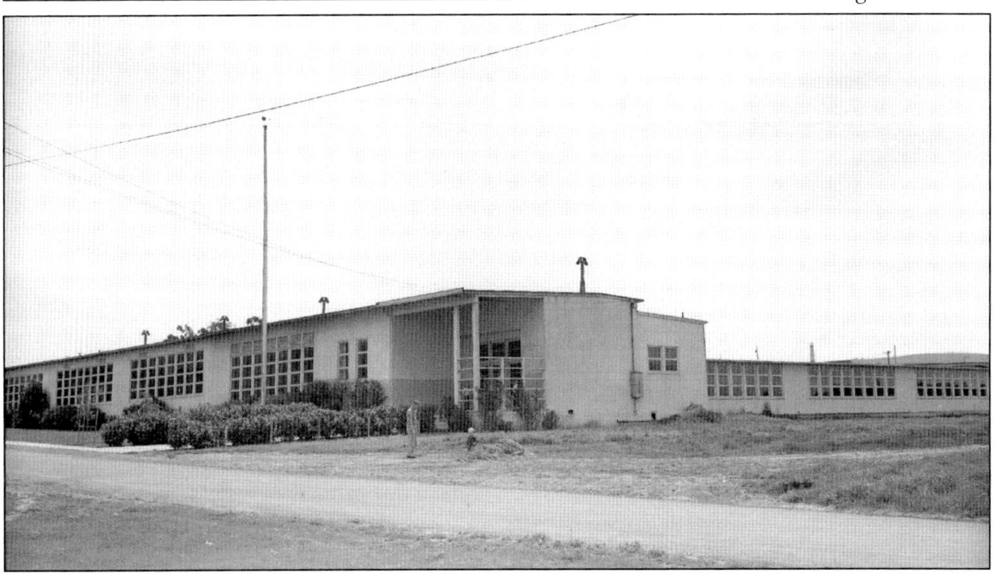

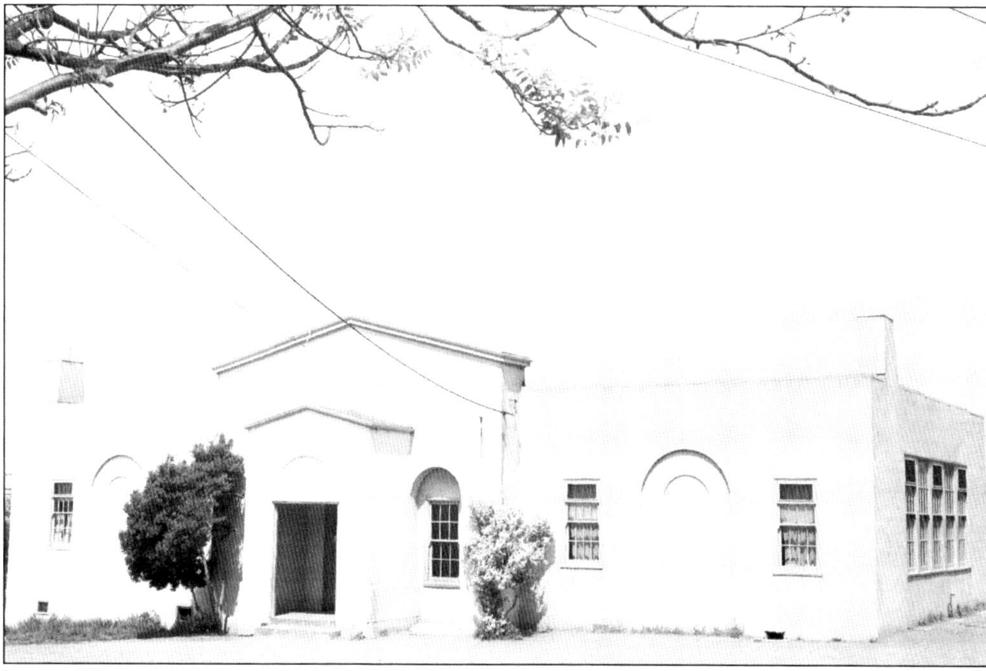

Many African American children who lived in North Vallejo attended this small two-room kindergarten on Holly Street. (Courtesy of the Vallejo Naval and Historical Museum.)

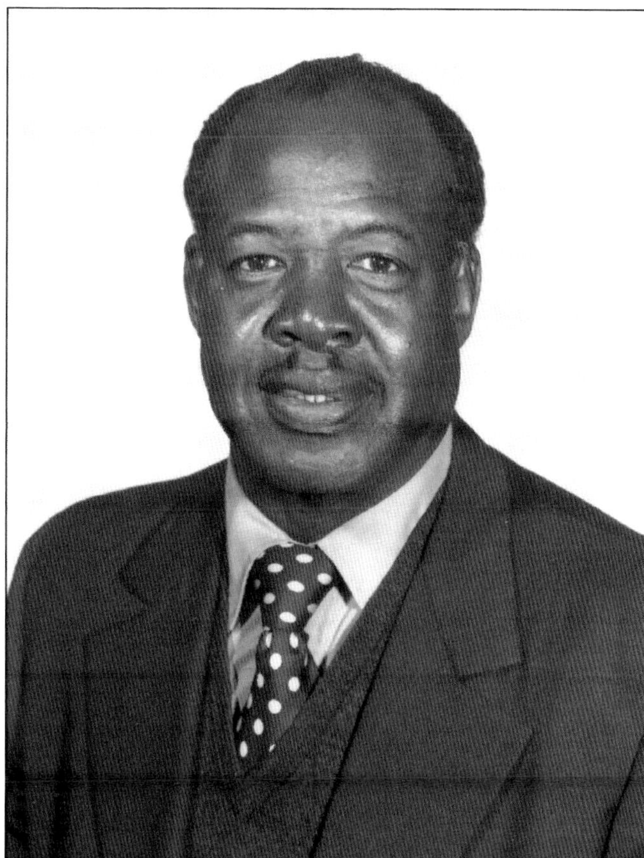

Frank Jackson came to Vallejo in the early 1940s and joined the NAACP shortly after arrival. Later, Jackson became president of the civil rights organization. (Courtesy of Vallejo Naval and Historical Museum.)

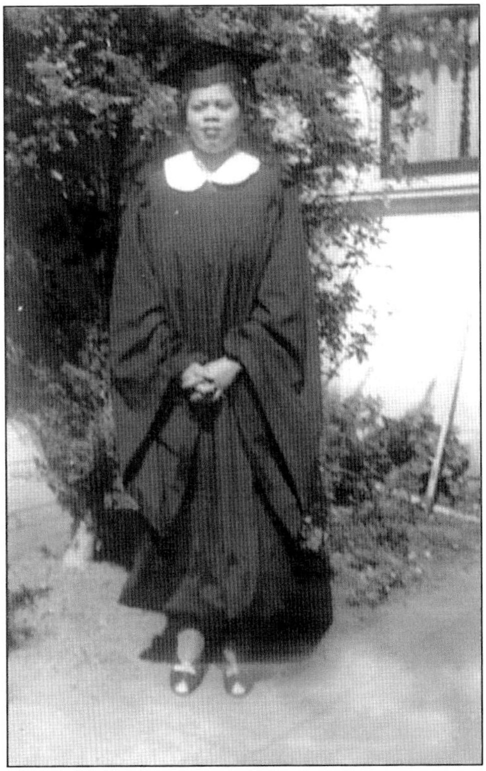

Grace Logan-Patterson, pictured here on the day she graduated from San Francisco State College in 1938, was Vallejo's first African American schoolteacher. Hired in 1949, Logan-Patterson was originally turned down by the Vallejo school district after being told by the city that it was "not ready to hire a Negro." In the 1980s, the Vallejo Unified School District named a South Vallejo elementary school after Logan-Patterson. (Courtesy of Jeannette Mohlson.)

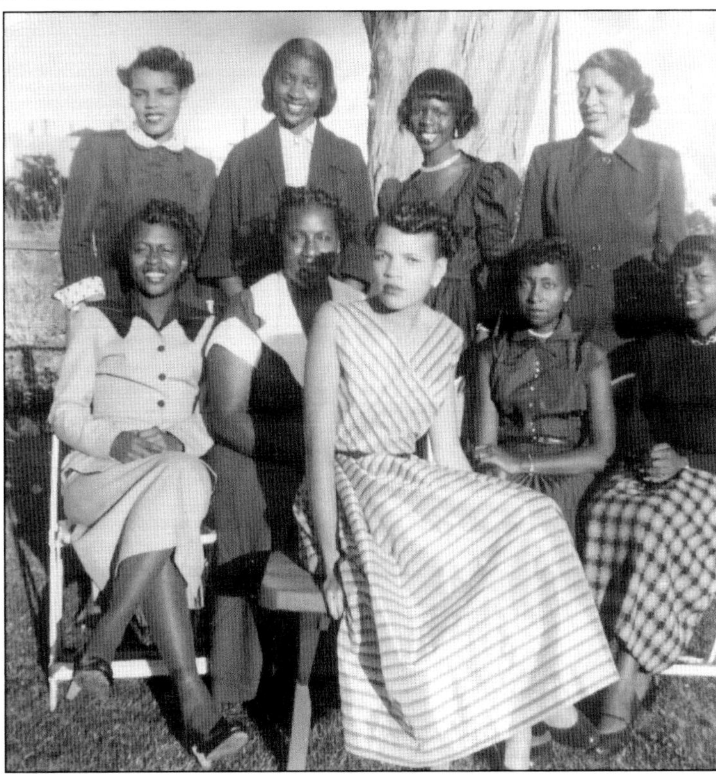

Some members of the 1940s 4UR Girls Club posed for a group shot. The young women were all students at Vallejo High School. Pictured are, from left to right, (sitting) Doris Oliver, Edith Austin, Arthene Day, Eunice Hicks, and Alvina Oliver; (standing) Arlene Day, unidentified, Robbie Henderson, and unidentified. Alvina Oliver, mother of the two Oliver girls pictured, organized the club. The club held dances at Firma Lodge No. 27 at 1209 Georgia and played softball against other clubs in Vallejo. (Courtesy of Robbie Henderson.)

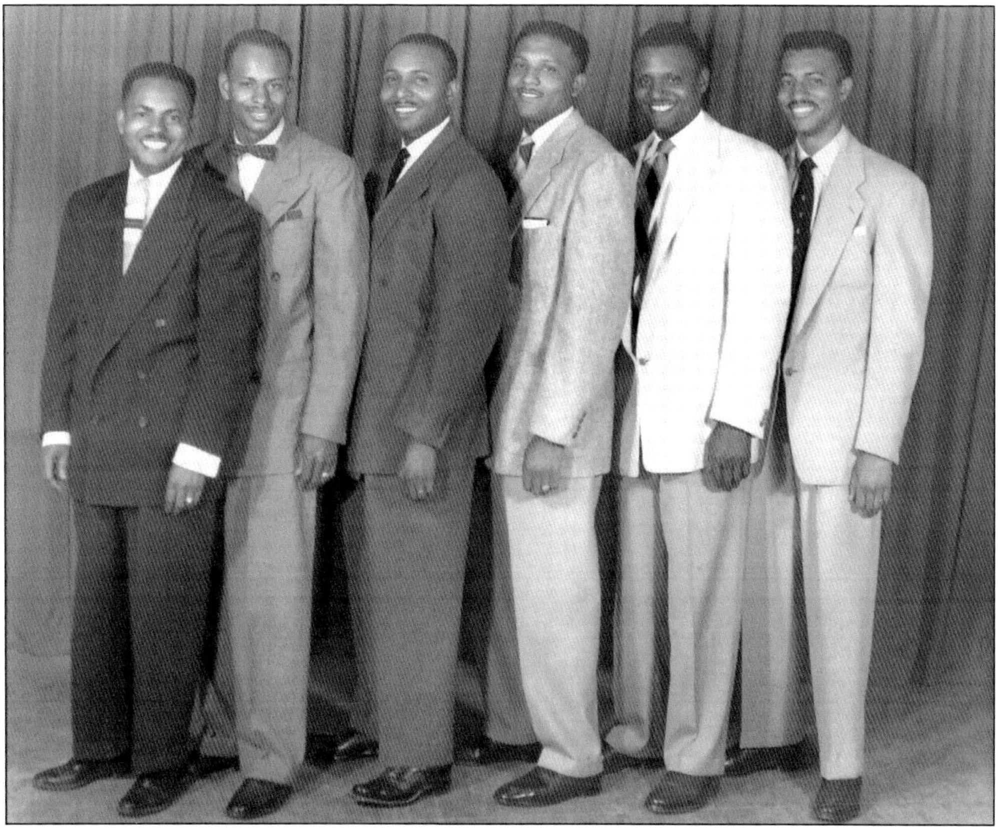

The Brown brothers, including Robert (far left) and Lewis (second from the left), pose for a family portrait. Hailing from Laurel, Mississippi, the brothers started making their way westward in the 1940s. Each brother has lived in Vallejo at some time.

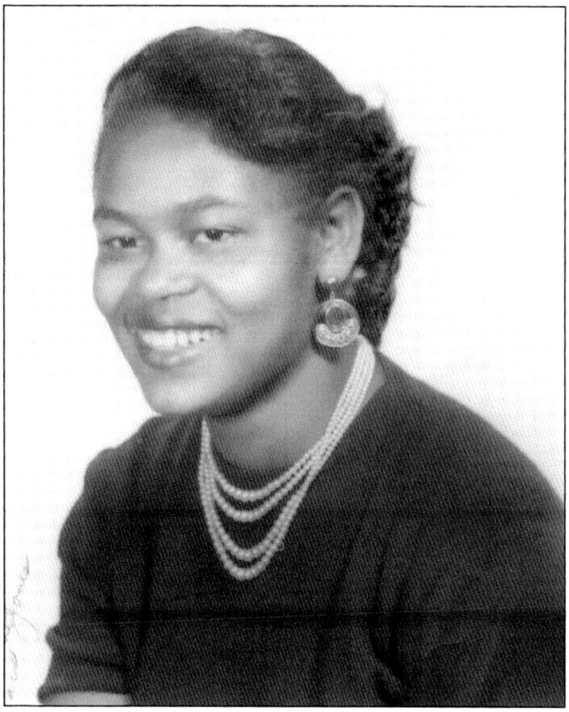

Gertrude Williams was 17 when this photograph was taken at J.C. Penney department store in downtown Vallejo during the 1950s. With a discount coupon for the photograph, she walked from her Arkansas Street home to the store, which was located on Georgia Street. It was not unusual for Vallejo residents—young and old—to walk long distances to get to their destinations. (Courtesy of Gertrude Williams Jones.)

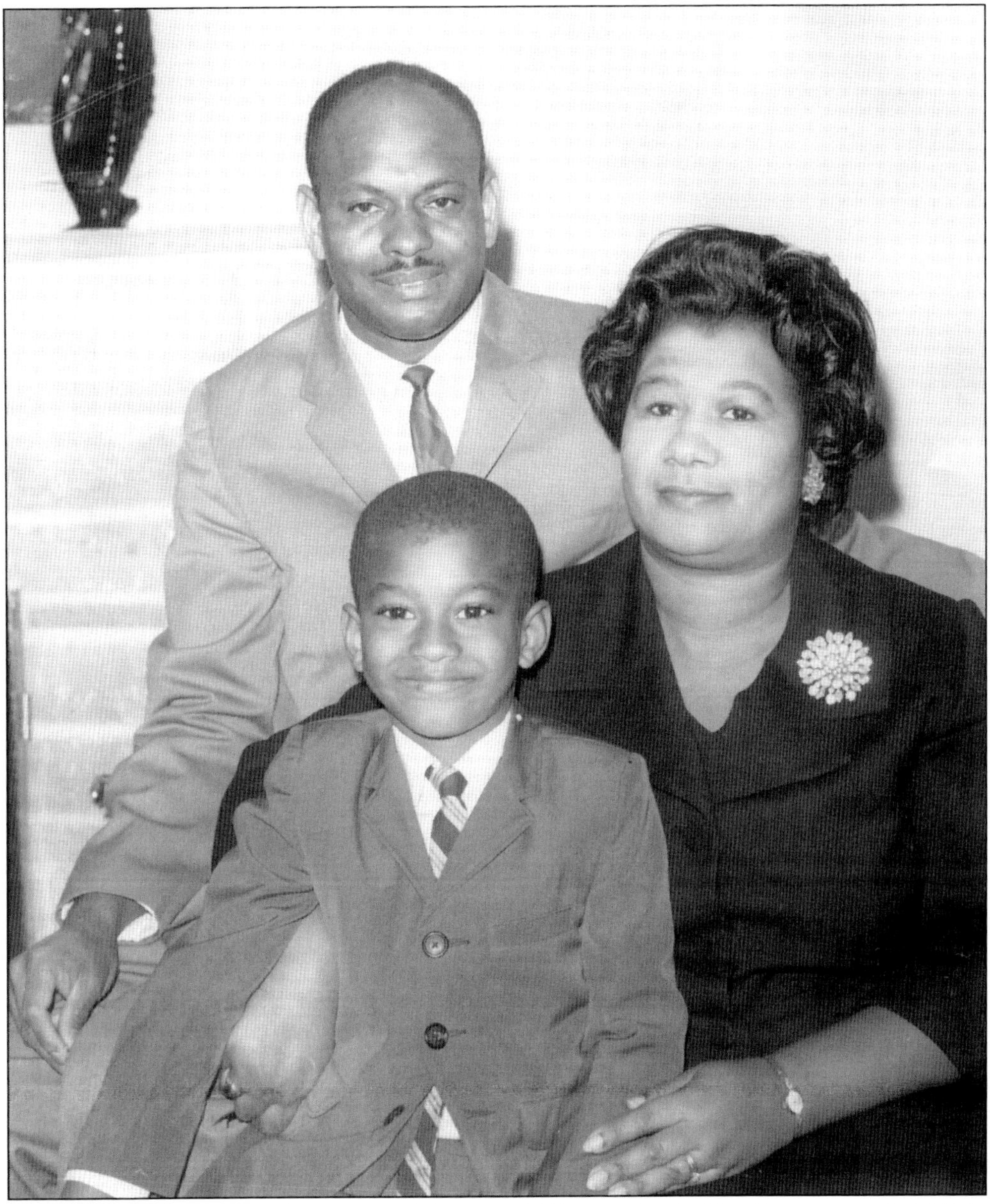

This is an early-1960s family portrait of the Lewis F. Brown family. The Browns met in Vallejo shortly after Mrs. Brown was hired as a kindergarten teacher for Flosden Elementary School. Lewis Brown Jr. sits on his mother's lap. (Courtesy of attorney Lewis F. Brown.)

Three

Creating Community

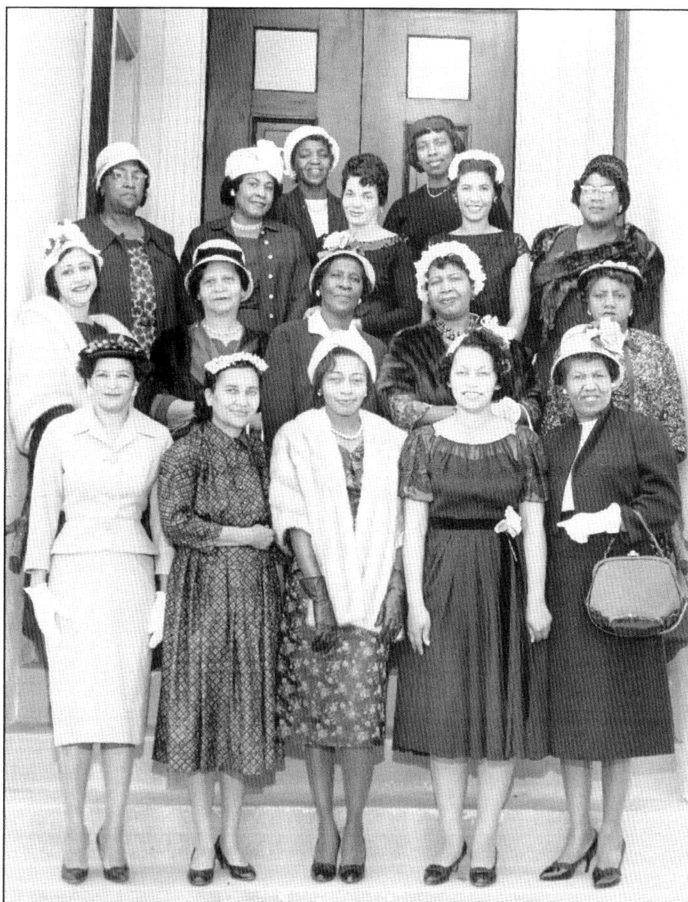

In this early-1960s William Banks photograph, members of the Vallejo chapter of the National Council of Negro Women stand proudly in front of Kyles Temple AME Zion Church. From left to right are (first row) Almada Gales, unidentified, Jesse Jones, Lucy Chatmon, and Queen Logan; (second row) Grace Sibley, Anna Hill, two unidentified women, and Maude James; (third row) Mamie Williams, two unidentified women, Sue King, and unidentified; (fourth row) unidentified and Millie Watson. The Vallejo chapter was chartered in the 1950s. (Courtesy of Verlady Banks.)

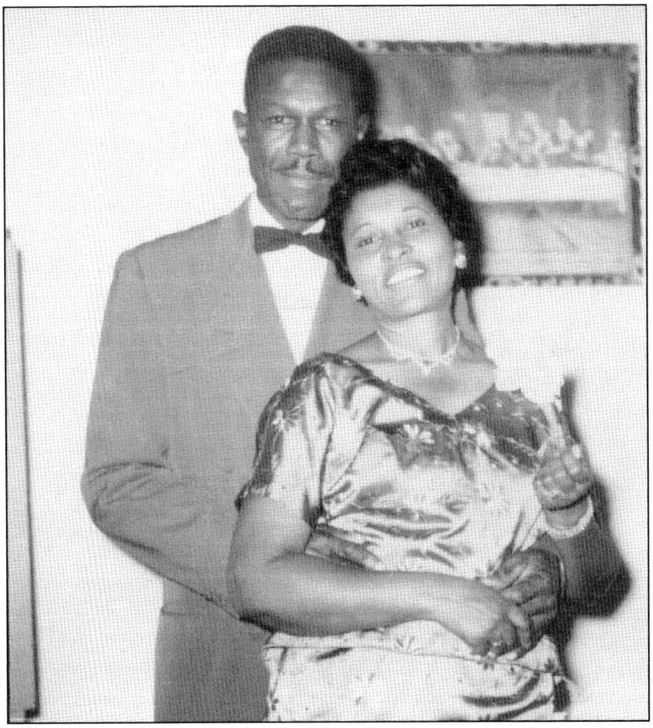

Georgia H. Brooks Solomon was one of the local African American photographers who helped illustrate the Great Migration story of the 1940s through the 1960s. A schoolteacher who worked in the East Bay, she lived on Teton Street in Chabot in the 1940s. *Vallejo Observer* publisher Arthur Scott also used his camera to tell the story of African Americans in Vallejo during the 1940s and 1950s.

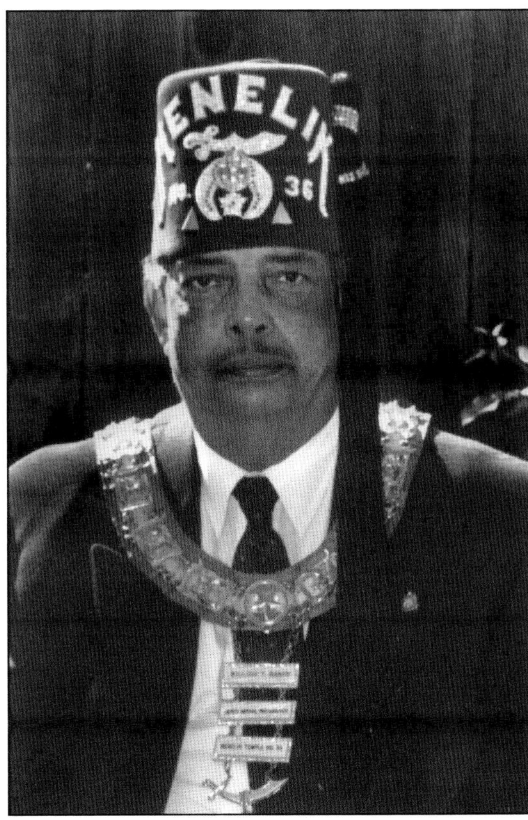

In the 1950s and 1960s, Williams Banks, with camera in hand, was a familiar sight at African American social events in Vallejo. The Memphis, Tennessee, native was the official photographer for local fraternal orders and the It Club, which sponsored cotillion balls for many years in the 1960s and early 1970s. (Courtesy of Verlady Banks.)

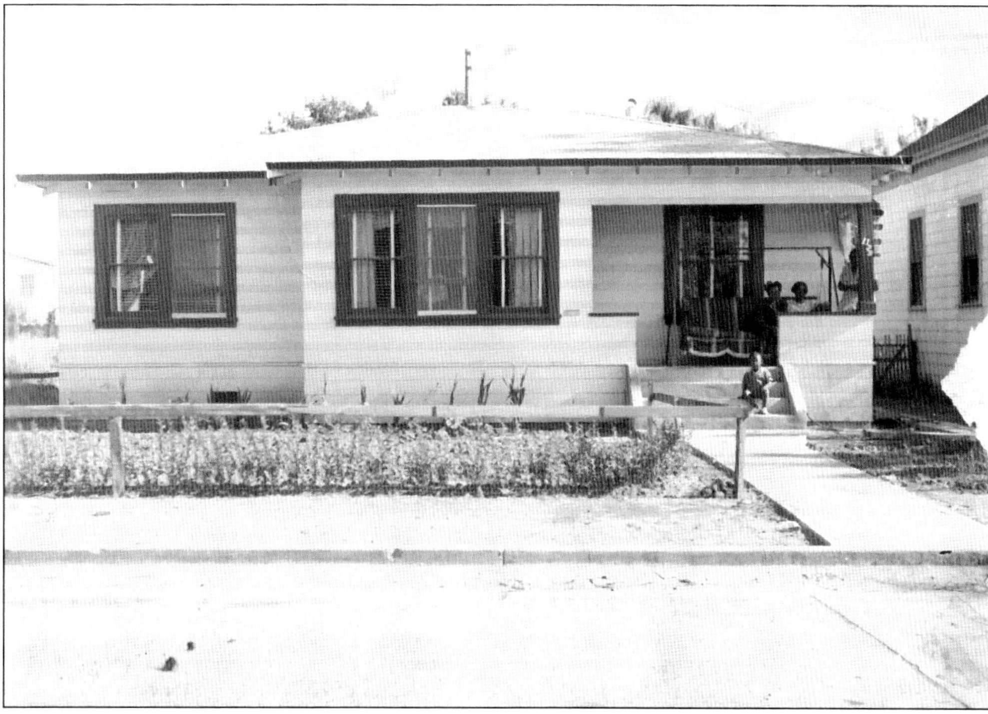

Here is Clara Pulley's Louisiana Street home. (Courtesy of the Boyden collection.)

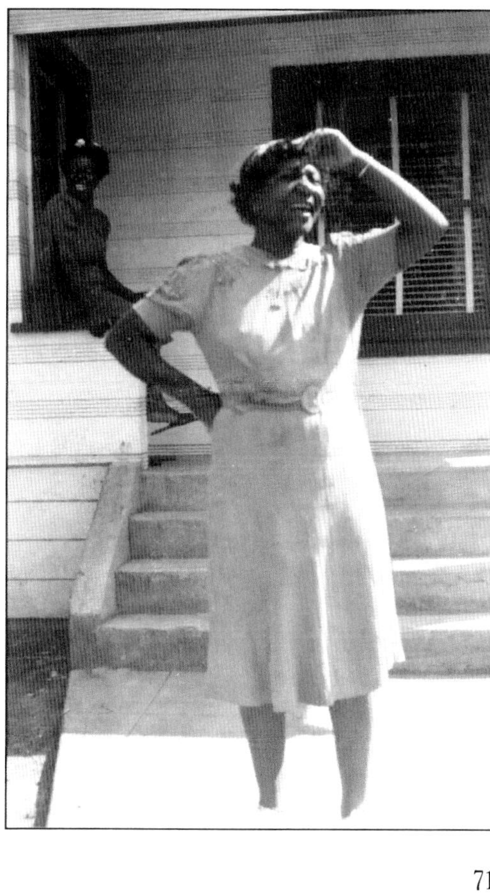

In the 1930s and after, Clara Pulley and her husband, Oscar, stayed in the 1100 block of Louisiana Street right off Broadway Street. This Vallejo neighborhood was one of a few enclaves built for and by African Americans between World War I and World War II. Other black neighborhoods included those near the old Kyles Temple AME Zion Church at Illinois Street and Sonoma Boulevard and the area near the Prince Hall Masonic Hall, Firma Lodge No. 27 at 1209 Georgia Street. Around the turn of the 20th century, most African Americans lived in downtown Vallejo. (Courtesy of the Boyden collection.)

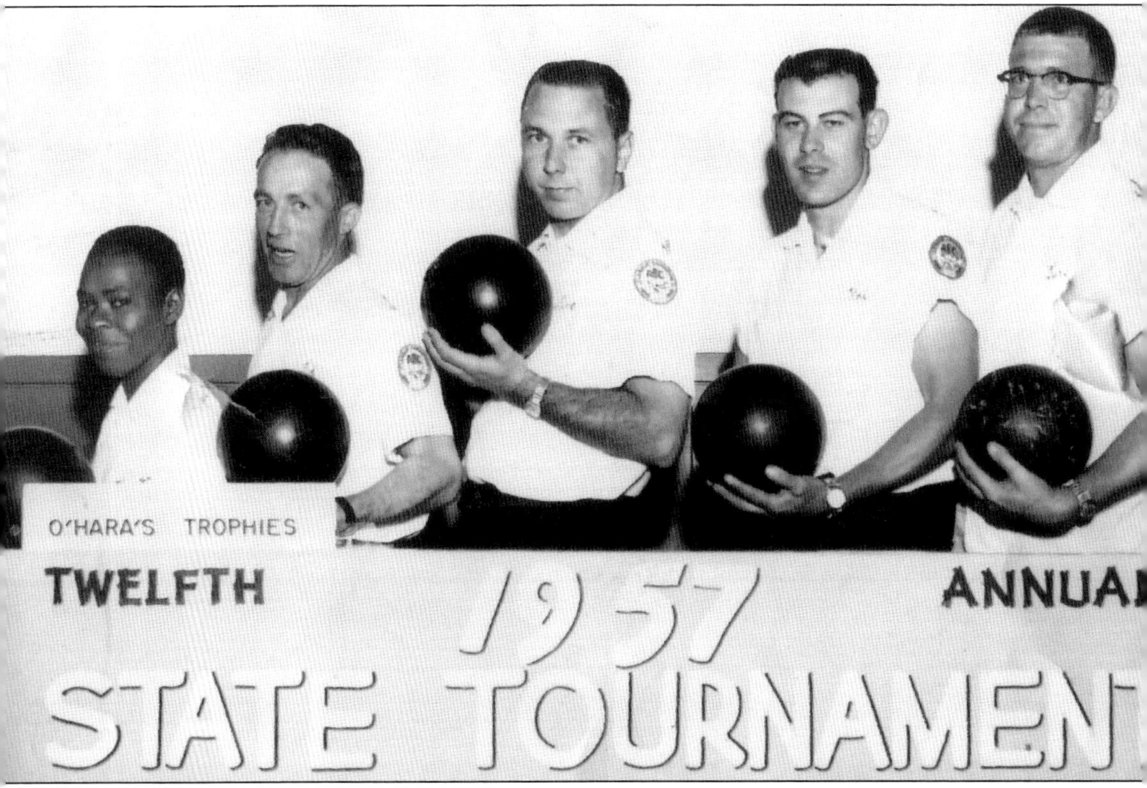

Curtis Wiggins, left, loved to bowl, but prior to the early 1950s, African Americans were banned from using Vallejo bowling lanes. Wiggins, a native of Missouri, did not let bigotry deter him. He traveled to Richmond and other Bay Area cities where African Americans were welcomed in bowling establishments. By the late 1950s, Vallejo's bowling lanes were integrated and Wiggins brought his bowling skills to the city. Pictured here with a Vallejo bowling league, Wiggins was named one of the top bowlers in Vallejo by a local bowling association in the early 1970s. (Courtesy of Curtis Thomas.)

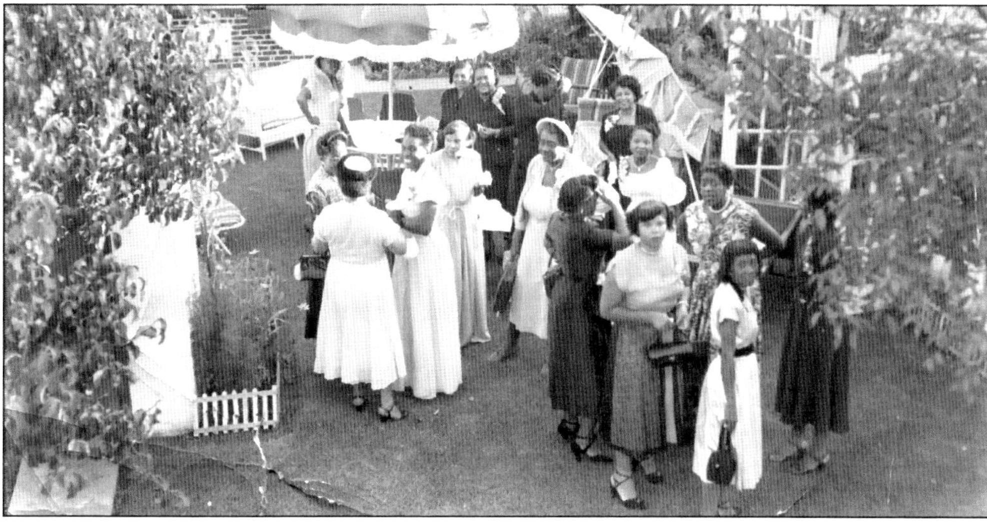

This photograph by Georgia H. Brooks was taken in the mid-1950s. Garden parties and teas were popular in the 1950s. Brooks, whose last name later became Solomon, was a much sought-after photographer in Vallejo during from 1940s through 1960s. She photographed social clubs and church events, especially those of Second Baptist Church where she was a member. (Courtesy of the Vallejo Naval and Historical Museum.)

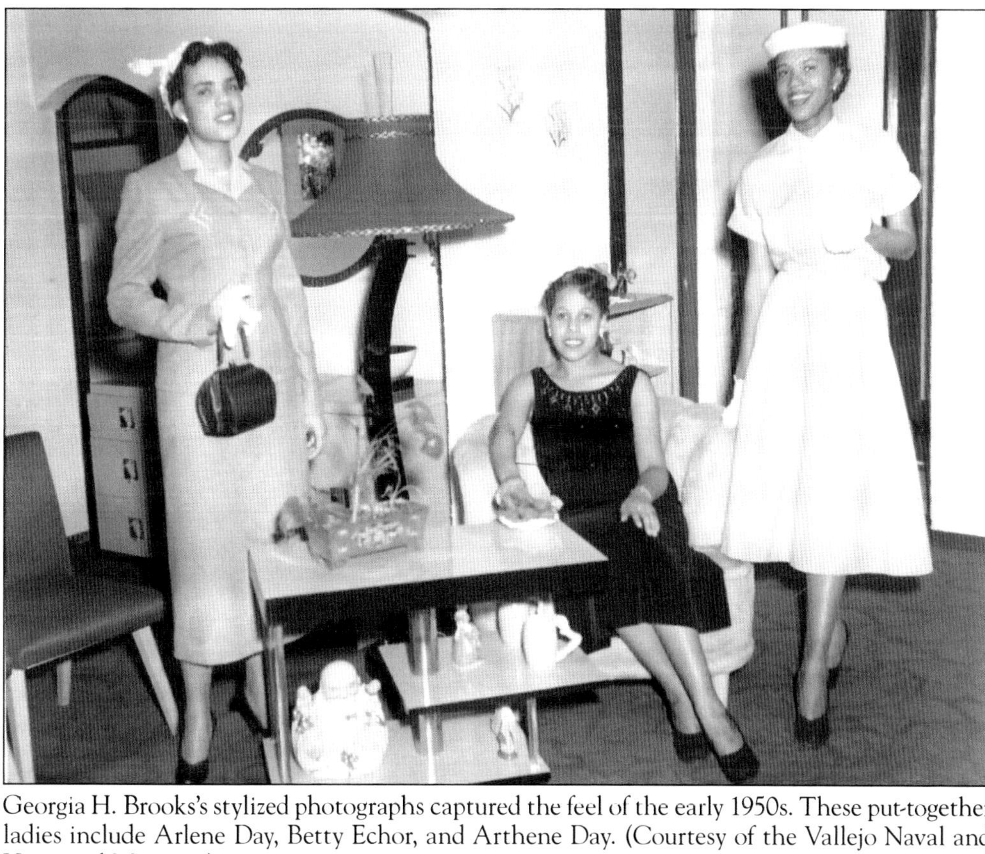

Georgia H. Brooks's stylized photographs captured the feel of the early 1950s. These put-together ladies include Arlene Day, Betty Echor, and Arthene Day. (Courtesy of the Vallejo Naval and Historical Museum.)

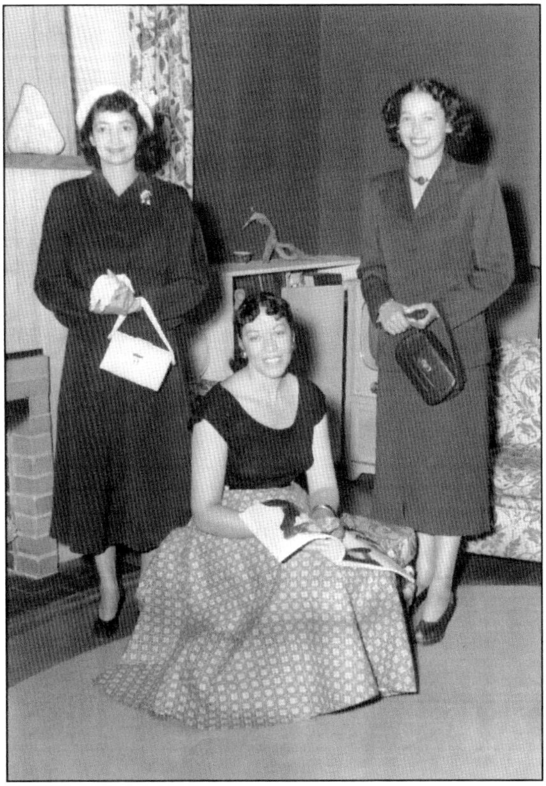

Yet another classic Georgia H. Brooks photograph shows Willie Bob Hill, on the left. Striking fashionable poses, the other two women are unidentified. Georgina H. Brooks resided on Teton Street in Chabot Terrace in the 1940s. (Courtesy of the Vallejo Naval and Historical Museum.)

Members of the Vallejo junior branch of the NAACP prepare for a Vocational Guidance Workshop at Vallejo Junior College—then located on Nebraska Street—in August 1951. Grace Logan-Patterson served as youth adviser of the NAACP youth group. Students included, from left to right, (first row) William Williams, Susie Hicks, and Robert Lavow; (second row) Norman Brown, Pearlie Tilman, Tomelia Williams, Dolores Owens, and Ella May Smith. (Courtesy of the Vallejo Naval and Historical Museum.)

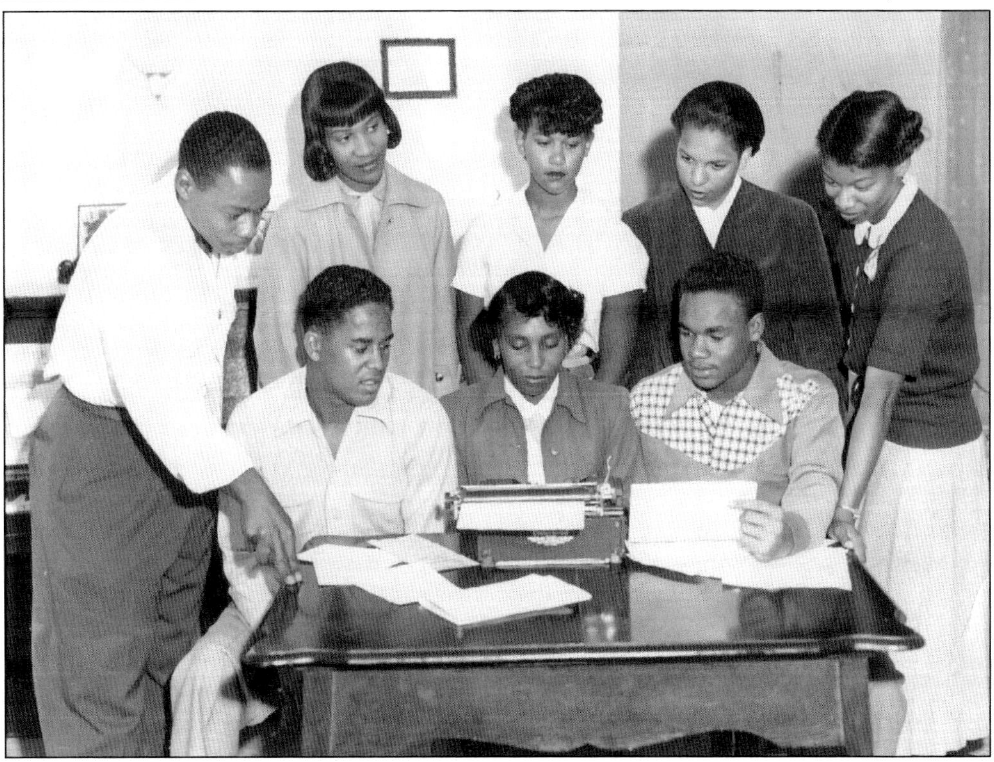

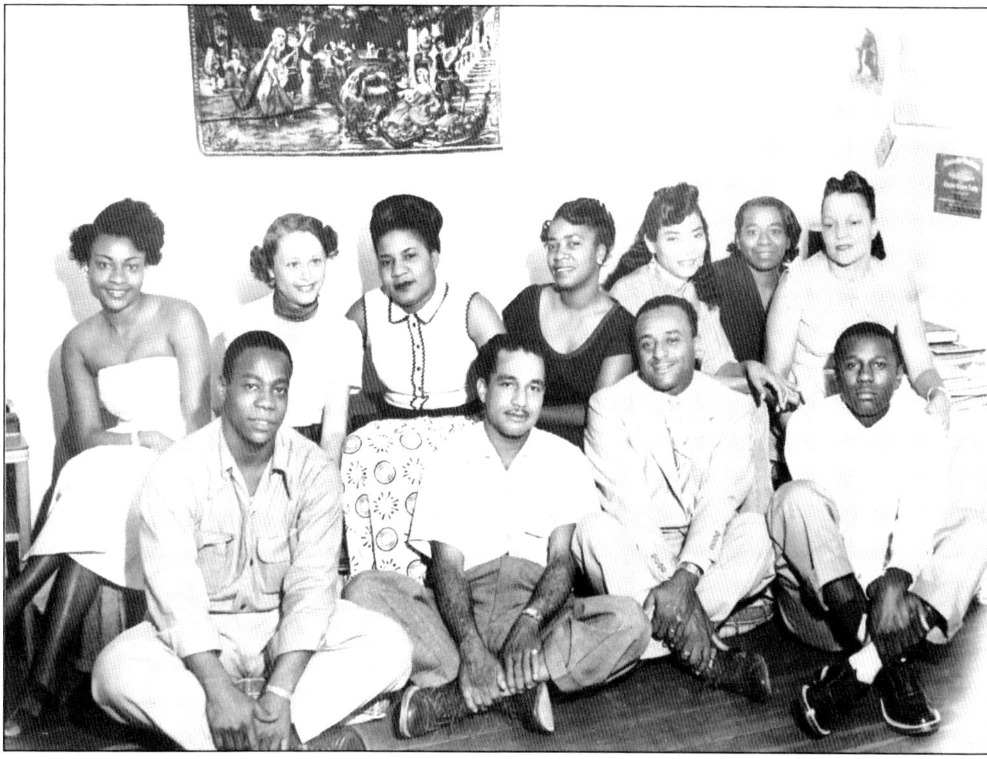

In this November 1952 photograph, a young group of Vallejo residents appears relaxed and ready to socialize at an NAACP event. From left to right are (first row) Norman Brown, Clarence Robinson, DuWane Hill, and Earl Smith; (second row) Ann Hill and Corinne Smith, fifth from the left. (Courtesy of the Vallejo Naval and Historical Museum)

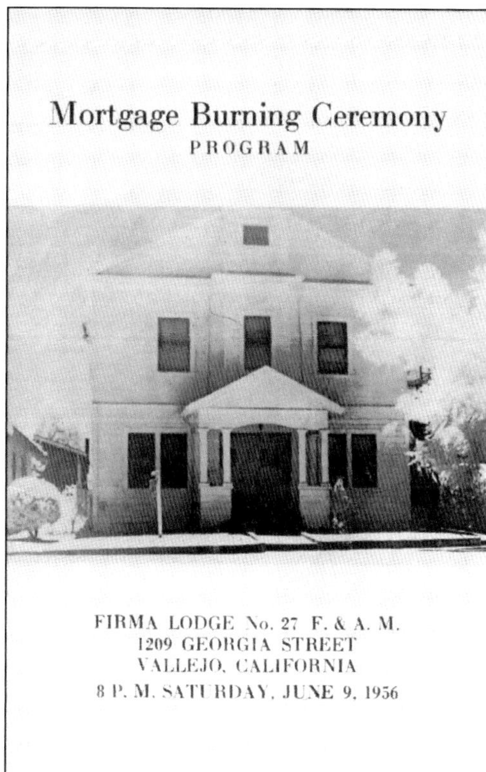

Mortgage Burning Ceremony
PROGRAM

FIRMA LODGE No. 27 F. & A. M.
1209 GEORGIA STREET
VALLEJO, CALIFORNIA
8 P. M. SATURDAY, JUNE 9, 1956

In 1956, Prince Hall Masons, Firma Lodge No. 27 held a mortgage-burning ceremony 10 years after purchasing the two-story building from the veterans and auxiliary hall association. The association represented the African American Spanish-American War veterans who built the lodge around 1916. The Masons, as well as other local fraternal orders, had met in the lodge hall since 1918. (Courtesy of Catherine Fulcher.)

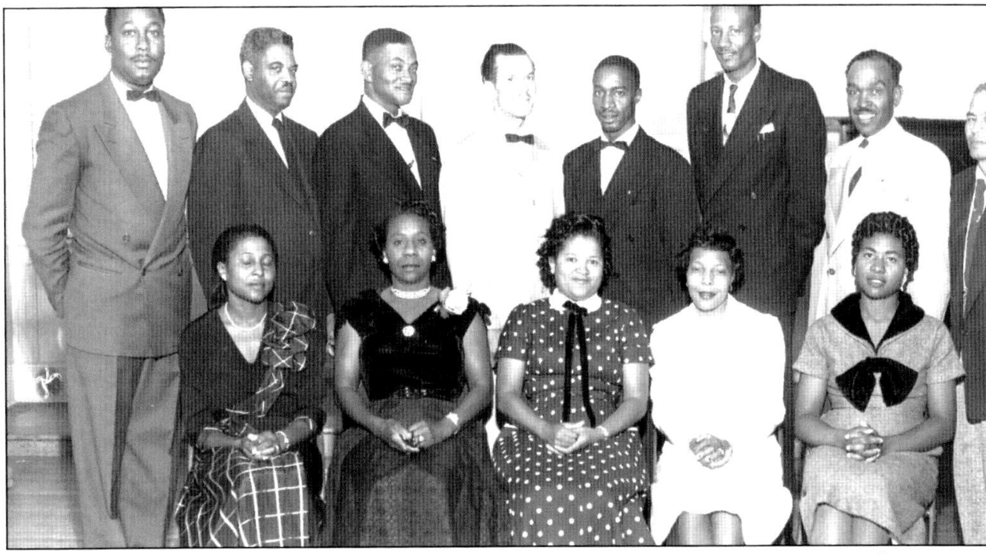

This 1950s photograph includes both Masons and members of the Eastern Star chapter. For many years, Frank Boone (standing, second from the right) served as historian for both the local and state lodges. In 1954, Firma Lodge No. 27 launched Prince Hall Credit Union No. 3. The credit union directors were Peter Larrieau and Lloyd Murray. (Courtesy of the Vallejo Naval and Historical Museum.)

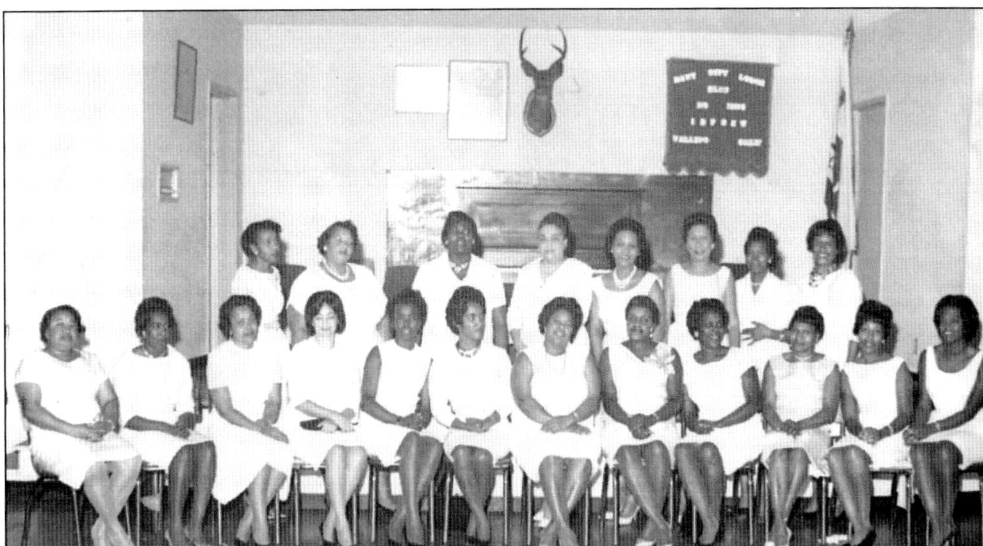

Benevolent societies have long played a role in the Vallejo African American community. Adele B. Ashford Temple No. 903, the female auxiliary of the local African American Elks Lodge, was established in the 1940s. This 1965 photograph of the installation ceremonies of the Adele B. Ashford Temple 903 includes a number of prominent Vallejo women who were founding members of the organization. From left to right are (first row) Josie Johnson, trustee; Della Stuman; Vera Toney; Bobbie Hill; Bessie Daney; Geneva Writt; Hazel Owens, daughter ruler; Kathryn Mathews; Leonna Sutton; Ethel Garner; Uldine Wroten; Ollie Jones; and Jesse Williams; (second row) McGilt on; Willie Mae Singleton, Maybelle Blake; Luthermae Adams; Ollie O. Cross; Mary Stephens; Leah Fuller; and Eva Williams. (Courtesy of the Vallejo Naval and Historical Museum.)

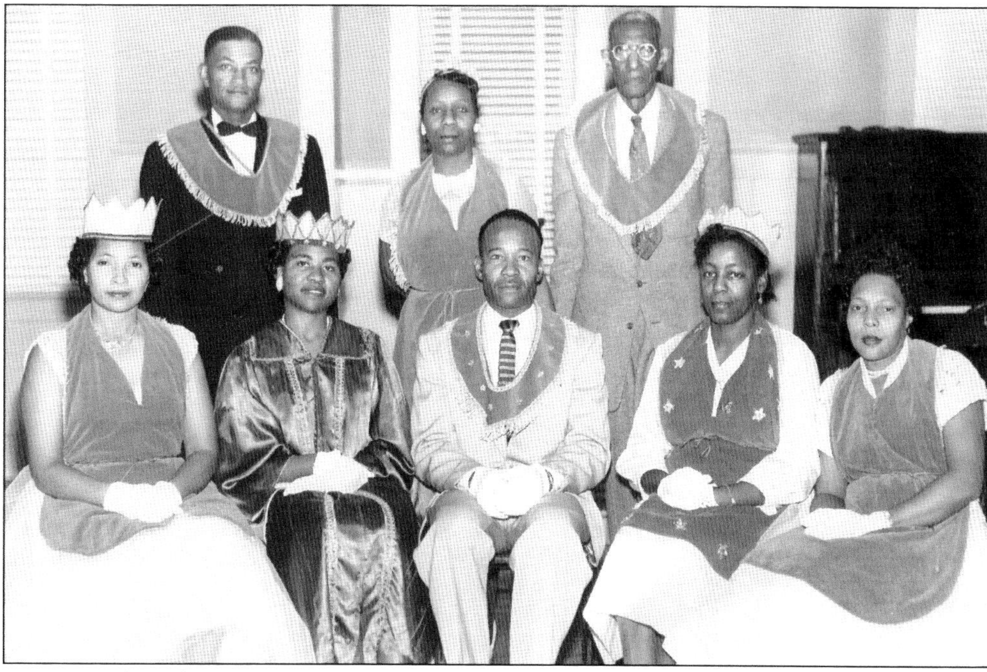

Heroines of Jericho, Harmony Court No. 18 was yet another group that met at 1209 Georgia Street. (Courtesy of the Vallejo Naval and Historical Museum.)

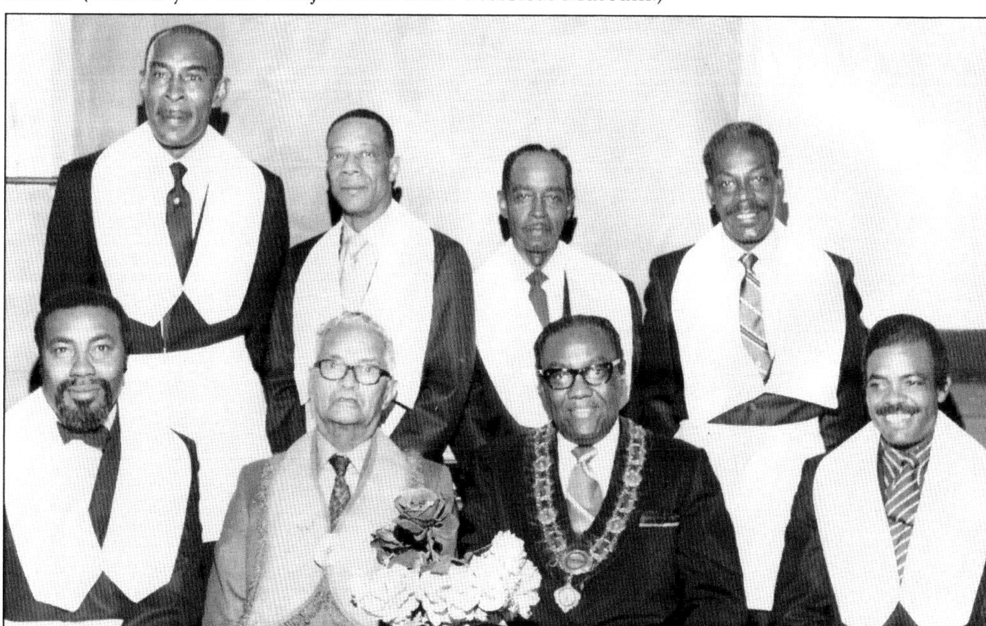

The Grand United Order of Odd Fellows formed a new chapter in Vallejo in the 1960s. In this photograph, the new officers included, from left to right, (sitting) Haskell Forte, president; C. Blackwell, district grand director; Hadley J. Simmons, Los Angeles district director; and William R. Neal Jr., vice president; (standing) Frank Dixon, secretary; Earl E. Harris, assistant secretary; Raymond E. Johnson, treasurer; and Malcolm Whaley, chaplain. In 1913, the Grand United Order of Odd Fellows, El Dorado Lodge No. 9429 was organized in Vallejo. (Courtesy of Haskell Forte.)

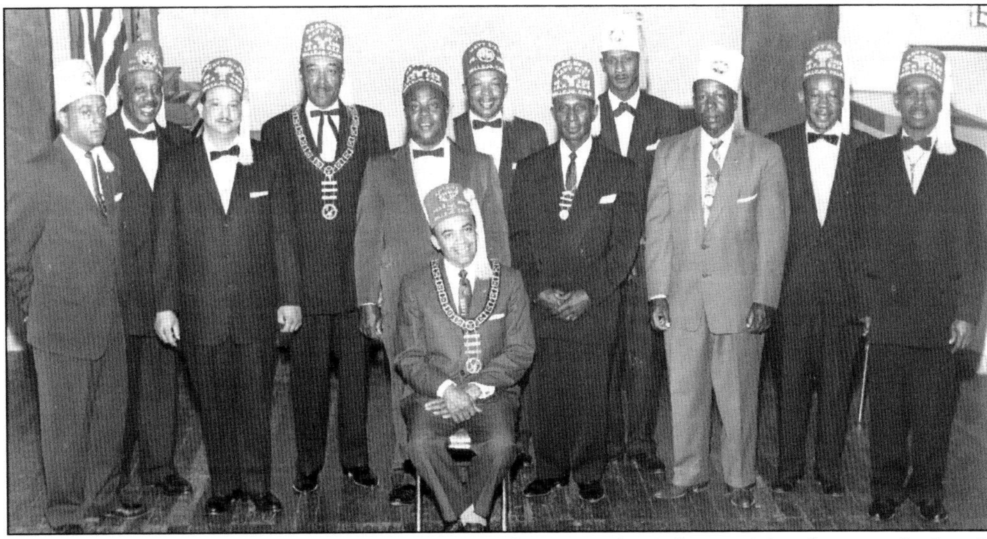

Members of the Navy City Lodge No. 1268 are shown in this July 21, 1961, photograph shortly after being installed. The Elks Lodge was then located in downtown Vallejo at 208 Georgia Street. Seated is Woodrow Tatum, exalted ruler. Standing from left to right are DuWane Hill, Jerry Martin, Louis Wiley, Charles Williams, Donald Woods, James Garner, Clyde Stephens, James McGee, Ashley Jones, Cornelius Toney, and John Dupar. (Courtesy of the Vallejo Naval and Historical Museum.)

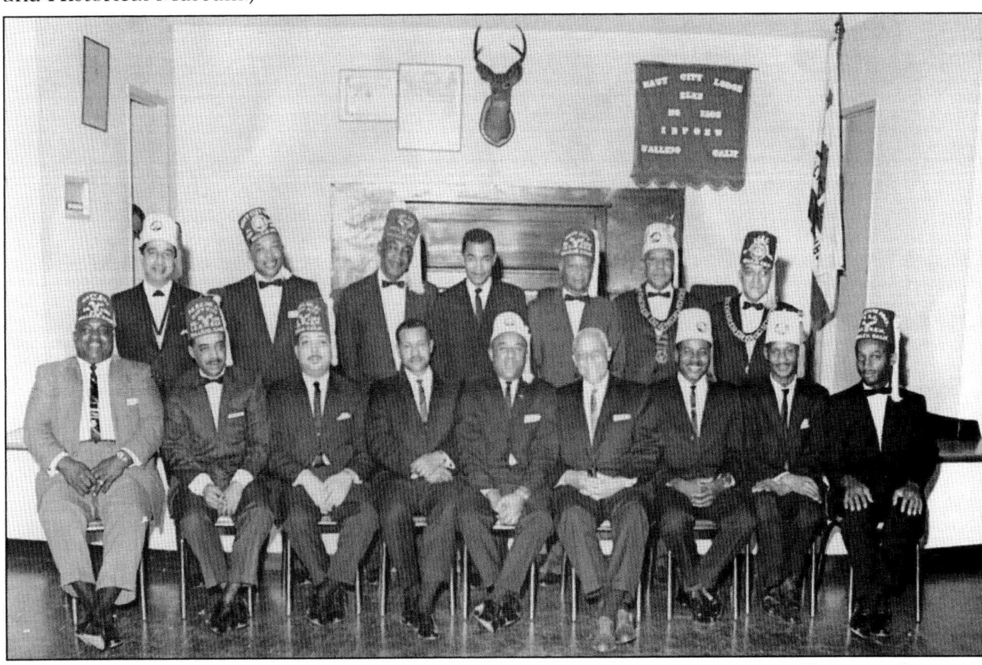

By 1964, as a result of redevelopment in downtown Vallejo, the Navy City Elks moved to 1020 Alabama Street. The elected officers included Jerry Martin, James McGee, Marvin Gaston, Homer Butts, Donald Woods, DuWane Hill, Floyd Williams, Robert Franklin, James Garner, B.W. Williams, John Duper, Clarence Robinson, Earl Batiste, Charles Wright, Frank Clark, Woodrow Tatum, Bert Braham, Spencer Davis, Leon Singleton, and Alvin Henderson. (Courtesy of the Vallejo Naval and Historical Museum.)

John Beverly (left), a founding member of the Navy City Elks, accepts a portrait from Rev. Victor Lawhorn, whose son painted the portrait. Beverly, a founding member of the Navy City Elks, was honored following the renaming of the lodge, John S. Beverly Lodge No. 1268.

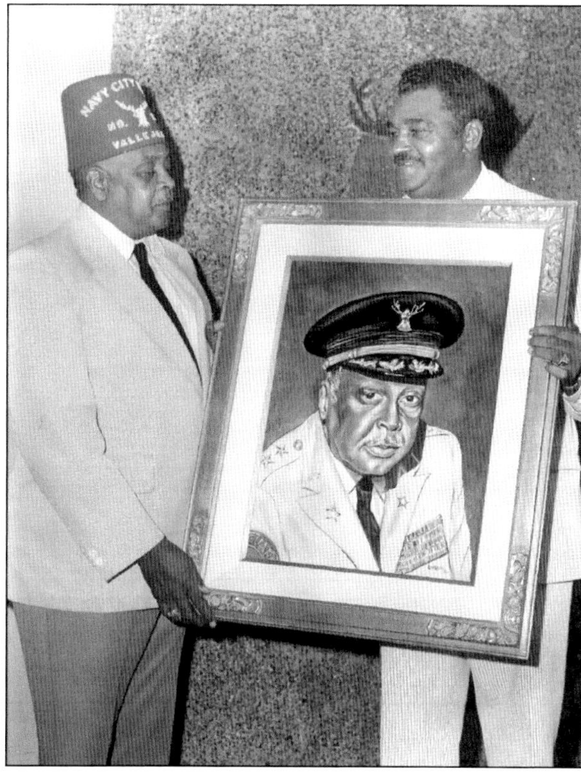

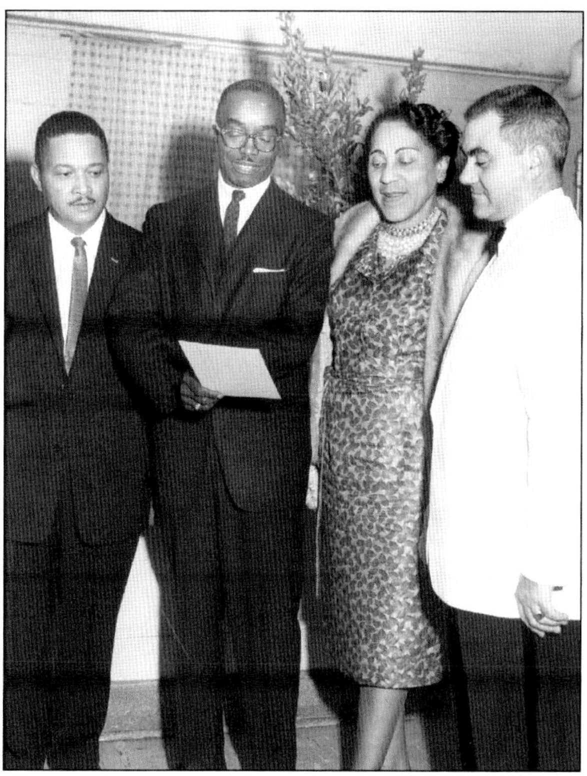

In the early 1960s, Tarea Hall Pittman, a well-known Bay Area radio personality and civil rights activist, was the guest speaker at a Vallejo NAACP dinner. Pittman hosted the popular syndicated radio program *Negroes in the News*. Pictured from left to right are Clarence Poche, Vallejo NAACP president; Judge Joseph Kennedy, San Francisco's first African American judge; Pittman; and Anthony Tasca. (Courtesy of the Vallejo Naval and Historical Museum.)

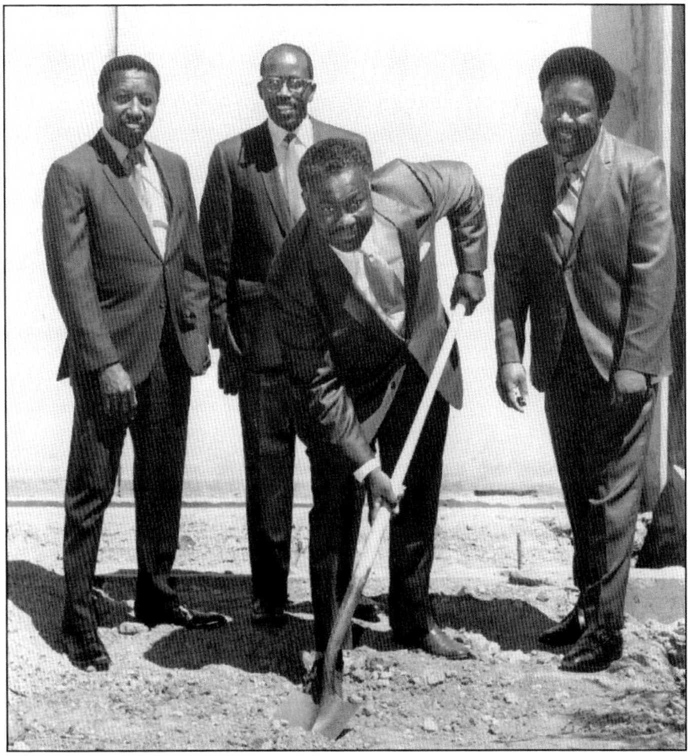

Rev. Boyd Rogers of the Second Baptist Church prepares to "bury" the church mortgage during a ceremony in the 1980s at the Benicia Road church. Looking on are Elijah Blocker, Benjamin Flippin, and Robert Hines. Second Baptist Church, the city's oldest formally organized African American church, moved to the Benicia Road location in 1963 in the wake of Vallejo's massive downtown redevelopment project. (Courtesy of the Vallejo Naval and Historical Museum.)

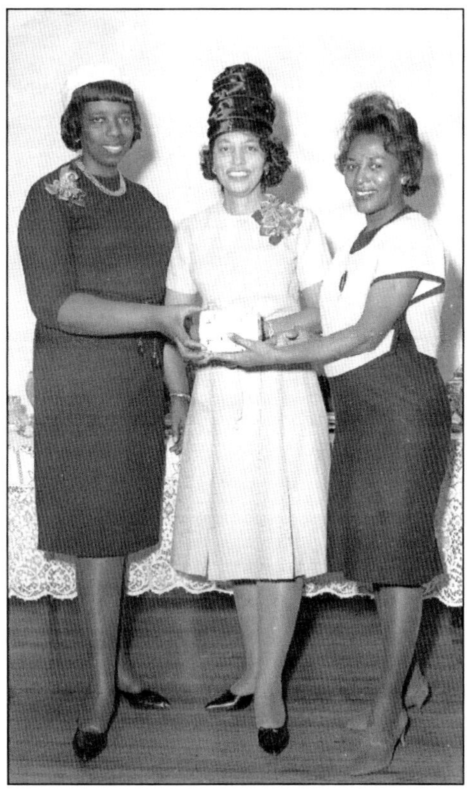

Lucy Chatmon (center) was a charter member of the National Council of Negro Women when it launched its Vallejo chapter in the 1950s. In this early 1960s photograph, Chatmon is presented a gift in recognition of her service to the organization. Mildred "Millie" Watson (left), who served as vice president; and Louise Bronson presented Chatmon with the gift. That year, attending the unveiling of the Mary McLeod Bethune Memorial in Washington, DC, Mildred Watson served as secretary to Mayor Florence Douglas, the first such position held by an African American. (Courtesy of the Vallejo Naval and Historical Museum.)

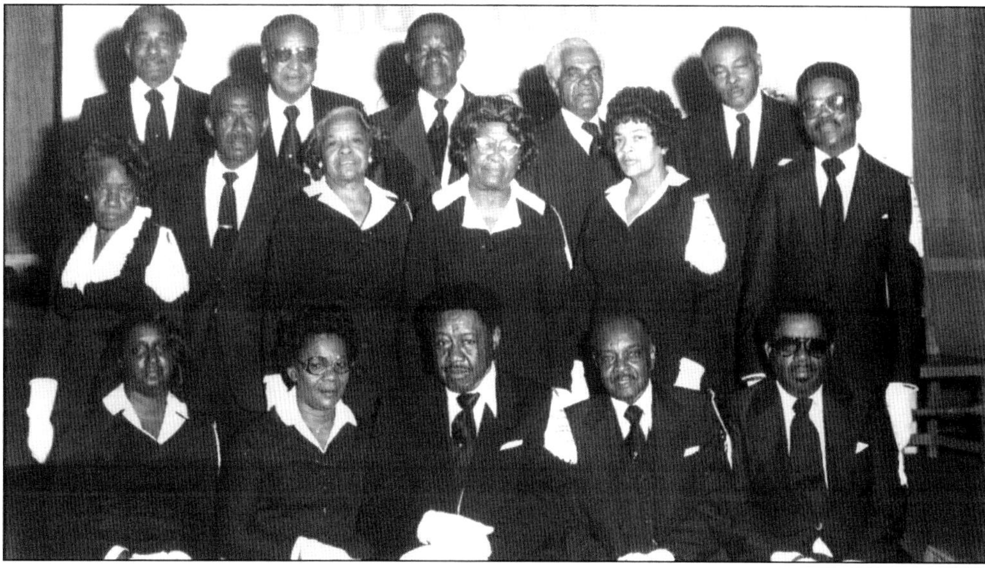

By the time this photograph of the Second Baptist Church Usher Board was taken, many of its members had belonged to the historic church for more than 40 years. Many joined as soon as they arrived in Vallejo from the south. Some of the members pictured include Dorothy Polk, Inez Smith, Tommy Lemmon, Ninus Harris, and Christine Smith. During the height of the Great Migration period of the 1940s, Second Baptist Church had so many people attending that Sunday services were standing room only. (Courtesy of Verlady Banks.)

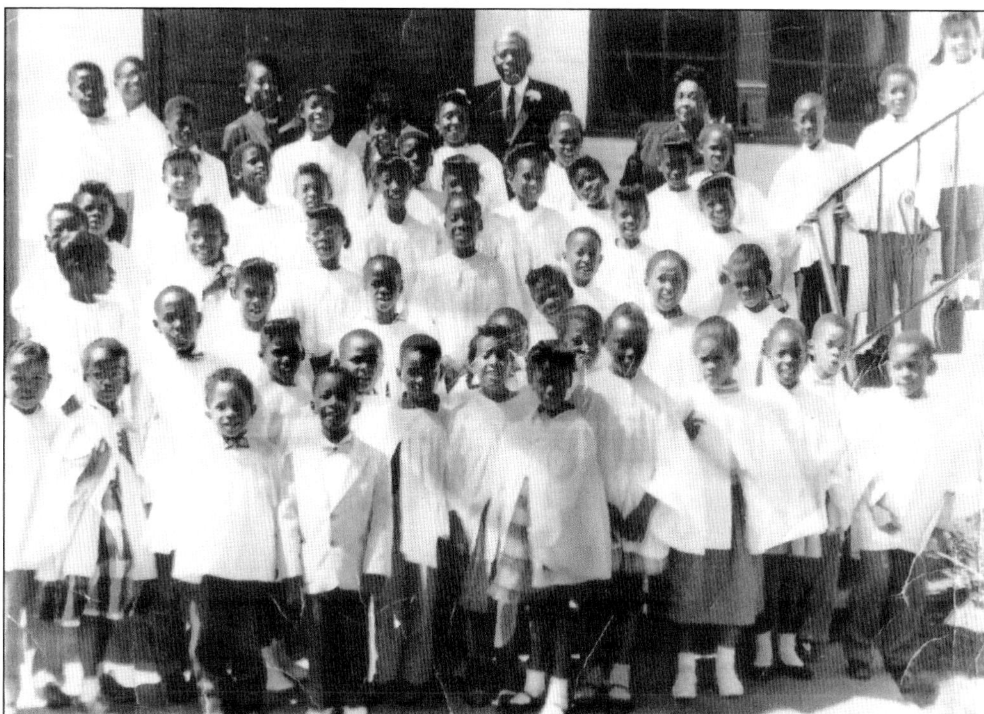

As young as two years old, children participated in the Cradle Choir of Second Baptist Church. (Courtesy of Carey Thompson.)

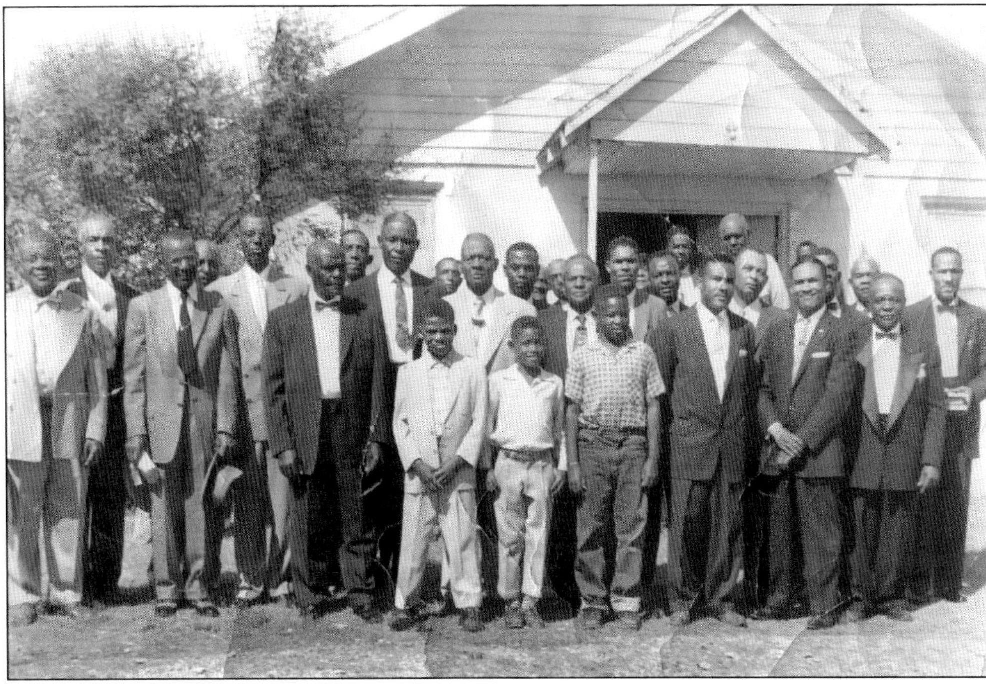

Many Vallejo residents kept close ties with out-of-state friends and relatives through regional church gatherings. In this photograph, a young Cherubim "Jake" Speaks (first row, fourth from left) attends a church meeting in Stroud, Oklahoma. (Courtesy of Cherubim "Jake" Speaks.)

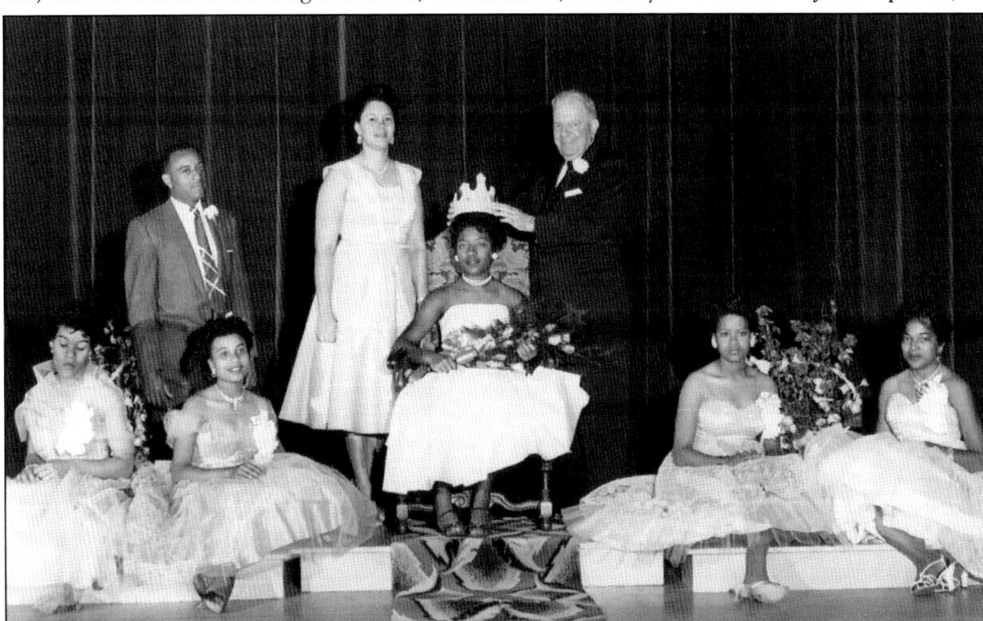

Azalee Pierce won the NAACP queen contest in May 1956. Assemblyman Samuel R. Geddes crowns Pierce, while NAACP president DuWane Hill and Doris Higgins, chairwoman of the contest, look on. Other contestants were, from left to right, Loretta Holt, JoAnn Crawford, Ann Louise Ray, and Gladys Hastings. (Courtesy of the Vallejo Naval and Historical Museum.)

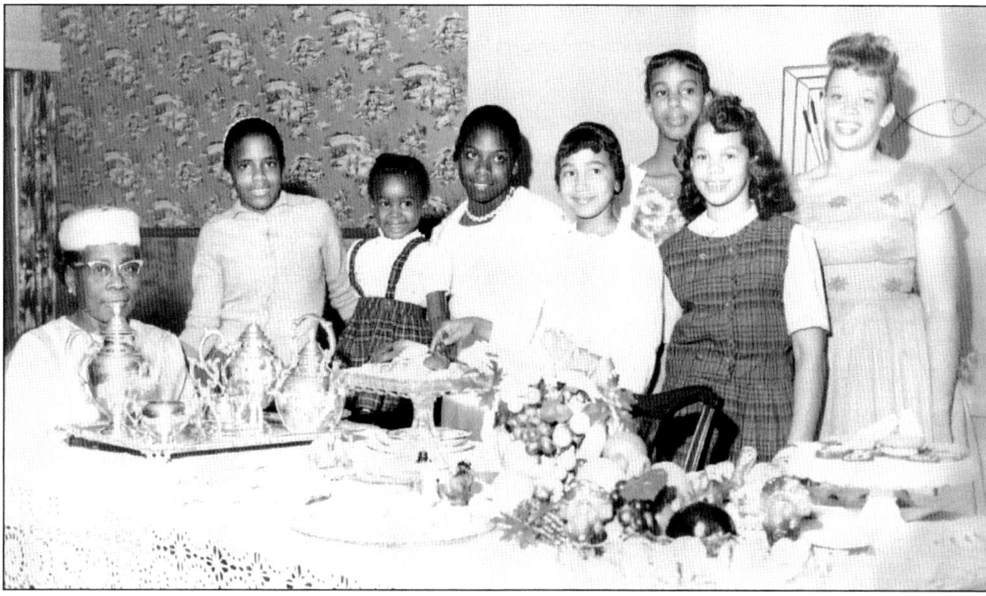

These young ladies were treated to refreshments during a tea in the late 1950s. Being served are Peggy Morris, unidentified, Patricia Morris, Nona Cohen, Darlene Love, Jimmy Esther, and Deborah Williams. (Courtesy of Althea Lett.)

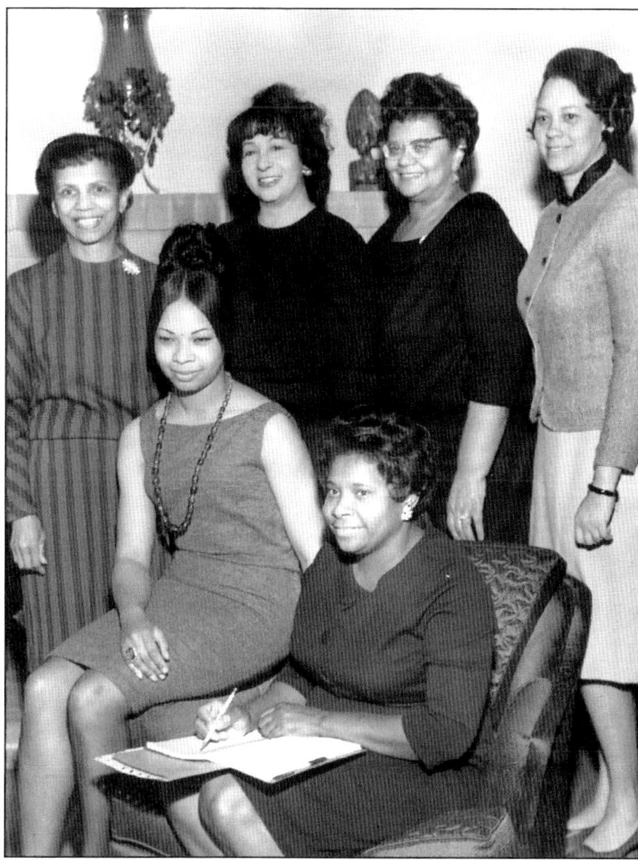

The It Club cotillion balls were the highlight of Vallejo's African American social scene in the 1960s. This 1964 photograph by William Banks shows members of the It Club's ball-planning committee. That year the ball was held at the Veterans Memorial Building. From left to right are (sitting) Barbara Wiggins and Gerti Thomas; (standing) Thelma Sayles, Aleane Curtis, Ernestine Ellis, and Doris Higgins. (Courtesy of the Vallejo Naval and Historical Museum.)

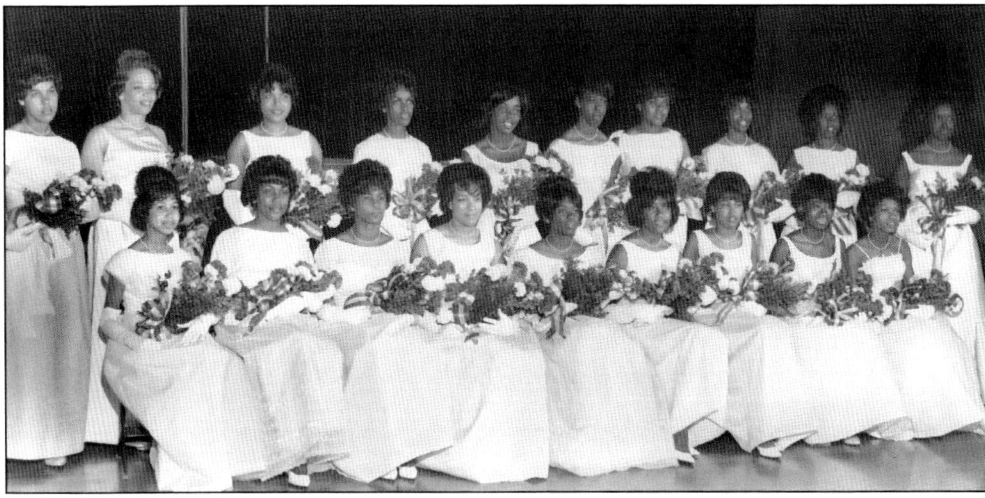

The 1964 debutantes presented by the Vallejo It Club included young ladies from both the local high schools and community college. (Courtesy of the Vallejo Naval and Historical Museum.)

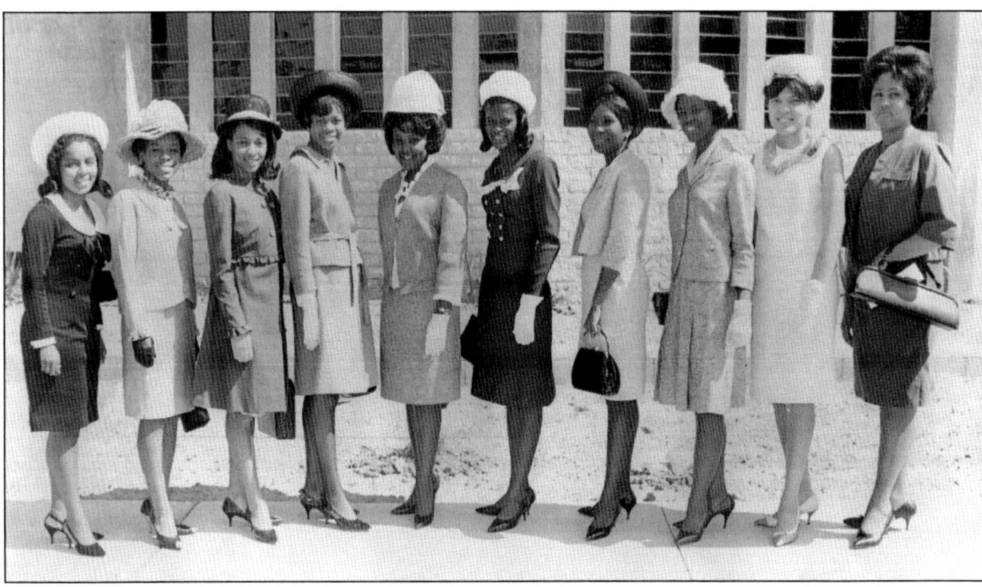

These young women were among those presented to Vallejo society in 1965. Standing in front of Second Baptist Church on Benicia Road are Patricia Bohannon, Sharon Alexander, Shirley Marsh, Yvonne Harris, Nancy Graham, Eileen Williams, Melody McGriff, Frankye Thurston, Vivian Owens, and Sharon Marley. Not pictured are Joan Bouldin, Sara Byrd, Elena Spencer, and Cheryl Taylor. (Courtesy of the Vallejo Naval and Historical Museum.)

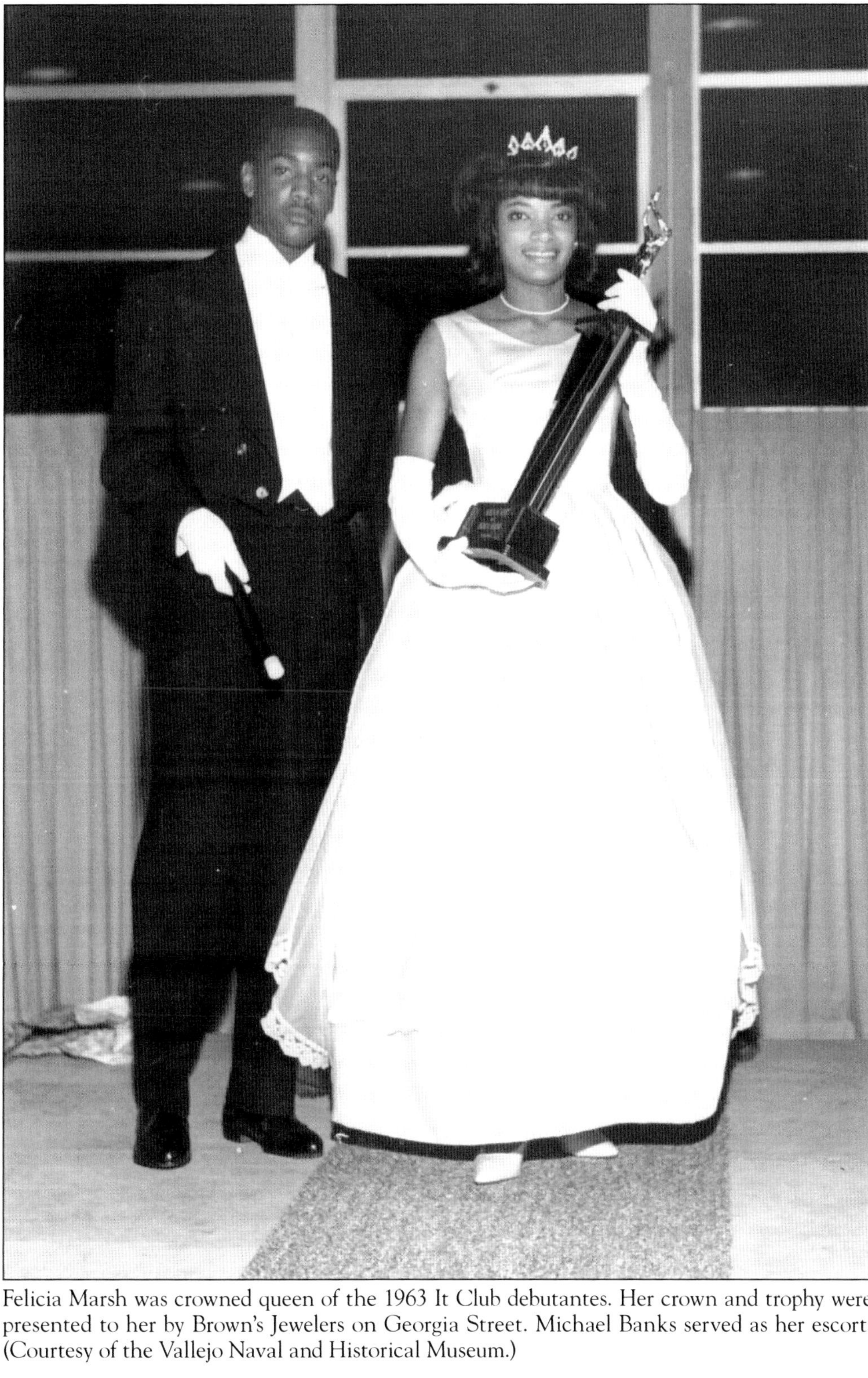

Felicia Marsh was crowned queen of the 1963 It Club debutantes. Her crown and trophy were presented to her by Brown's Jewelers on Georgia Street. Michael Banks served as her escort. (Courtesy of the Vallejo Naval and Historical Museum.)

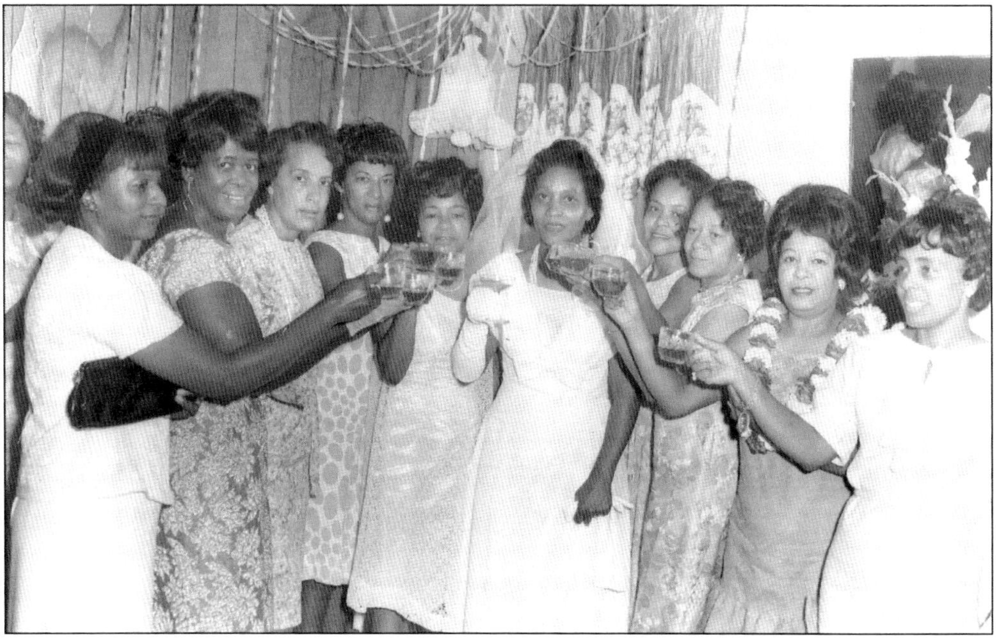

Ollie Cross, center, was an active member of the Navy City Elks Club and was a longtime resident of Vallejo. (Courtesy of Verlady Banks.)

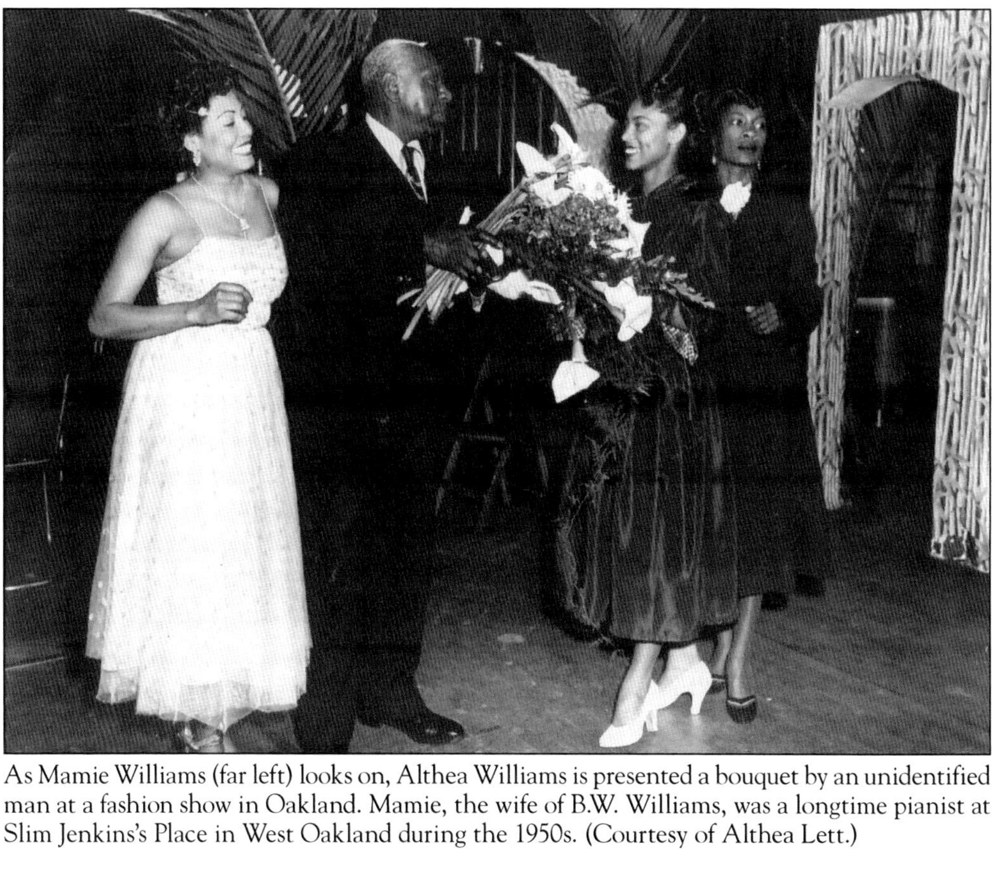

As Mamie Williams (far left) looks on, Althea Williams is presented a bouquet by an unidentified man at a fashion show in Oakland. Mamie, the wife of B.W. Williams, was a longtime pianist at Slim Jenkins's Place in West Oakland during the 1950s. (Courtesy of Althea Lett.)

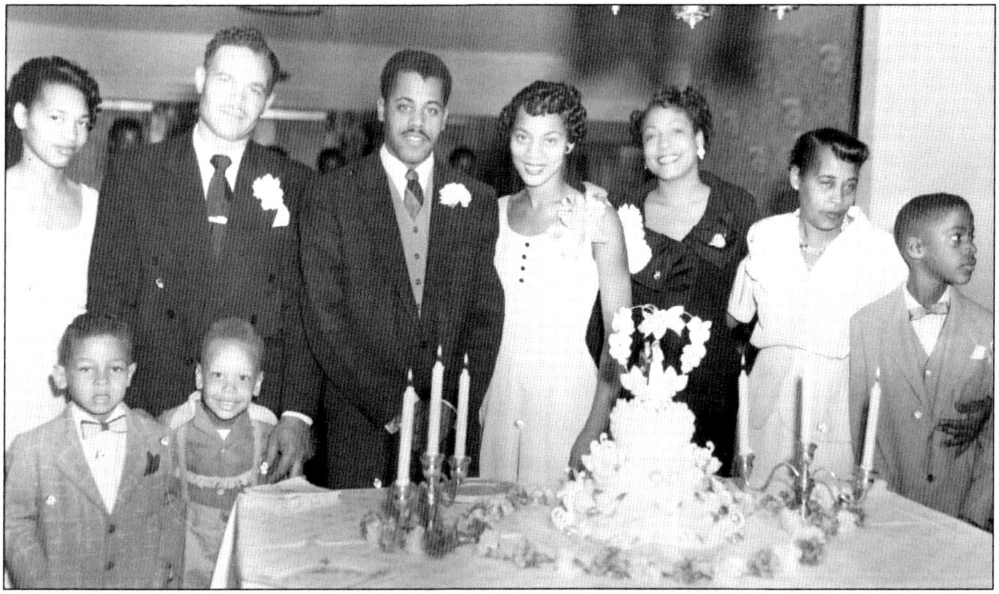

Althea Williams Wiggins, center, beams during a reception following her marriage to Hilliard Wiggins in the mid-1950s. Pictured on either side of the happy couple are B.W. Williams and Mamie Williams. Also at the festive occasion, Beaneathes "Butchie" Williams Jr. stands in the front. (Courtesy of Althea Lett.)

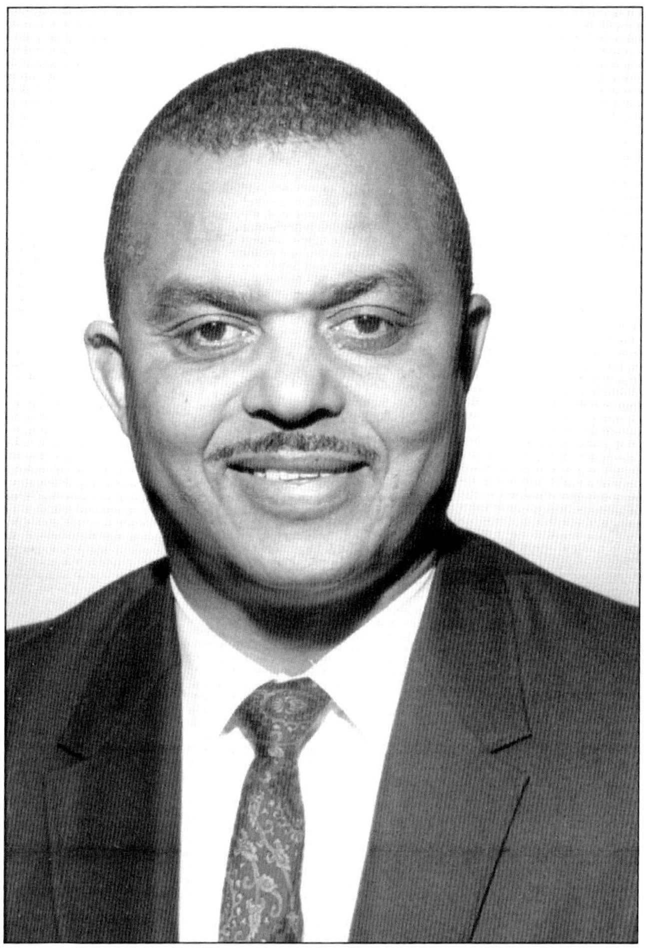

Calvin Elam was a well-known local businessman who owned the Calvin Elam Bail Bond service. Originally located on the lower end of Georgia Street, Elam moved to his business to Capitol Street. (Courtesy of the Vallejo Naval and Historical Museum.)

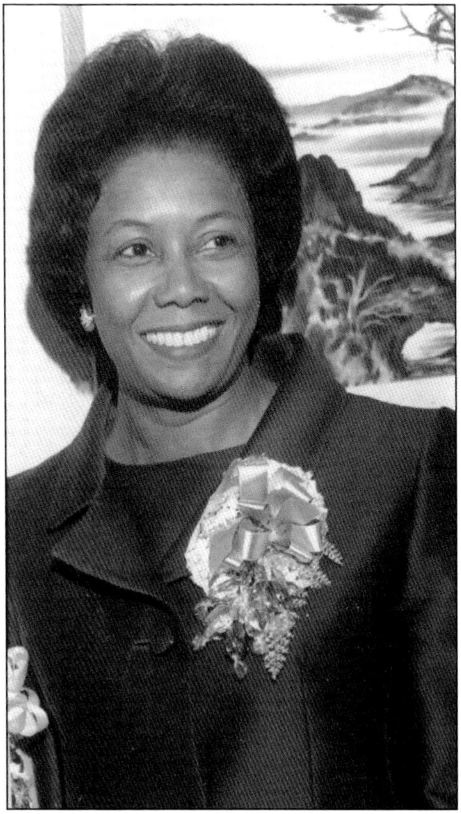

The late Thelma Brown was actively involved in a variety of organizations in Vallejo and the county, including the Solano County Democratic Central Committee. For a number of years, she was a staff member of assemblyman Thomas Hannigan. In 1984, Brown launched the Girls and Boys Club of Vallejo, Inc., which was housed at the former Grant Elementary School in South Vallejo.

Segregated housing in Vallejo neighborhoods during the 1950s and 1960s helped create schools that had large African American enrollments. These schools included Flosden and Olympic elementary schools. This Olympic Elementary School photograph from the late 1950s includes students who lived in the neighborhoods of Lofas-Lakeside, Country Club Crest, Flosden Acres, and Floyd Terrace. (Courtesy of the author.)

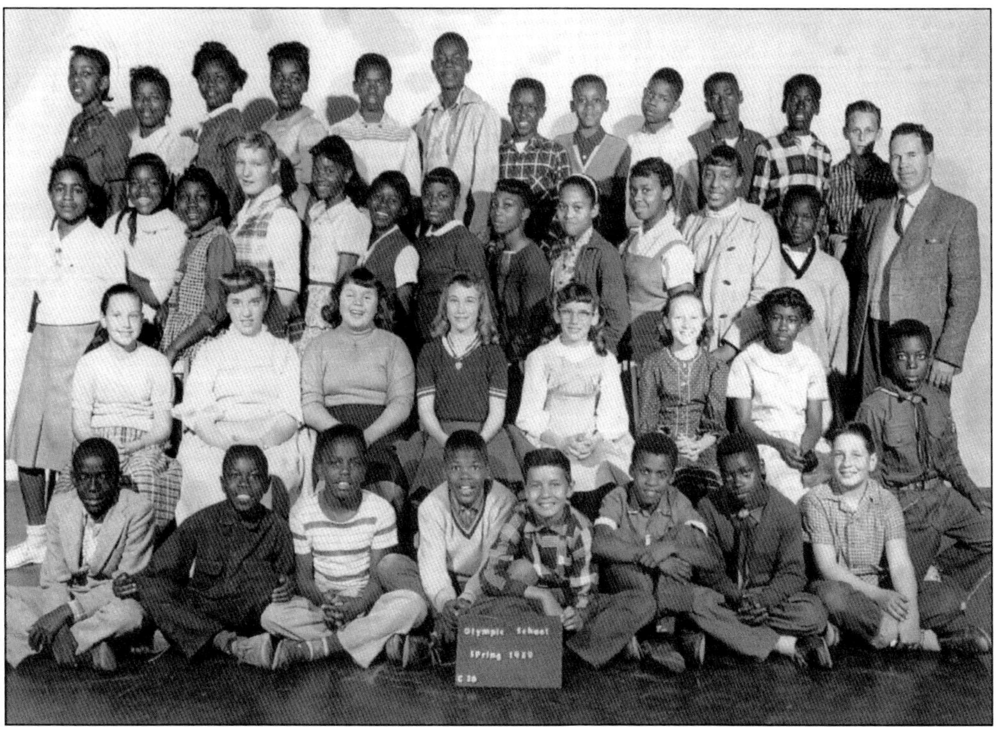

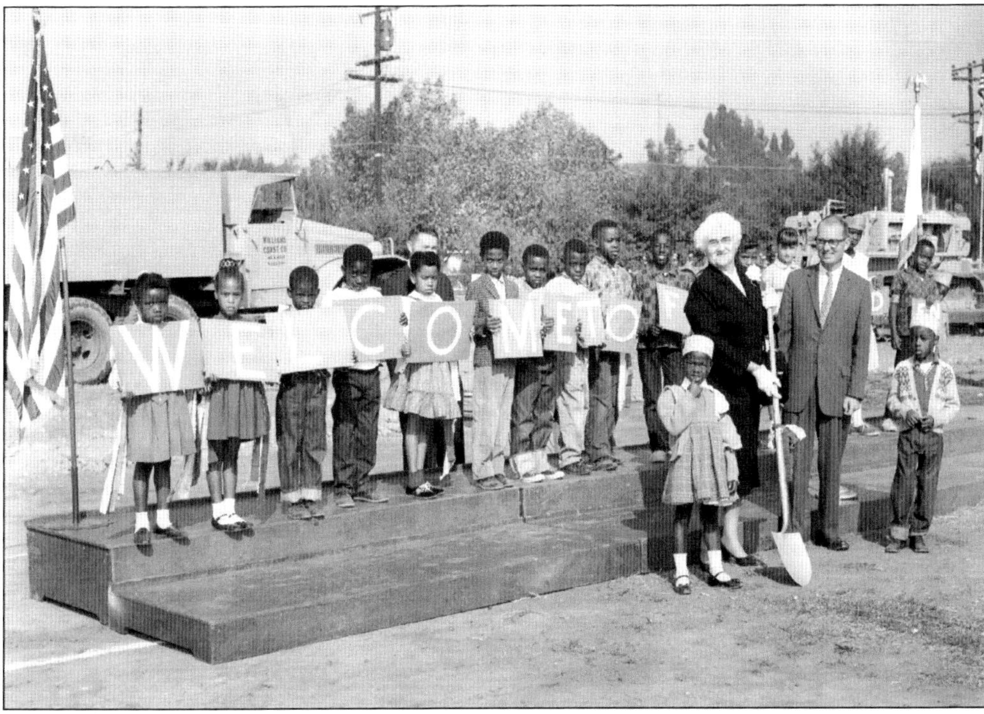

These 1961 Flosden Elementary school youngsters welcome visitors to the North Vallejo school. Construction was underway to add extra buildings to accommodate an expanding attendance. (Courtesy of the Vallejo Naval and Historical Museum.)

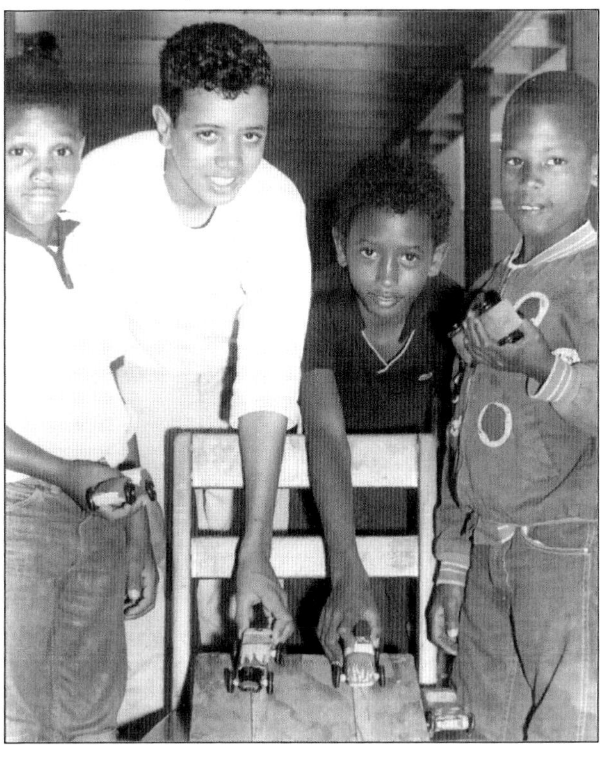

Churches, social clubs, and other groups sponsored events for children throughout the year. The Greater Vallejo Recreation District hosted flag football, baseball, basketball, and marble tournaments for youngsters. In this photograph, Michael Gaines, Carlos and Howard Cusseaux, and Reginald Carter prepared for an upcoming drag strip race at the all city finals. (Courtesy of the Vallejo Naval and Historical Museum.)

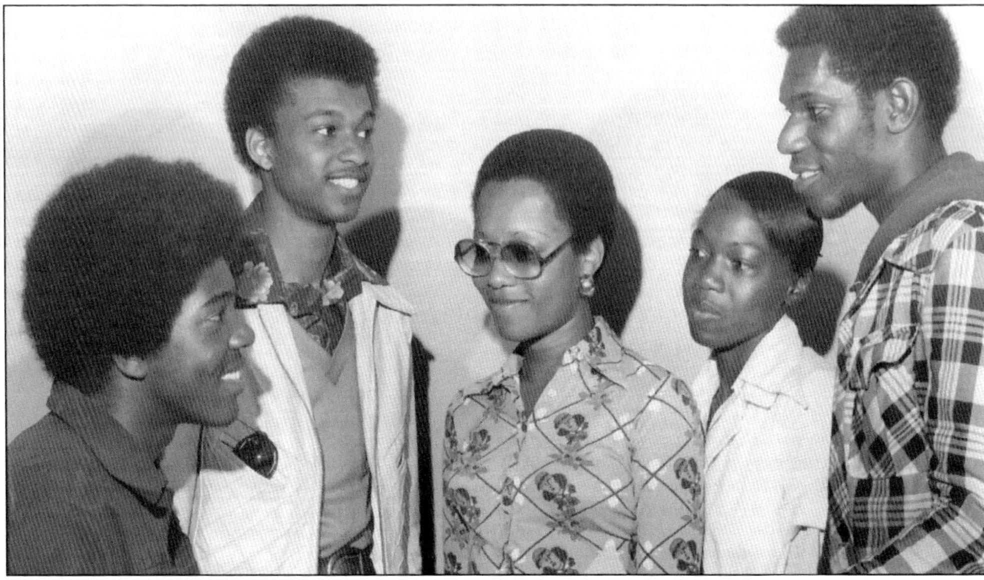

These Vallejo high school and junior college students gathered to plan a career-awareness day, titled "Be Watcha' Wanna Be." Students included Julian Carroll, Lewis Brown Jr., Angela Green, Cheri Jackson, and Phillip McFarland.

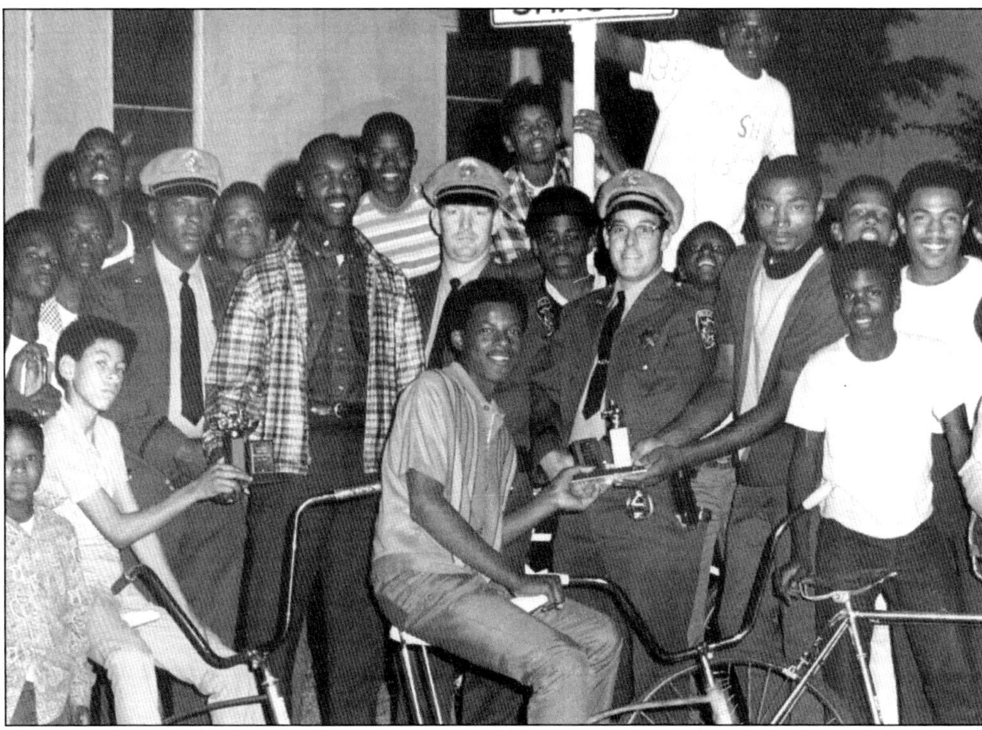

Philmore Graham, in the plaid shirt, was the founder of the Continentals of Omega Boys Club in the early 1960s. In this photograph are the winners of a "wheelstand" contest, sponsored by the Continentals of Omega Boys Club. Winners included Joey Jackson, Maceo Houston, and Raymond Charlton. Patrol officers who participated in the contest were John Williams, William Barber, and James Stollery. (Courtesy of the Vallejo Naval and Historical Museum.)

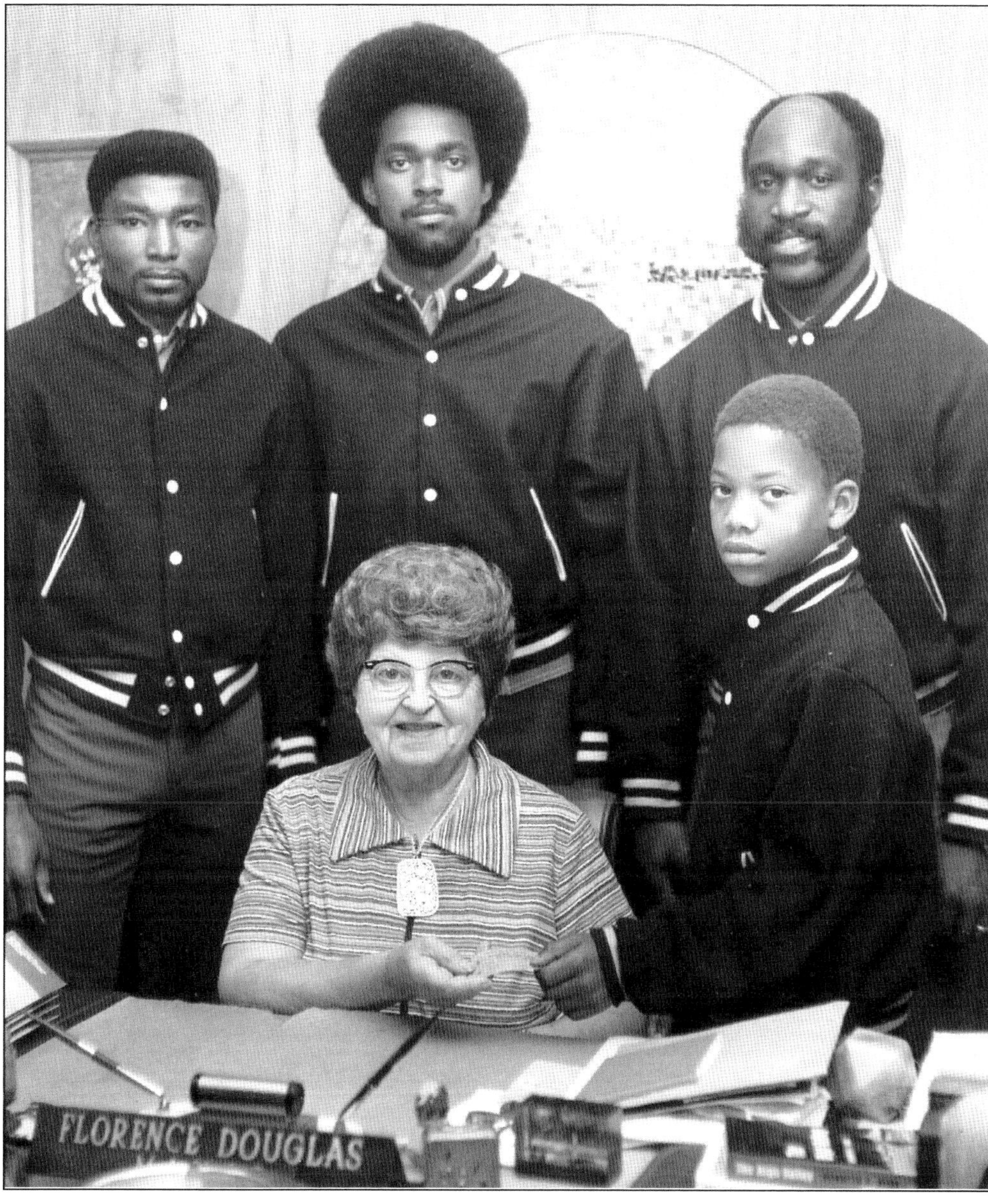

In the early 1970s, Mayor Florence Douglas gave her support at an awards and recognition dinner hosted by the Continentals of Omega Boys Club. Former San Francisco Warriors coach Al Attles served as guest speaker of the event, which was a major fundraiser for the club. Rickey Benjamin, (right foreground) sells Mayor Douglas a ticket, while James Swindle, John Jones, and Philmore Graham look on. (Courtesy of the Vallejo Naval and Historical Museum.)

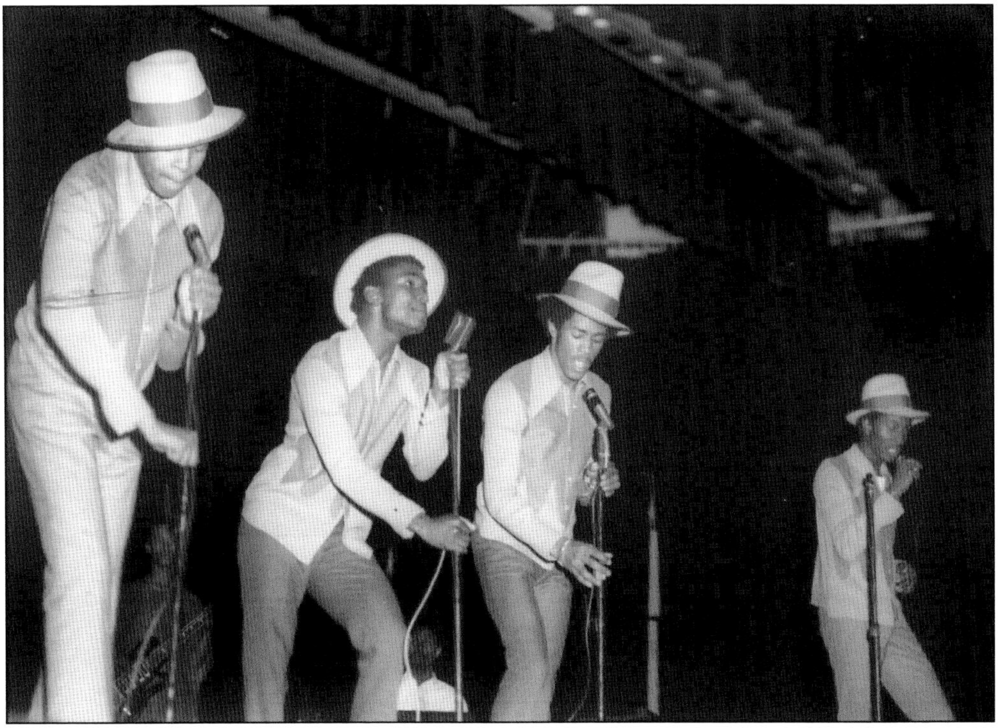

The rousing climax to a talent show presented as part of Vallejo High School's black history week festivities in the early 1970s was provided by the popular Techniques singing group. They are, from left to right, Overton Claborne, Victor McClane, Fred Gums, and Larry Pratt. (Courtesy of the Vallejo Naval and Historical Museum.)

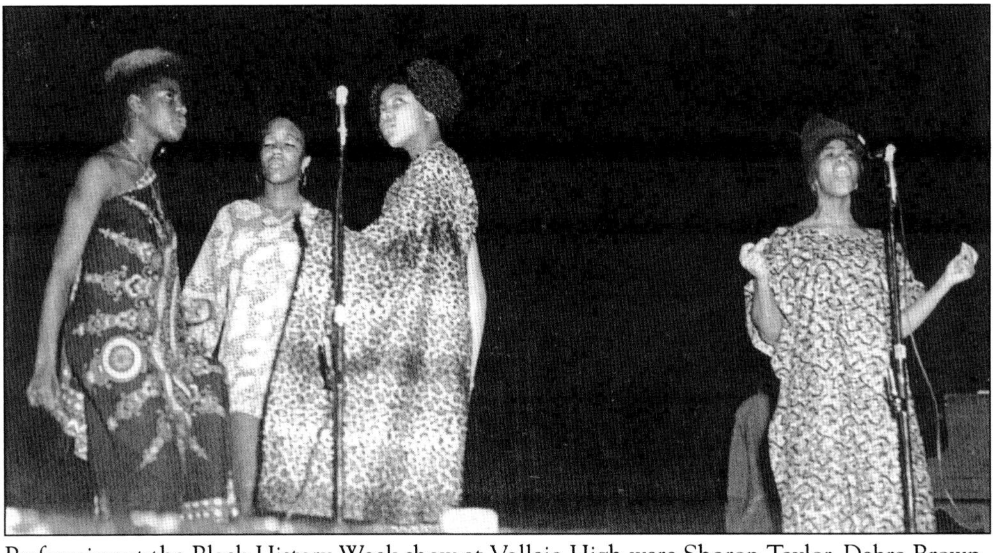

Performing at the Black History Week show at Vallejo High were Sharon Taylor, Debra Brown, Pam Nickolas, and Lynn Nickolas. (Courtesy of the Vallejo Naval and Historical Museum.)

Four

CHANGE AND BEYOND

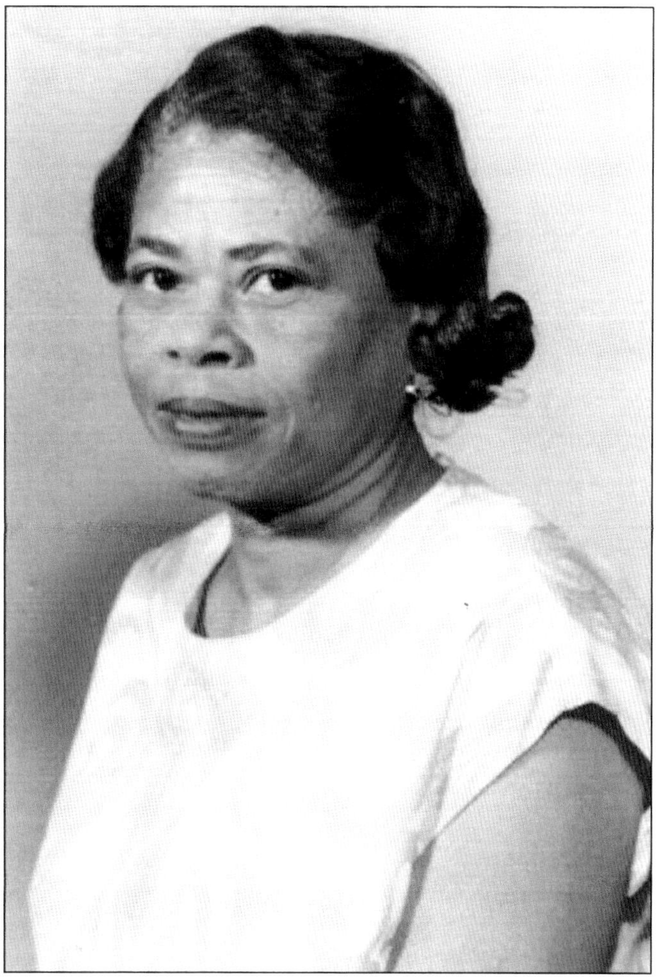

In 1949, Grace Logan (later Patterson) was hired as Vallejo's first African American schoolteacher. This remarkable and long-awaited event marked a watershed moment in the areas of racial and political change in Vallejo. Years before, Logan, who had earned her degree in education at San Francisco State College in the late 1930s, was turned down by Vallejo school officials who told her they were "not ready to hire a Negro" teacher. Logan and the Vallejo NAACP persevered and pushed for her hiring. She served as a Vallejo schoolteacher for 25 years. In 1989, in recognition of her service to the city, the Vallejo Unified School District named an elementary school in her honor. (Courtesy of Jeannette Mohlson.)

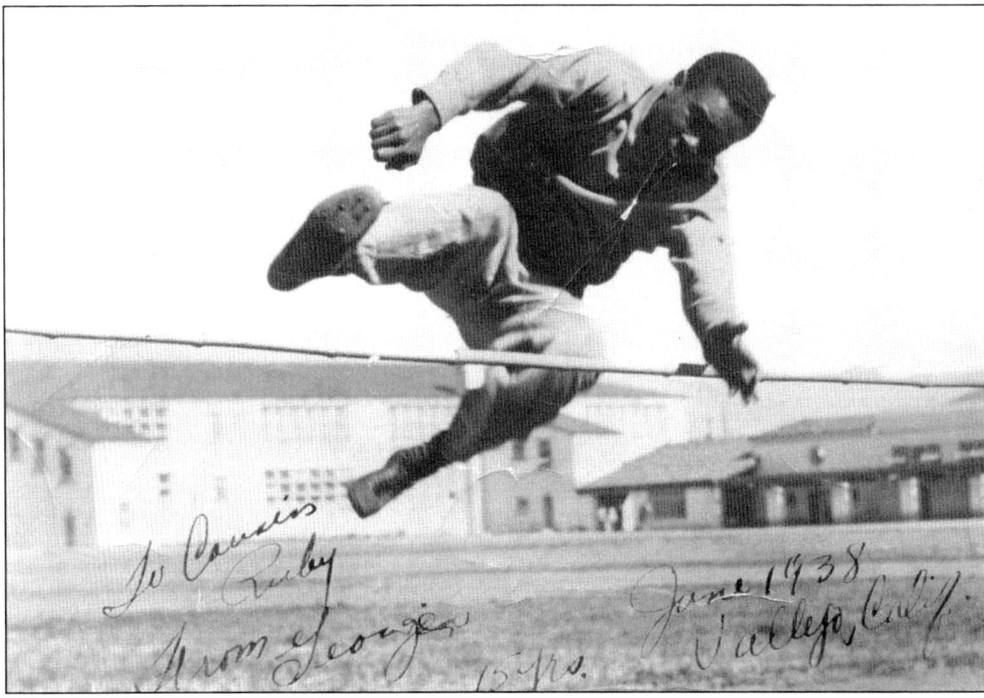

George Malcolm was an outstanding Vallejo High School athlete who was versatile in a number of sports, including track and field and football. The 1937 Vallejo High School graduate held the rushing record at the school until the mid-1950s, when Dick Bass broke his record.

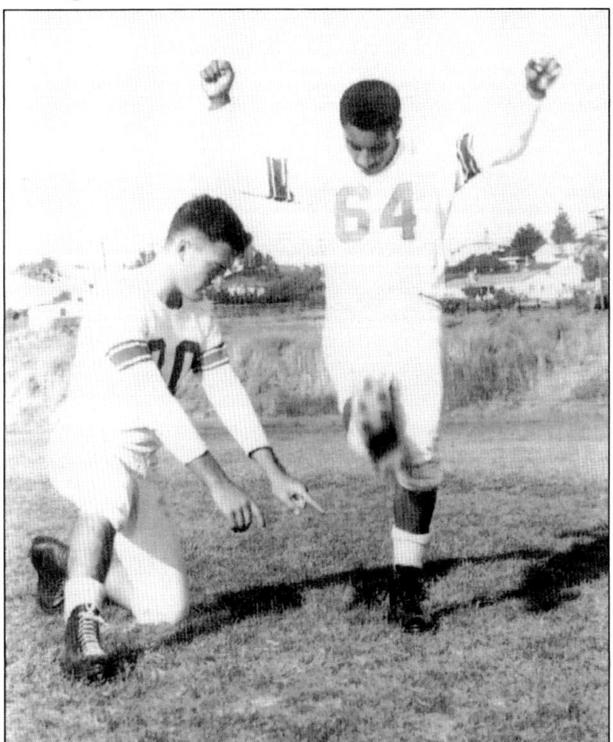

Richard "Dick" Bass excelled at all sports at Vallejo High School in the early 1950s. Raised on Sacramento Street in Vallejo, Bass was born in Georgetown, Mississippi. He scored a state-record 37 touchdowns in 1954, when he led the Vallejo Apaches to an undefeated season at 9-0. The team averaged 54 points per game in 1954. He was a 1955 Vallejo High School graduate. Following graduation, Bass went on to play at the College of the Pacific and was later drafted by the Los Angeles Rams. Bass's brother Norman was an outstanding athlete in his own right. In the early 1960s, he was starting pitcher for the Kansas City Athletics. In May 2012, a Vallejo High School practice field was named for Dick Bass. (Courtesy of the Greater Vallejo Recreation District.)

Alfred Robinson was Vallejo's first African American police officer when he was hired in 1946. Because of racial prejudice, his position in local law enforcement was short-lived. A native of New Orleans, Robinson moved to Vallejo in 1941 to seek a better future for his young family. He found a job as a janitor in the Vallejo Police Department, where he cultivated a friendship with then police chief Earl Dierking. In 1946, Dierking promoted Robinson to the position of police officer. Robinson proudly wore police badge no. 176. Within two weeks of Robinson's hiring, Vallejo city leaders, fearful of a black man holding a law enforcement position, ordered Dierking to remove Robinson from his new post. Robinson, with a family to feed, returned to his position as VPD custodian, a job he held until his death in 1968. Robinson's son Herman is a sergeant in the Vallejo Police Department. Leon Wilson was Vallejo's first permanent African American police officer when he was hired by the VPD in the early 1960s. (Courtesy of Sgt. Herman Robinson.)

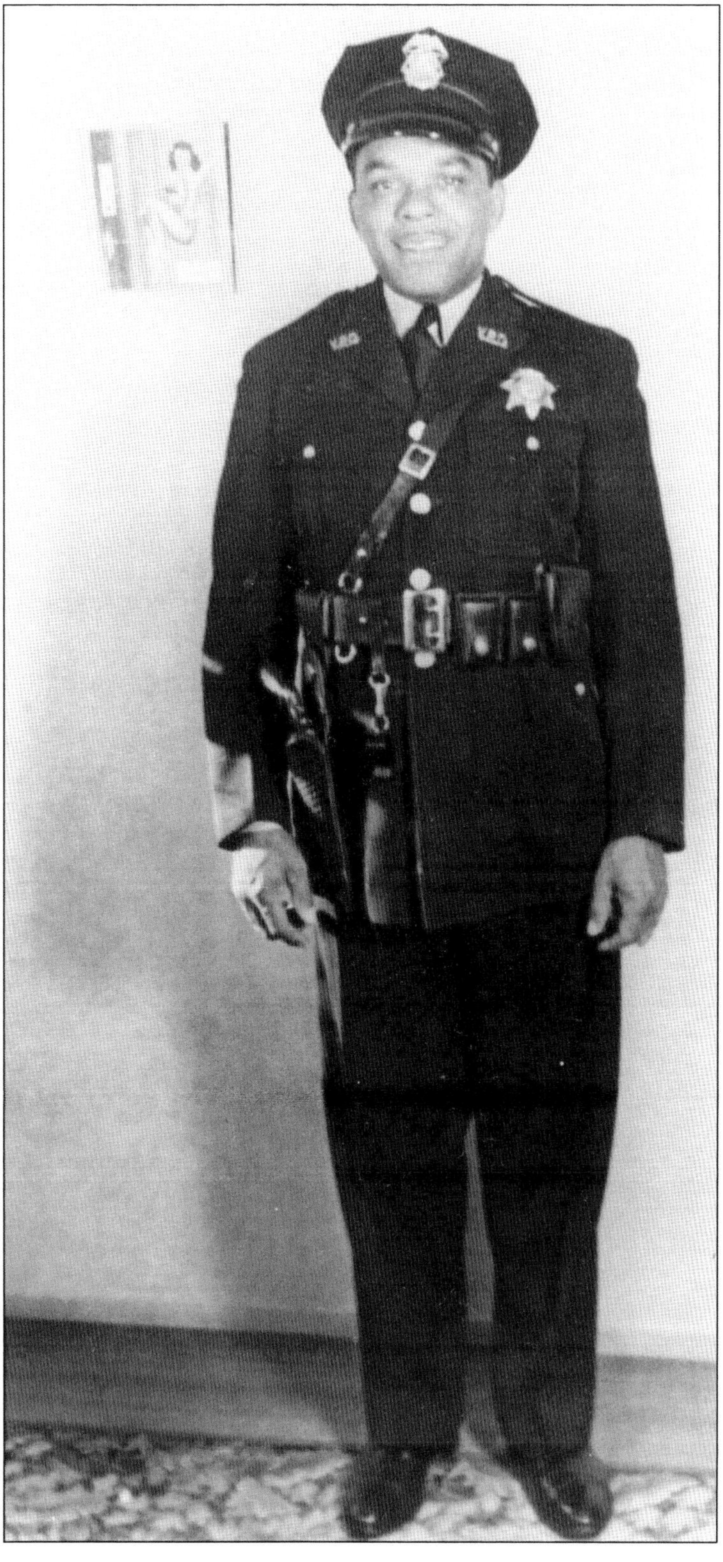

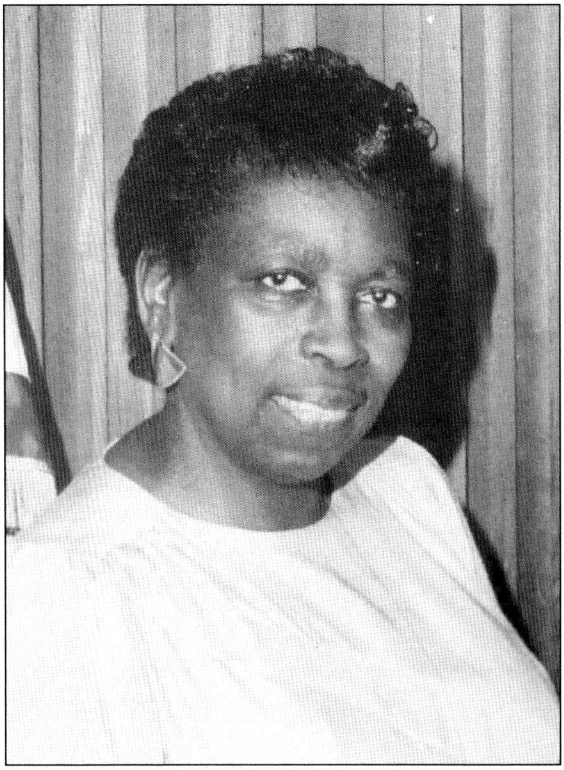

In 1961, Mildred "Millie" Watson was hired as a secretary by the city of Vallejo, making her the first African American to work in that capacity and the second black person to ever work at Vallejo City Hall. Watson was later named Vallejo city clerk, another first for an African American. William Jones, a longtime Vallejo resident, worked as a janitor at city hall for more than 20 years, starting in the late 1940s. Vallejo City Hall was then located at 734 Marin Street. (Courtesy of the Vallejo Naval and Historical Museum.)

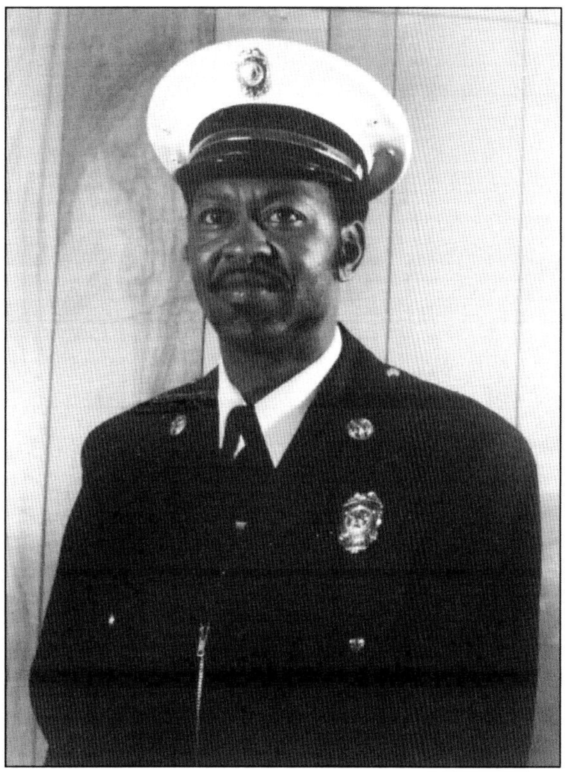

In 1964, John Wells became Vallejo's first African American firefighter. A native of Mississippi, Wells came to Vallejo in 1954 to be near his sister and complete high school. Working as a barber for many years, Wells was approached by the Reverend Horace J. Morris of Friendship Missionary Baptist Church to apply for the position. Wells rose through the VFD ranks, eventually retiring as a department captain. (Courtesy of John Wells.)

Bill Thurston was a native of Logtown, Mississippi. His family moved to California in 1944, and at age 17 Thurston joined the military. He served in Korea, Germany, the Philippines, and Okinawa before leaving the service in 1964. A longtime history and political science teacher at Solano Community College, he was the first African American president of the Academic Senate of SCC. Thurston was also the first African American chair of the Solano County Democratic Central Committee. (Courtesy of the Vallejo Naval and Historical Museum.)

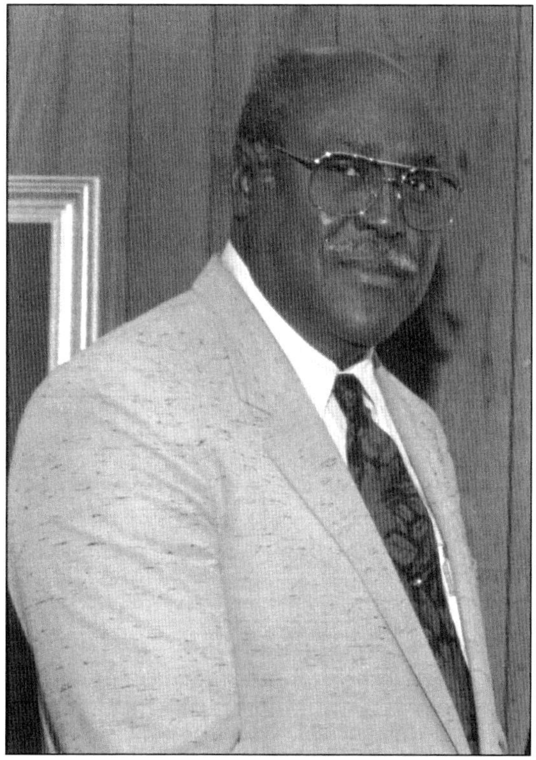

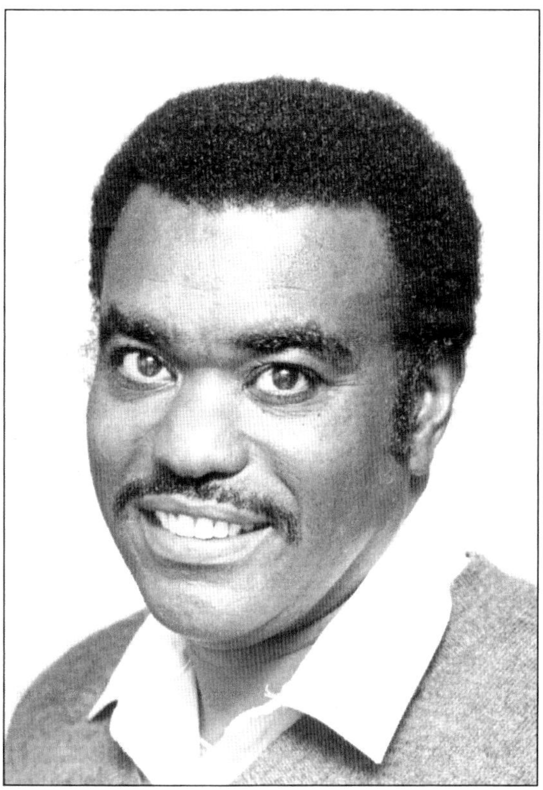

Willie B. Adkins became Vallejo's first African American school principal in 1969. A native of Mississippi, Adkins joined the Vallejo school district in 1961 after being discharged from the Army. (Courtesy of the Vallejo Naval and Historical Museum.)

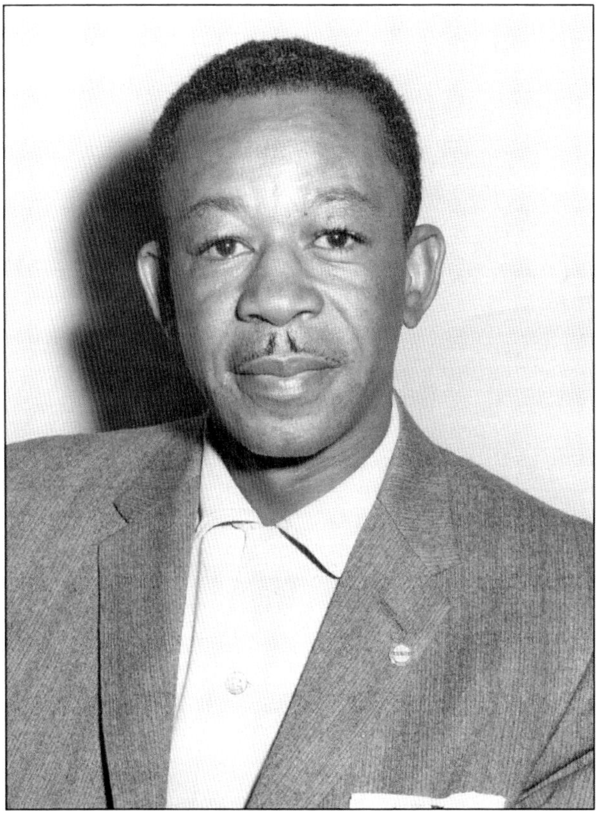

Cornelius Toney was among the earliest African American realtors in Vallejo when he opened his North Bay real estate office. At a time when overt racial discrimination in Vallejo housing was rampant, Toney helped African Americans purchase homes. He also owned Toney's Insurance Agency. Toney was active in city and county Democratic circles and was the grandson of Rev. C.H. Toney, founder of the Vallejo Industrial and Normal School. (Courtesy of the Vallejo Naval and Historical Museum.)

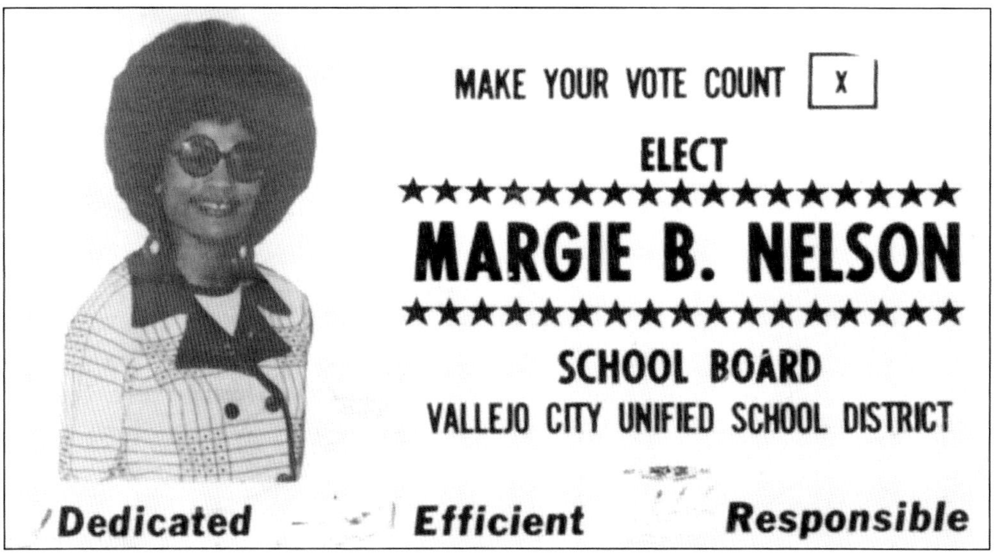

By the early 1960s, Margie Nelson, a young mother of four, was disillusioned with the "cultural insensitivity" shown by the Vallejo Unified School District toward African American children. In 1963, Nelson threw her hat in the ring and ran for the Vallejo school board, making her one of the earliest black women to run for office in the city. While she did not win, Nelson said that her stepping forward to run for office raised important issues regarding the education of minority children that had long been ignored. (Courtesy of Margie Nelson.)

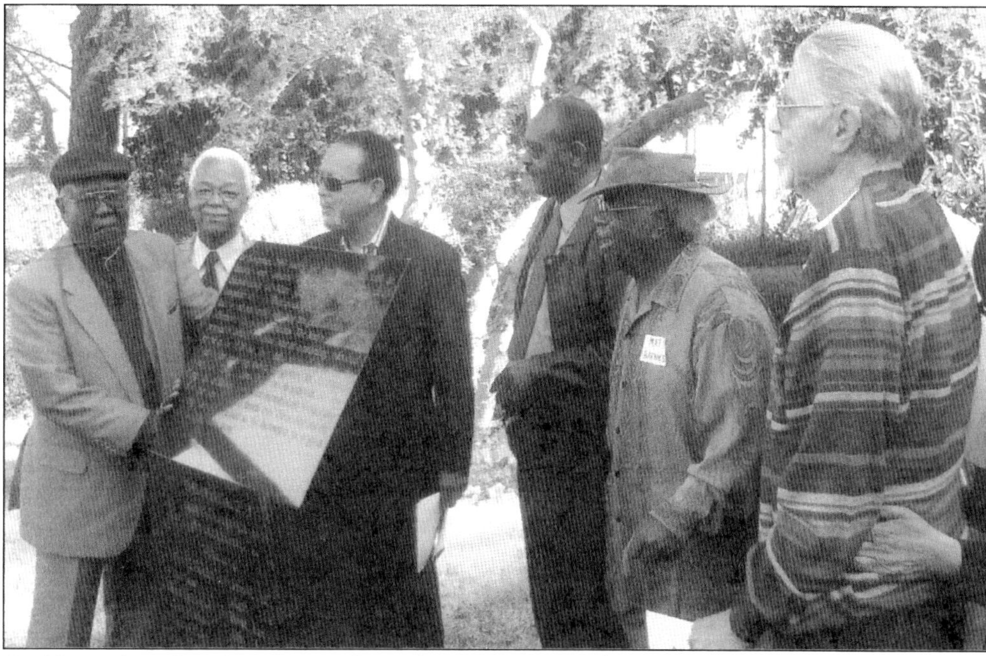

On November 17, 1961, a group of 21 African American shipyard workers at Mare Island filed a racial discrimination complaint with the Committee on Equal Employment Opportunity; in the complaint, the men outlined nine allegations of racial discrimination in employment at Mare Island and requested that the committee investigate and correct the deplorable conditions at the yard. The complaint, along with other similar actions, led to an acknowledgment by then defense secretary Robert McNamara in 1963 that employment discrimination based on race existed in the military. Their filing of the complaint brought about promotions for many of the original 21 members and other qualified African Americans at the Navy yard.

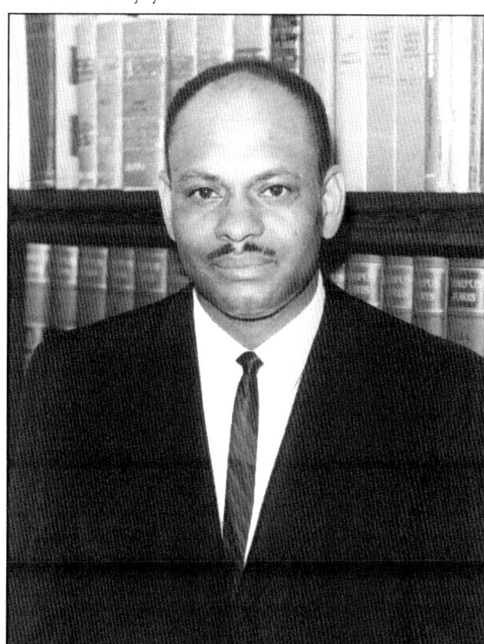

In 1964, Lewis F. Brown was elected Vallejo's first African American city councilman. In 1967, he achieved yet another distinction when he was chosen as Vallejo's first black vice mayor. (Courtesy of Lewis F. Brown.)

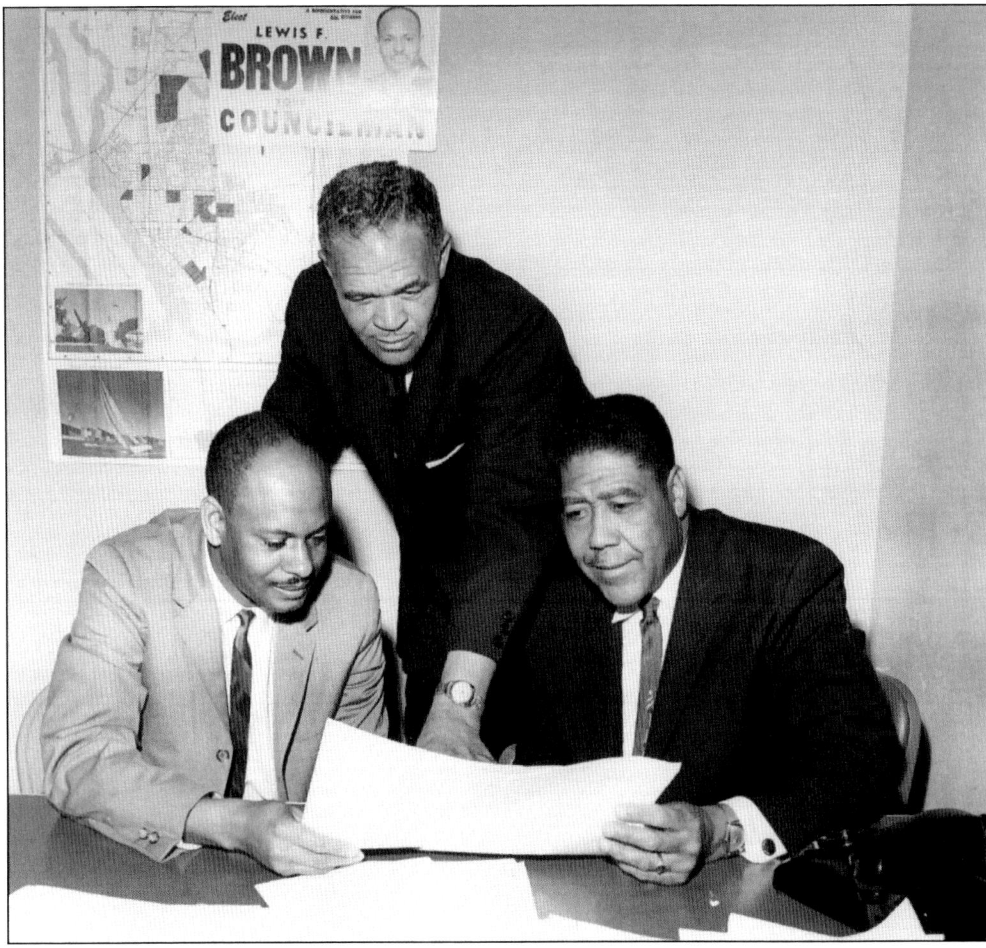

From left to right, Lewis Brown and campaign managers B.W. Williams and Charles Logan attend to final strategic details before the November 1964 election. (Courtesy of Lewis F. Brown.)

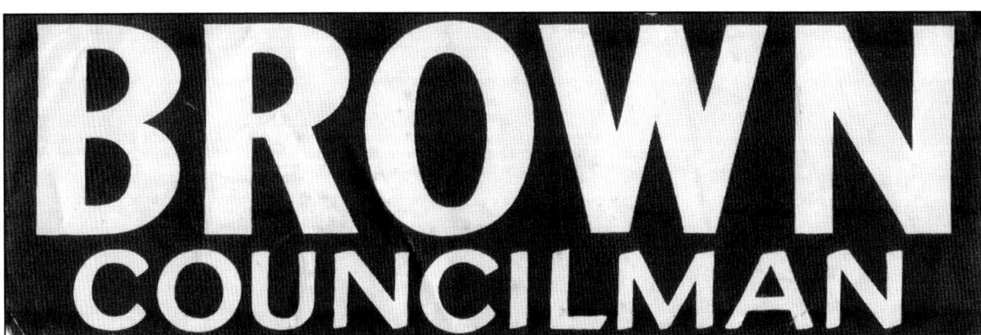

This Brown-for-Councilman bumper sticker from the 1964 campaign was appropriately colored brown. (Courtesy of Lewis F. Brown.)

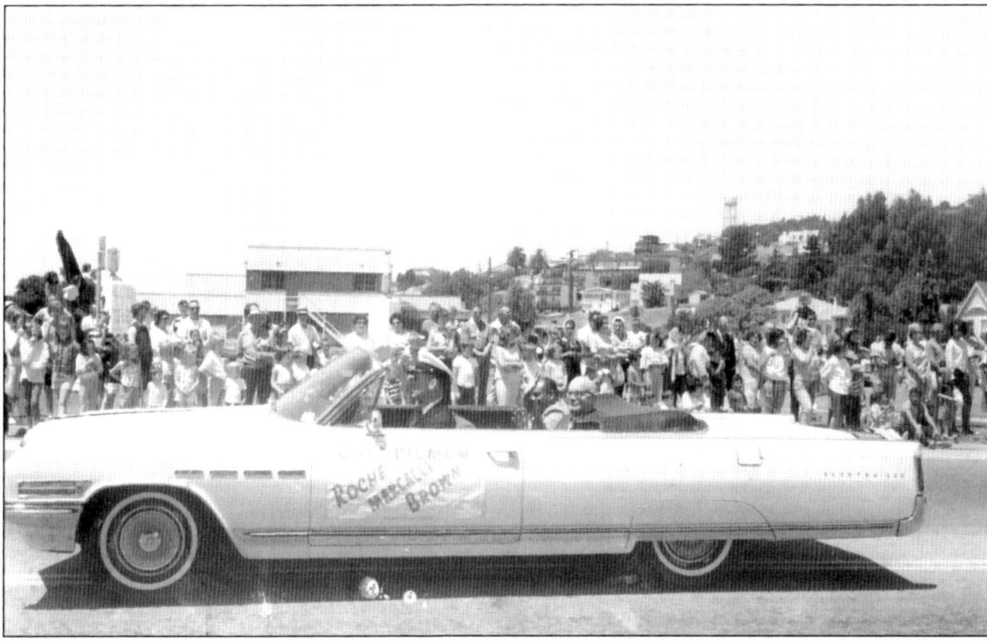

Councilman Lewis Brown rides through Vallejo during a 1960s Fourth of July parade. (Courtesy of Lewis F. Brown.)

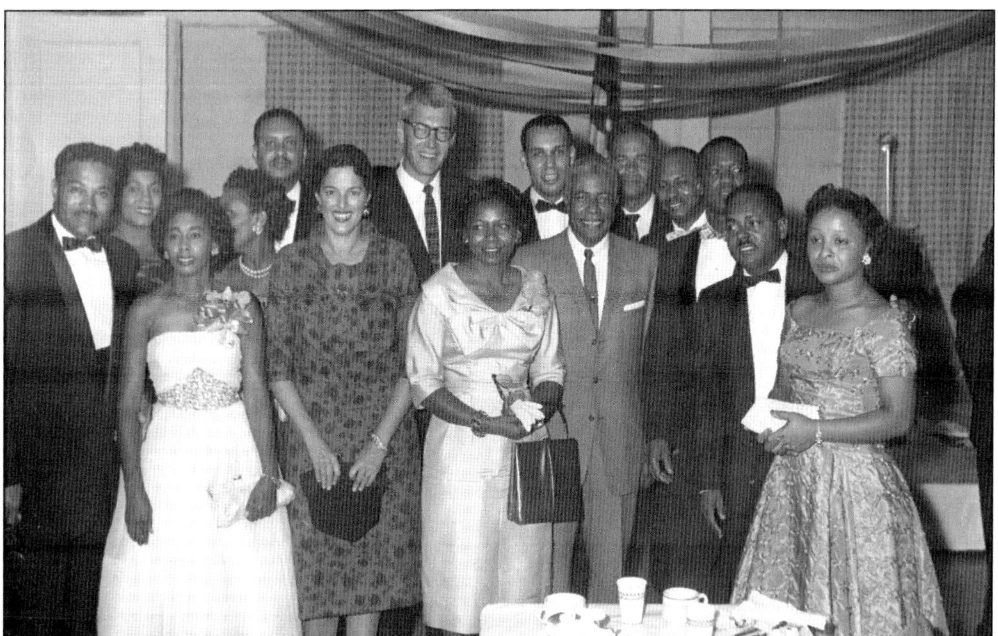

Wooing the African American vote has been a long-standing tradition with political candidates seeking elected office. In the early 1960s, a number of Vallejo's prominent African Americans attended a fundraiser for a candidate seeking statewide office. (Courtesy of Lewis F. Brown.)

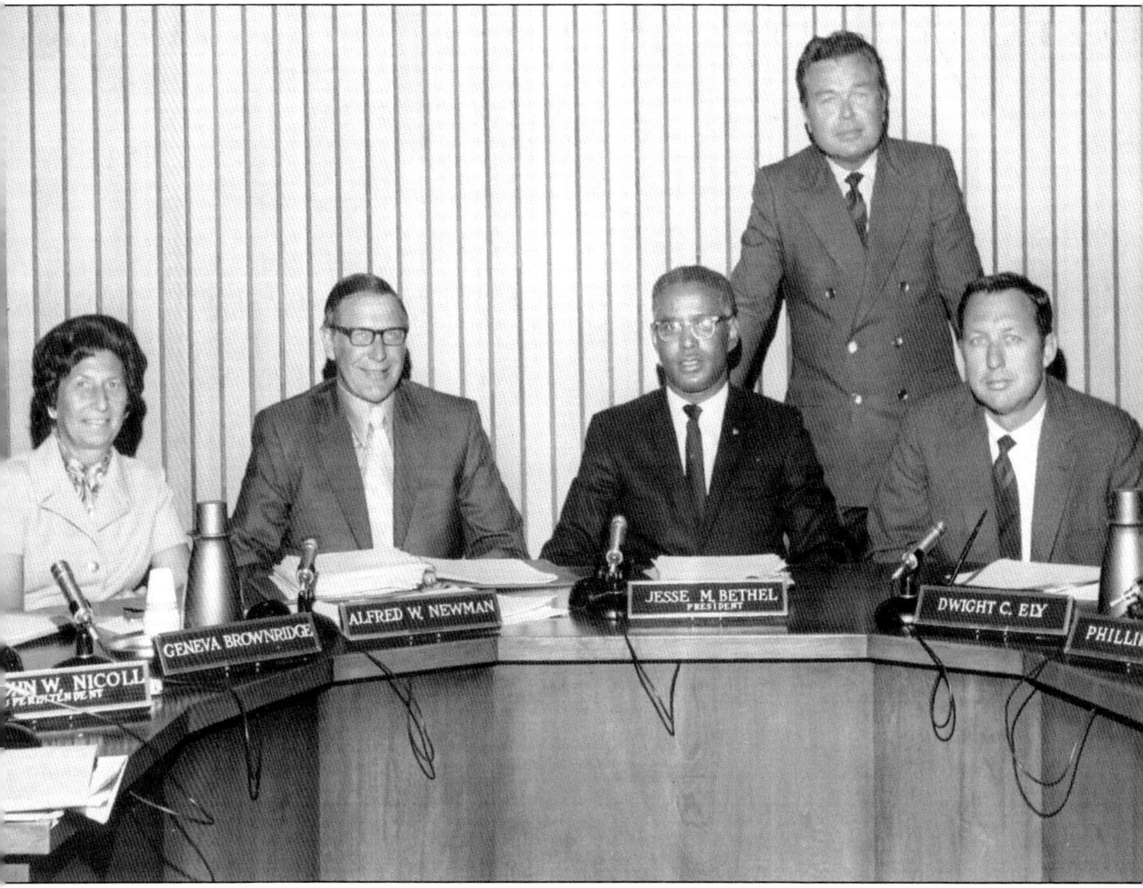

History was made in 1968 when Jesse Bethel was elected to the Vallejo City Unified School District Board of Directors. A chemist at Mare Island Naval Shipyard, Bethel would serve on the board for more than 16 years. A New York City native, Bethel was raised in Ohio, Arkansas, and Oklahoma. He moved to Vallejo in 1944. (Courtesy of Vallejo Naval and Historical Museum.)

Al Morrow was an African American who sought political office in Vallejo in the 1960s and 1970s. He served as president of the Vallejo NAACP twice, from 1965 to 1968 and from 1981 to 1982. It was under Morrow's leadership the NAACP pursued a joint labor-industry effort to enroll African American youth in apprenticeship programs. (Courtesy of the Vallejo Naval and Historical Museum.)

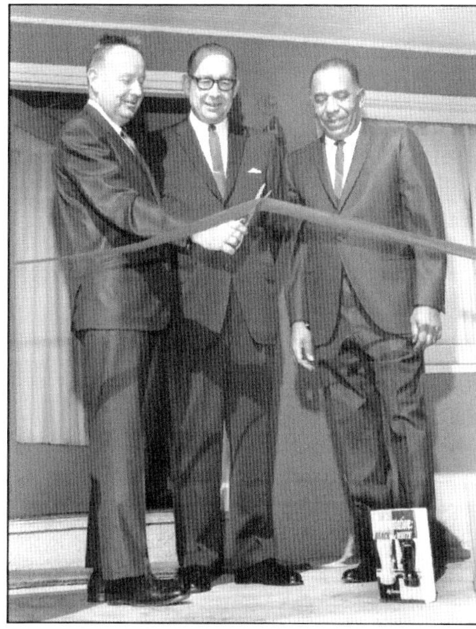

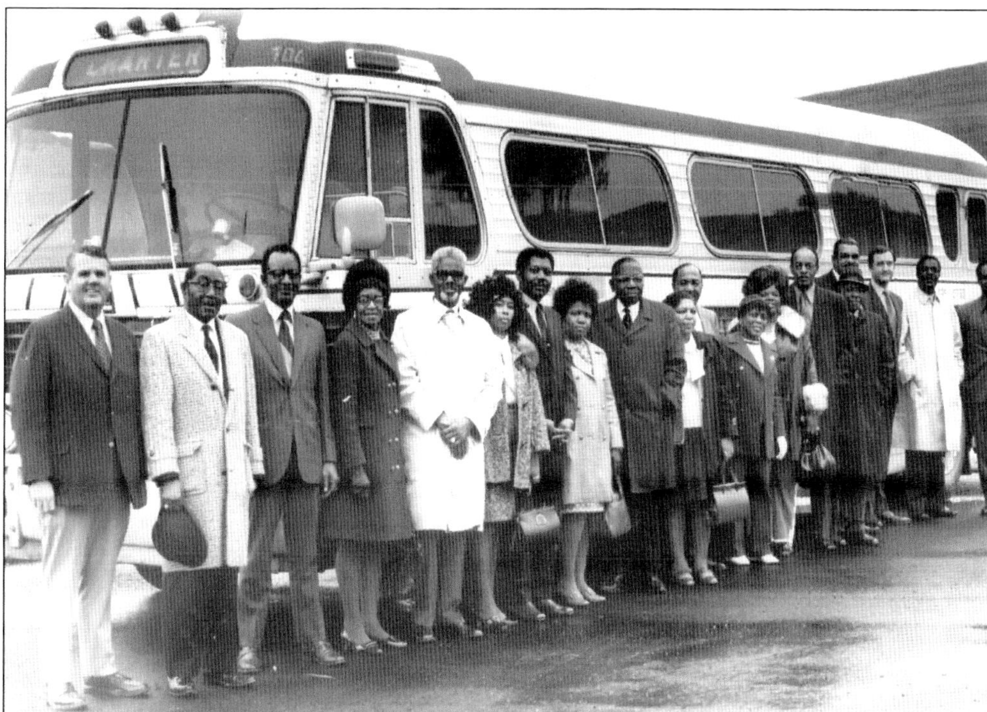

In this early 1970s image, members of the Country Club Crest Improvement Association prepare to leave on a bus tour of the Pacific Telephone Company's Sacramento facility. Taking part in the tour were Jim Morrish and Robert Whyte, telephone company officials; and Country Club Crest residents including the Rev. Leroy McGrue, Hurne Kersee, Vernon Lawhorn, Horace Morris, John Morrison, John McGlothin, Calvin Miller, Eugene Anderson, Mr. and Mrs. Melvin F. Thompson, Mr. and Mrs. Percy Carter, Mr. and Mrs. John LeGrande, Mrs. Mergareta Lawhorn, Jean Anderson, Mrs. Scott, and Bobby Vales. (Courtesy of the Vallejo Naval and Historical Museum.)

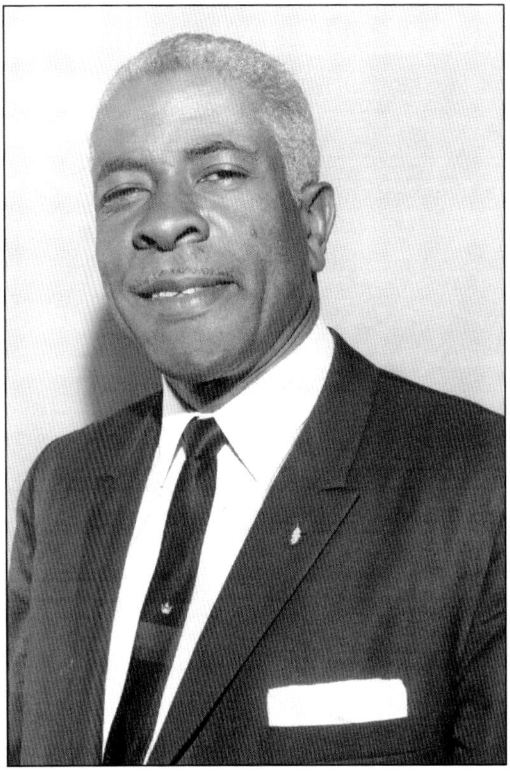

The Reverend Horace J. Morris, pastor of Friendship Missionary Baptist Church, was a dynamic leader of Vallejo's African American community from the late 1940s through 1960s. In the mid-1960s, Morris, along with the NAACP, led the fight against discrimination in local housing and employment. Reverend Morris led Friendship from its beginning in April 1948 until his death on June 4, 1973. (Courtesy of the Vallejo Naval and Historical Museum.)

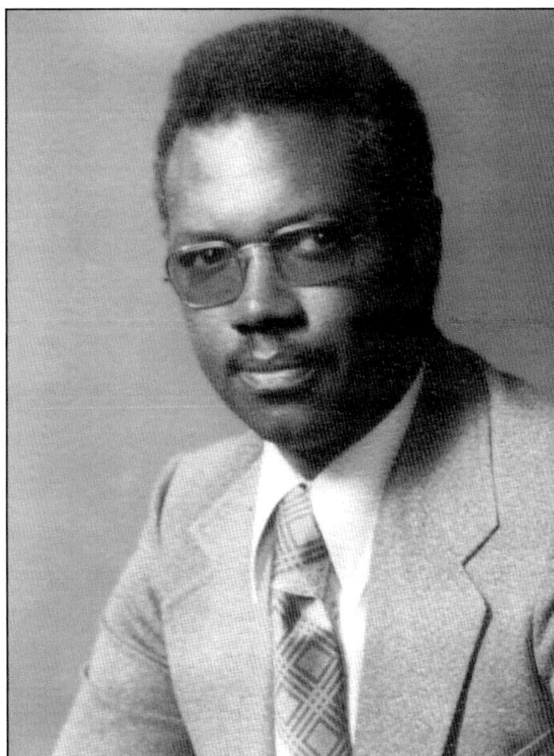

In the early 1960s, Dr. Oscar Jackson started his Vallejo practice on Broadway in Vallejo, making him one of the few African American physicians in Vallejo at the time. A graduate of Howard University's medical school, Jackson served in the Air Force prior to moving to the Bay Area.

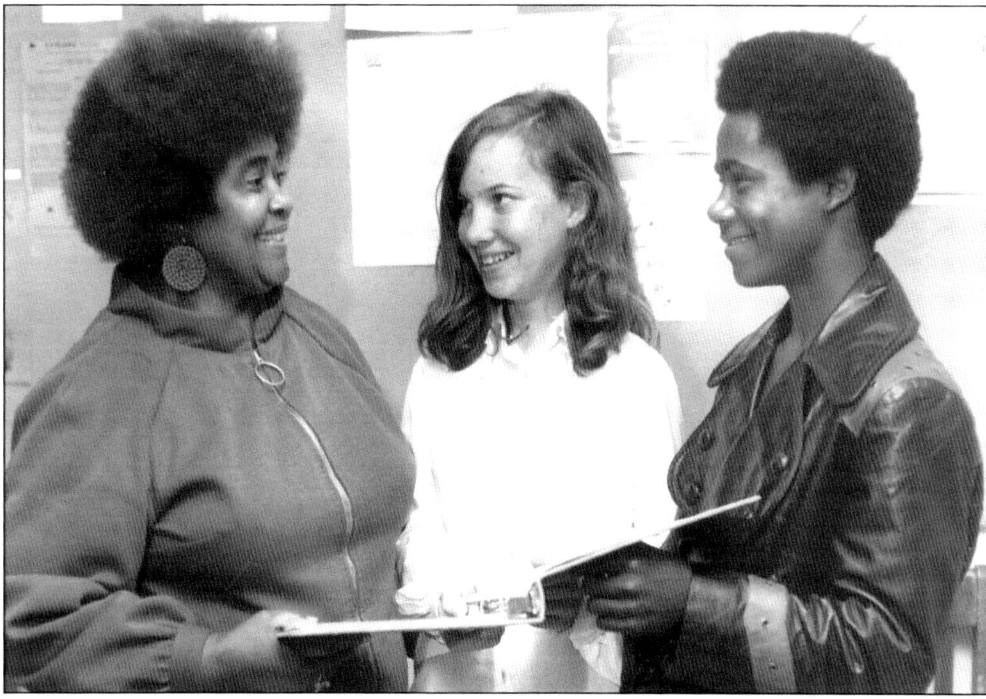

The antipoverty programs of the 1960s and 1970s helped not only with training and employing young African Americans but also organizing communities. In the 1960s, hundreds of young people were hired in the Big Brother Big Sister Program, a mentoring program that paired older youths with younger youths. In this 1971 photograph are Ceola Wade, who had worked with the local antipoverty program from its beginning in the mid-1960s; Stanley Carter; and an unidentified girl. (Courtesy of the Vallejo Naval and Historical Museum.)

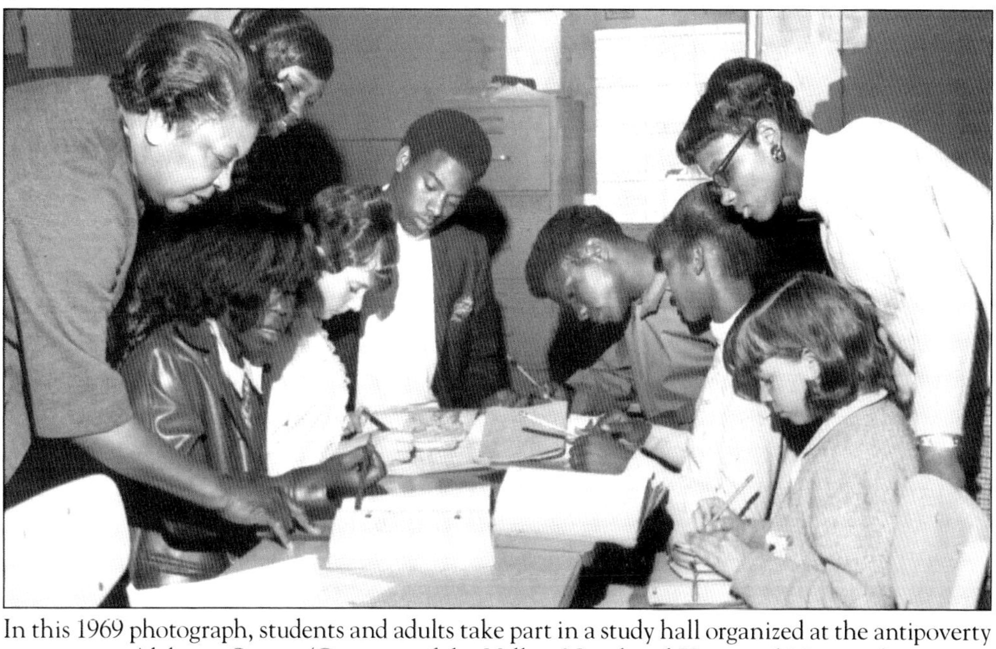

In this 1969 photograph, students and adults take part in a study hall organized at the antipoverty program on Alabama Street. (Courtesy of the Vallejo Naval and Historical Museum.)

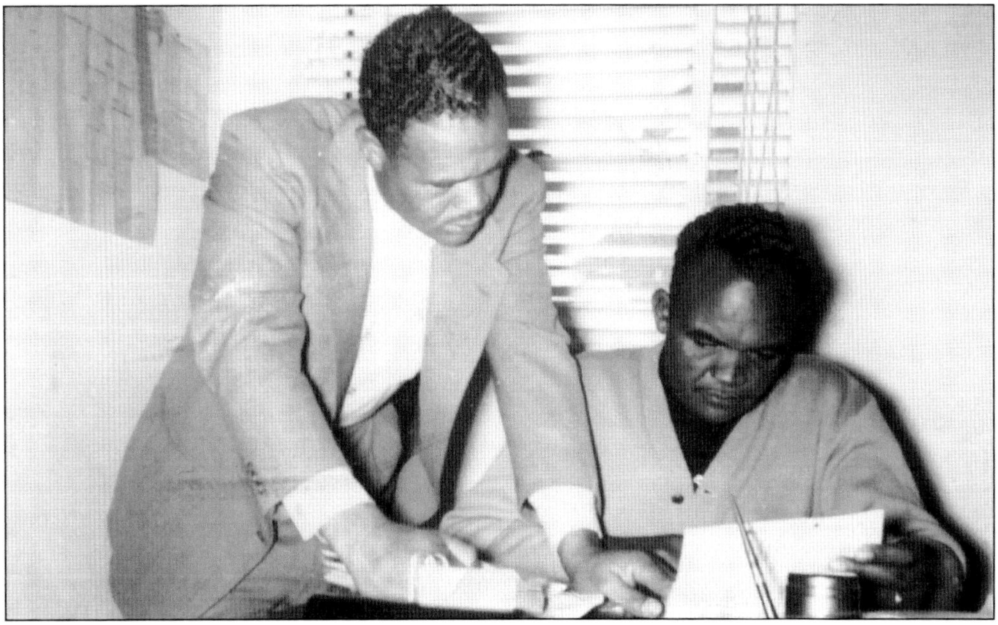

B.W. Williams, left, and his brother James go over plans for a new housing development. Williams and Jones Construction Company, formed in the 1940s, built houses for African Americans in Arizona; New Mexico; Pittsburg, California; and Richmond, California. The company also built dozens of houses in the College Park subdivision in Vallejo in the early 1960s. (Courtesy of Althea Lett.)

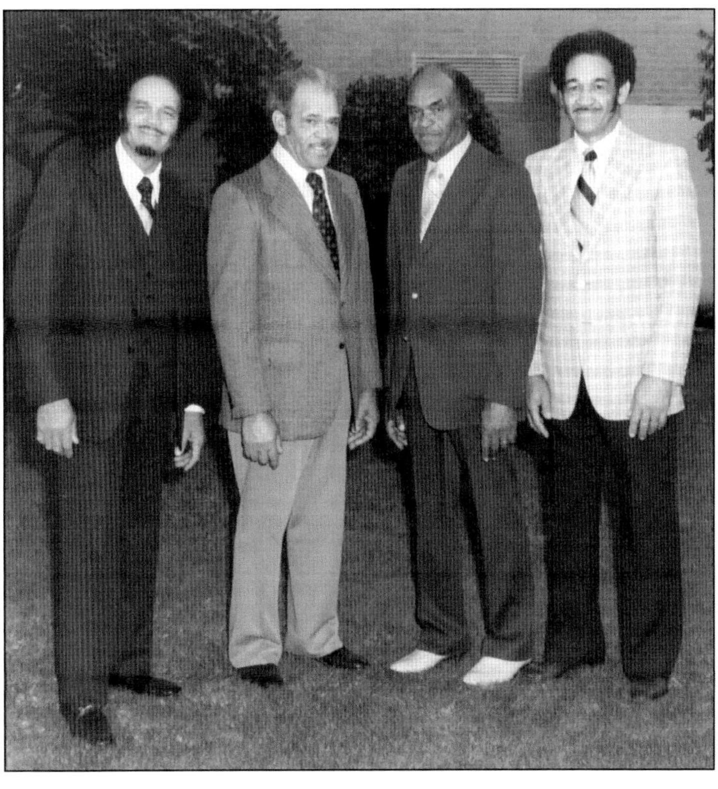

In the early 1970s, B.W. Williams, James, Dareman, and Travis Williams pose in front of the Lofas Place-Lakeside home built by their family business, the Williams and Jones Construction Company. The brothers were all successful in their own right. B.W. and James ran the Williams and Jones Construction Company in Vallejo, while Dareman and Travis operated the company in Arizona. (Courtesy of Althea Lett.)

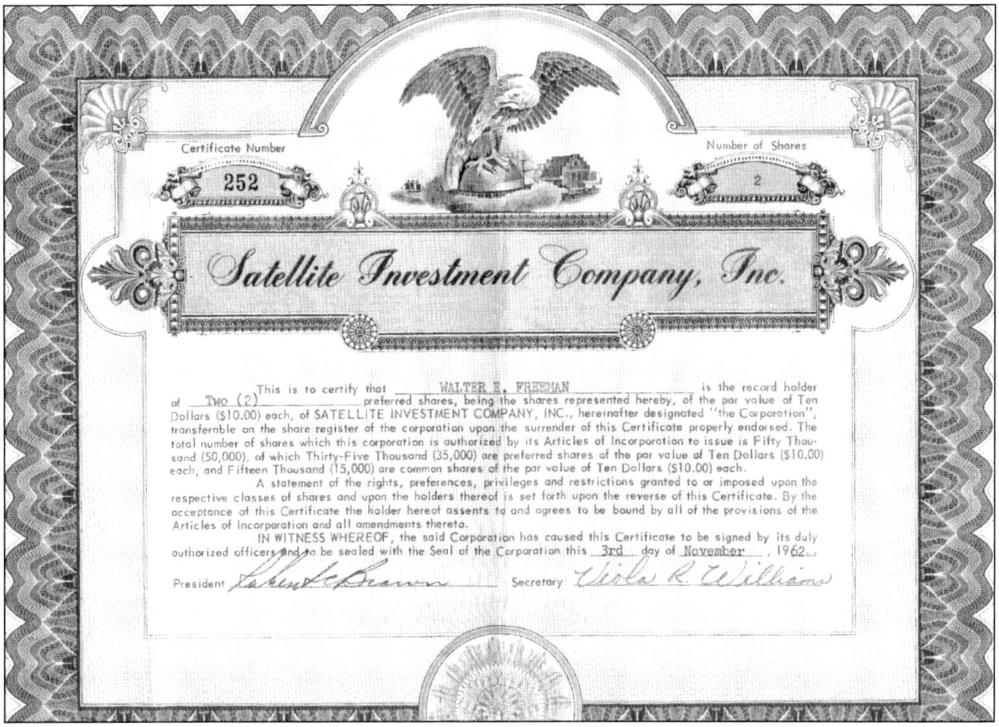

Certificate Number

252

Number of Shares

2

Satellite Investment Company, Inc.

This is to certify that WALTER E. FREEMAN is the record holder of Two (2) preferred shares, being the shares represented hereby, of the par value of Ten Dollars ($10.00) each, of SATELLITE INVESTMENT COMPANY, INC., hereinafter designated "the Corporation", transferable on the share register of the corporation upon the surrender of this Certificate properly endorsed. The total number of shares which this corporation is authorized by its Articles of Incorporation to issue is Fifty Thousand (50,000), of which Thirty-Five Thousand (35,000) are preferred shares of the par value of Ten Dollars ($10.00) each, and Fifteen Thousand (15,000) are common shares of the par value of Ten Dollars ($10.00) each.

A statement of the rights, preferences, privileges and restrictions granted to or imposed upon the respective classes of shares and upon the holders thereof is set forth upon the reverse of this Certificate. By the acceptance of this Certificate the holder hereof assents to and agrees to be bound by all of the provisions of the Articles of Incorporation and all amendments thereto.

IN WITNESS WHEREOF, the said Corporation has caused this Certificate to be signed by its duly authorized officers and to be sealed with the Seal of the Corporation this 3rd day of November, 1962.

President [signature] Secretary Viola R. Williams

In an effort to raise money to construct the Lofas-Lakeside housing development, B.W. Williams established the Satellite Investment Company and sold shares to Vallejo residents. (Courtesy of Althea Lett.)

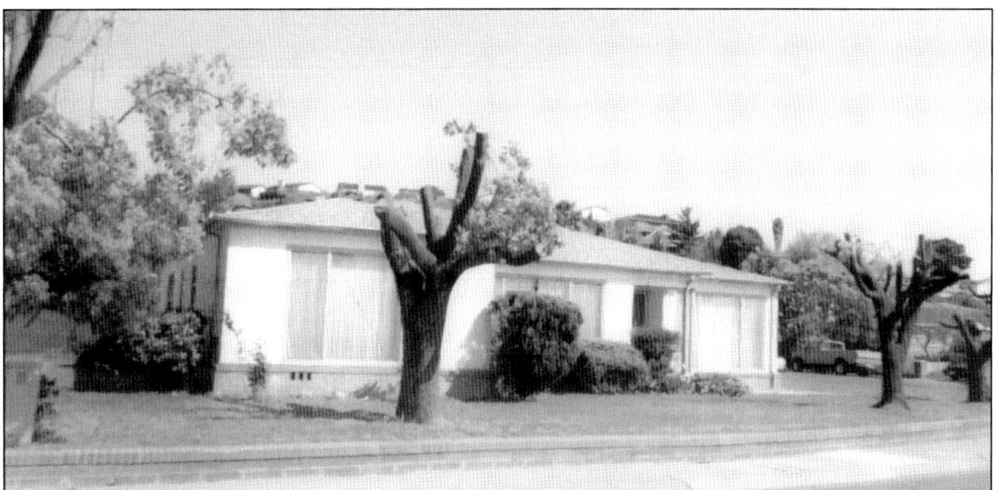

Here is the home of building contractor B.W. Williams at the corner of Walnut and Encerti Streets in 1952. While Williams brought his building skills to Vallejo in the 1950s, James Owens, a former Buffalo Soldier who came to Vallejo around 1902 after the Spanish-American War, was one of Vallejo's earliest-known African American building contractors. Owens may have helped in the construction of the Spanish-American War Veterans Hall at 1209 Georgia Street, which later became the meeting place for Prince Hall Masons, Firma Lodge No. 27. (Courtesy of Althea Lett.)

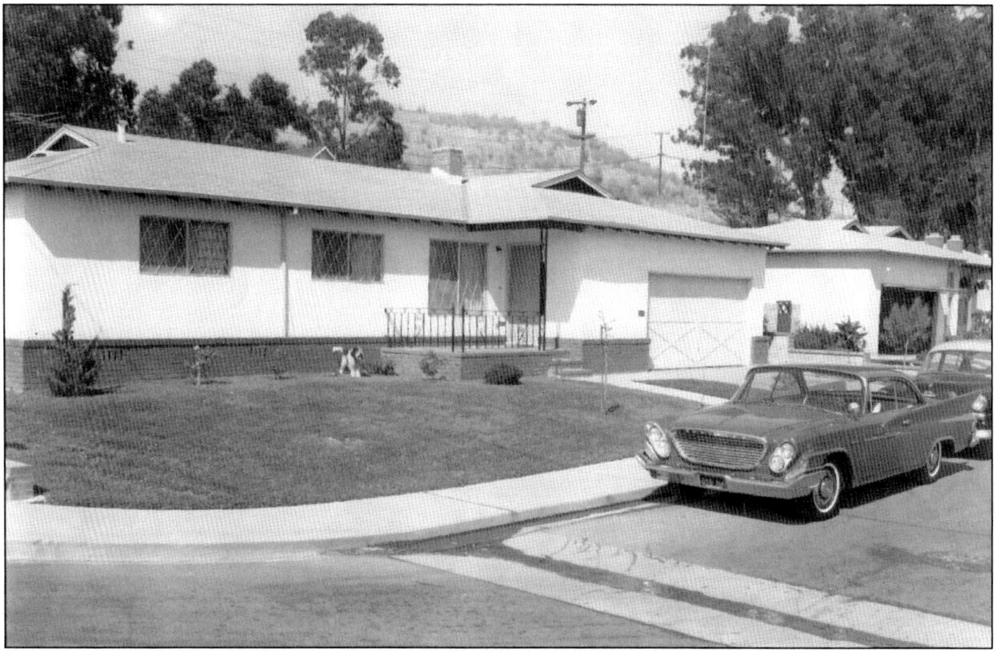

The Lewis F. Brown home, built in the 1960s, is yet another example of a Williams and Jones Construction Company home. The Vallejo City Council voted to name the street that runs past his home for the former city councilman and attorney. Brown's father, Frank, who lived in Laurel, Mississippi, and brother Dr. Willie Brown, of Fresno, have streets named for them in their cities. (Courtesy of Lewis Brown.)

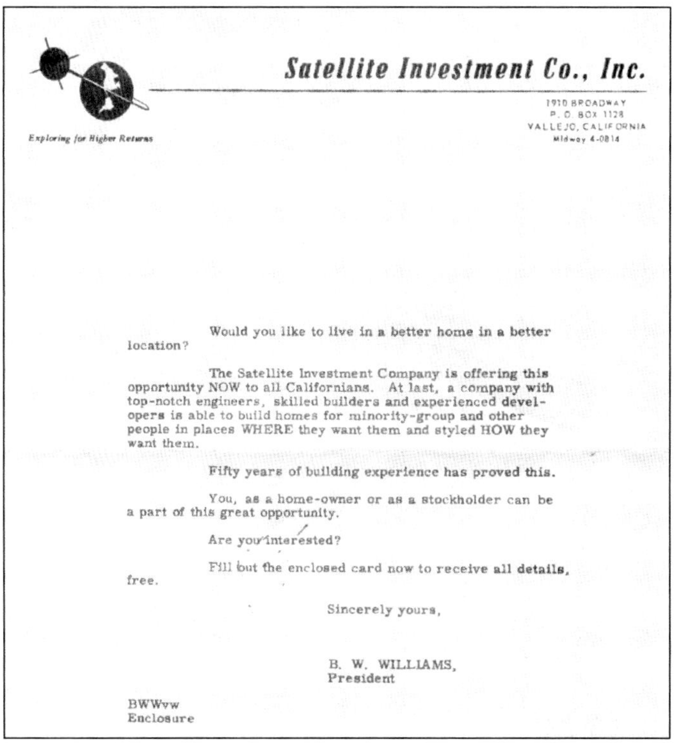

Satellite Investment Co., Inc.

1910 BROADWAY
P. O. BOX 1128
VALLEJO, CALIFORNIA
MIdway 4-0814

Exploring for Higher Returns

Would you like to live in a better home in a better location?

The Satellite Investment Company is offering this opportunity NOW to all Californians. At last, a company with top-notch engineers, skilled builders and experienced developers is able to build homes for minority-group and other people in places WHERE they want them and styled HOW they want them.

Fifty years of building experience has proved this.

You, as a home-owner or as a stockholder can be a part of this great opportunity.

Are you interested?

Fill out the enclosed card now to receive all details, free.

Sincerely yours,

B. W. WILLIAMS,
President

BWWvw
Enclosure

This 1950s letter encouraged potential investors and homeowners to invest in the Satellite Investment Company. It states, "At last, a company with top-notch engineers, skilled builders and experienced developers is able to build homes for minority-group and other people in places *where* they want them and styled *how* they want them." (Courtesy of Althea Lett.)

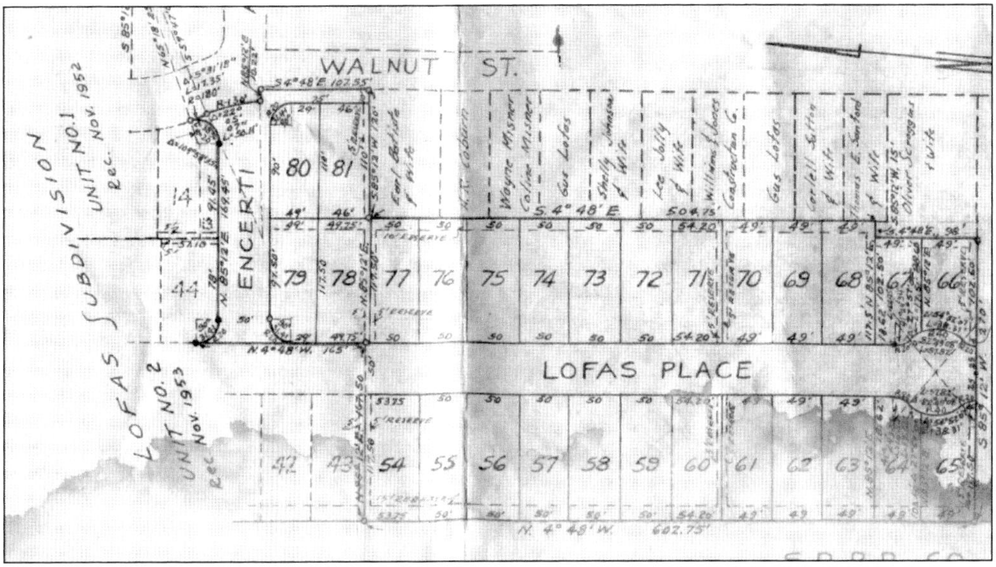

Here is a detailed section from the 1952 building plans for the Lofas-Lakeside subdivision. In the 1800s, Charles and Henry Hannibal owned the land where Lofas-Lakeside and the Country Club Crest housing subdivision are located. The 1880 census lists the brothers as mulatto, with Henry working as a farmer and Charles listed as a carpenter. (Courtesy of Althea Lett.)

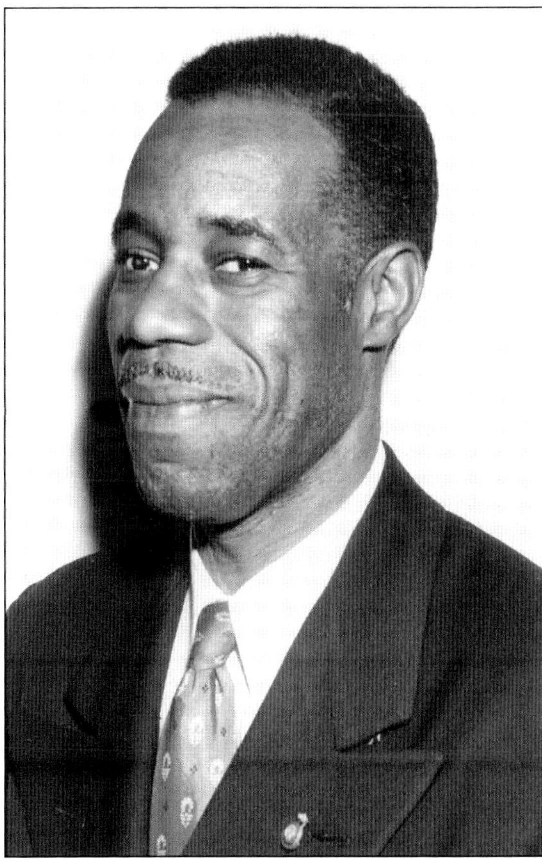

Walter Freeman was born and raised in Stockton, California, and moved to Vallejo with his young family in the 1940s. The family stayed in Chabot Terrace. For several years, he worked at Mare Island but eventually took a job as the Vallejo agent of Golden State Mutual Insurance, an African American insurance company based in Los Angeles. Freeman played a significant role in getting the word out about the new housing development that would become the Lofas-Lakeside subdivision. As an insurance agent, Freeman spoke to countless African American families on a daily basis. During those meetings with families, he made it known that the impending North Vallejo area was their opportunity to become homeowners and to have a neighborhood of their own. The Freeman family, who lived on Walnut Street (later renamed B.W. Williams Drive), was one of the first families to move into the Lofas-Lakeside subdivision. (Courtesy of the Vallejo Naval and Historical Museum.)

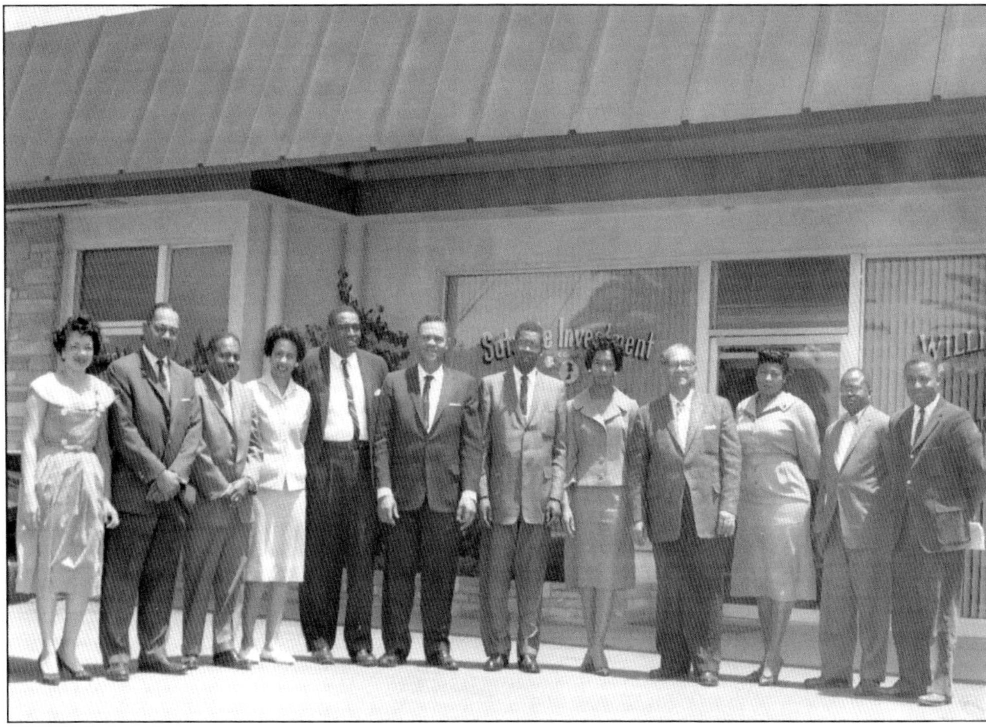

Members of the Williams and Jones Construction Company, including B.W. Williams, center; the Satellite Investment Company Board of Directors; and residents of the newly completed second phase of the Lofas-Lakeside subdivision on Pepper Drive stand outside the Satellite Investment Company's headquarters on Broadway. In addition to other office space in the building, the Satellite Building had a laundromat. (Courtesy of Althea Lett.)

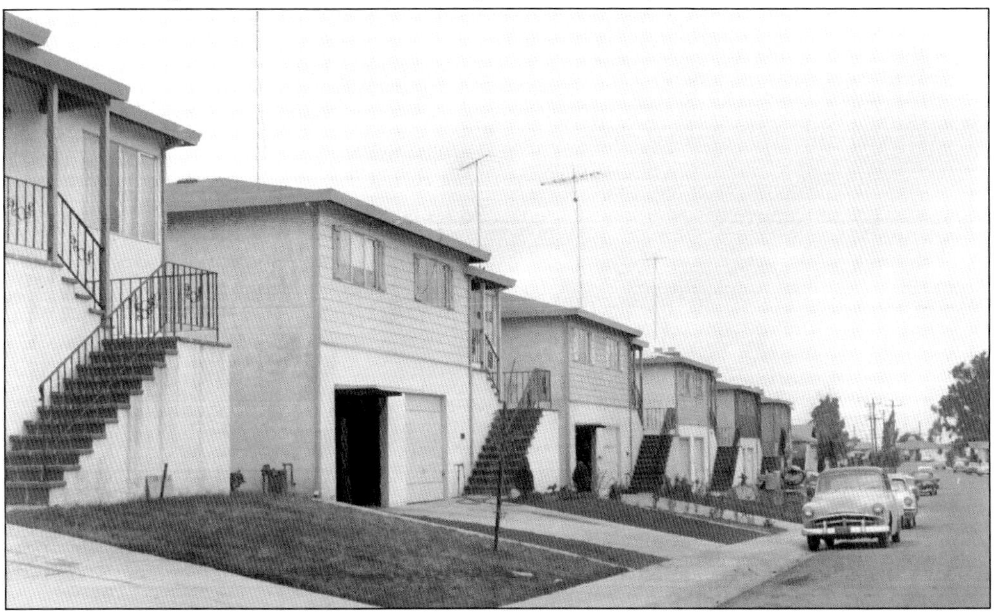

The newly completed Pepper Drive housing tract, built in the early 1960s, has both two- and one-story homes. (Courtesy of Althea Lett.)

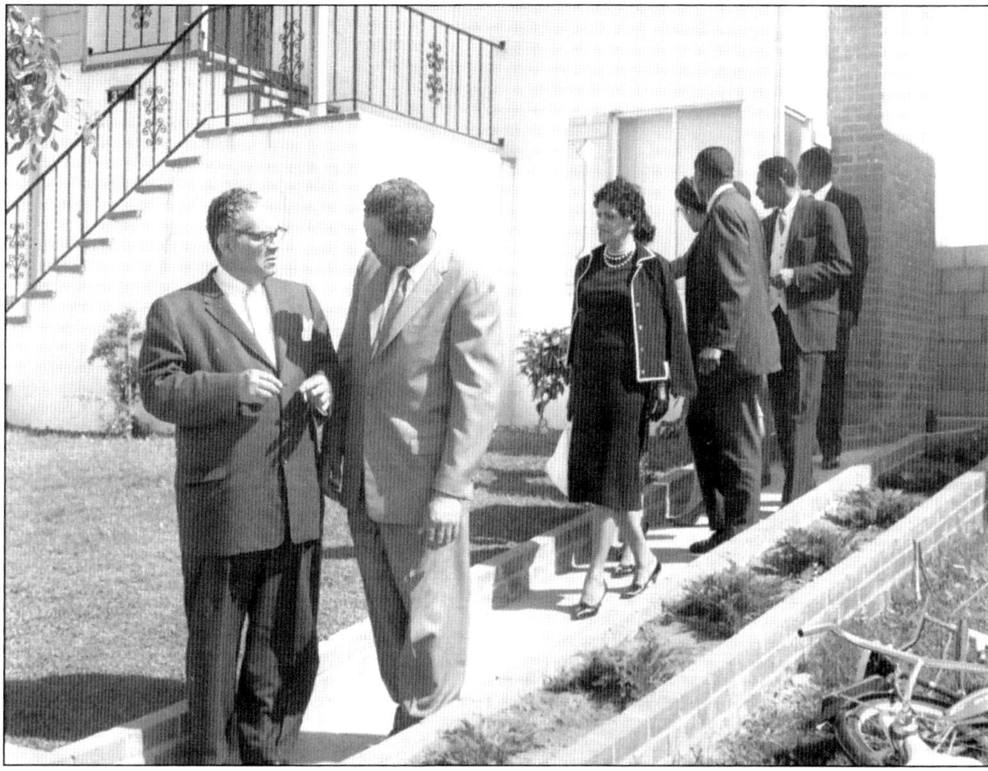

Potential homebuyers are seen touring the newly built homes on Pepper Drive. Harry Fox, a noted African American photographer from San Francisco, documented the tour. (Courtesy of Althea Lett.)

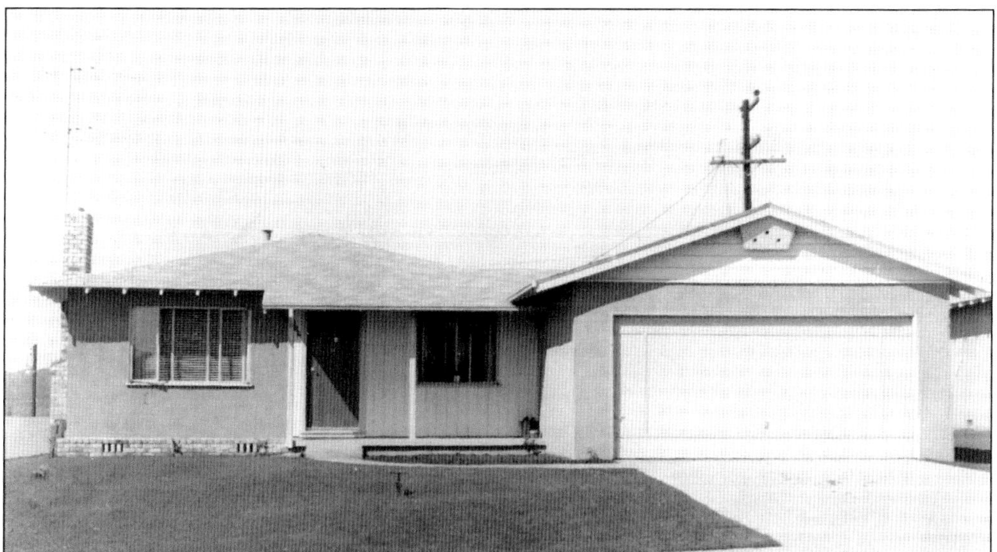

Around the same time the Lofas-Lakeside subdivision was being built, another subdivision, Country Club Crest Estates, was constructed. Many of the families who moved to "the Crest" in the late 1950s and early 1960s were former residents of neighborhoods throughout Vallejo, including Floyd Terrace. Many moved to the Crest from the East Bay. (Courtesy of Althea Lett.)

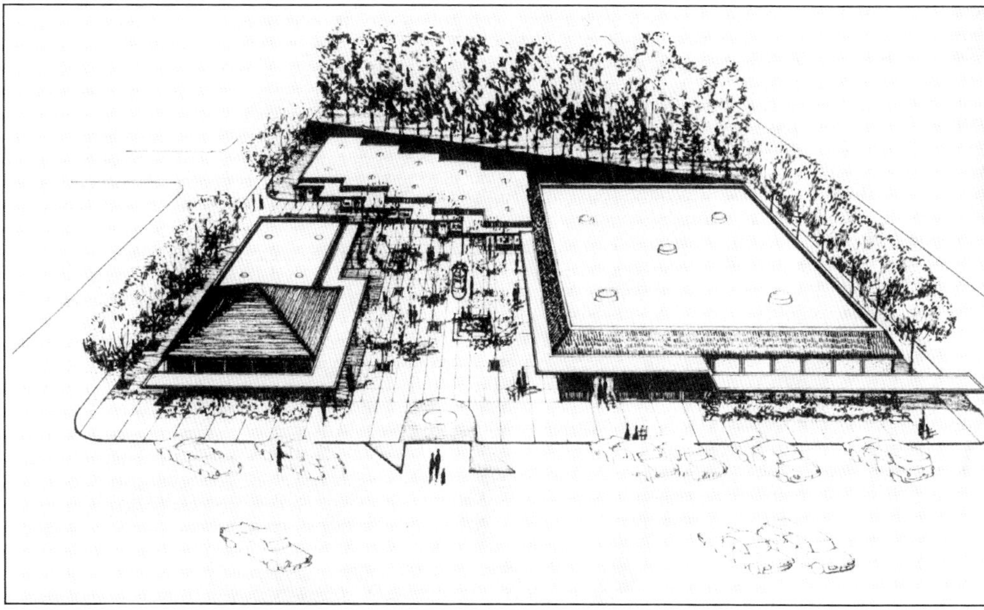

In the late 1960s and early 1970s, residents of Country Club Crest started developing plans for a shopping center near their housing development. (Courtesy of the Vallejo Naval and Historical Museum.)

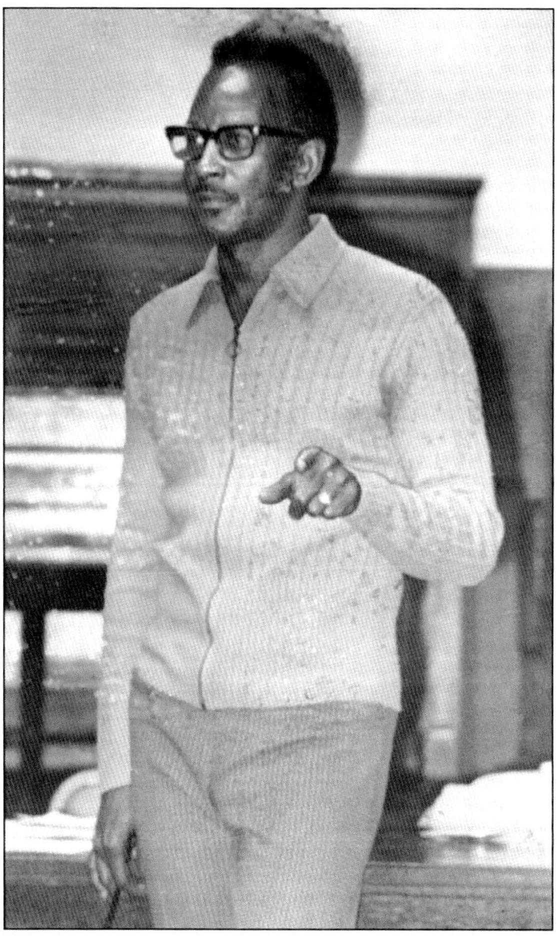

Melvin Thompson, longtime president of the Country Club Crest Improvement Association, pushed for greater recognition and city services for the North Bay neighborhood. (Courtesy of the Vallejo Naval and Historical Museum.)

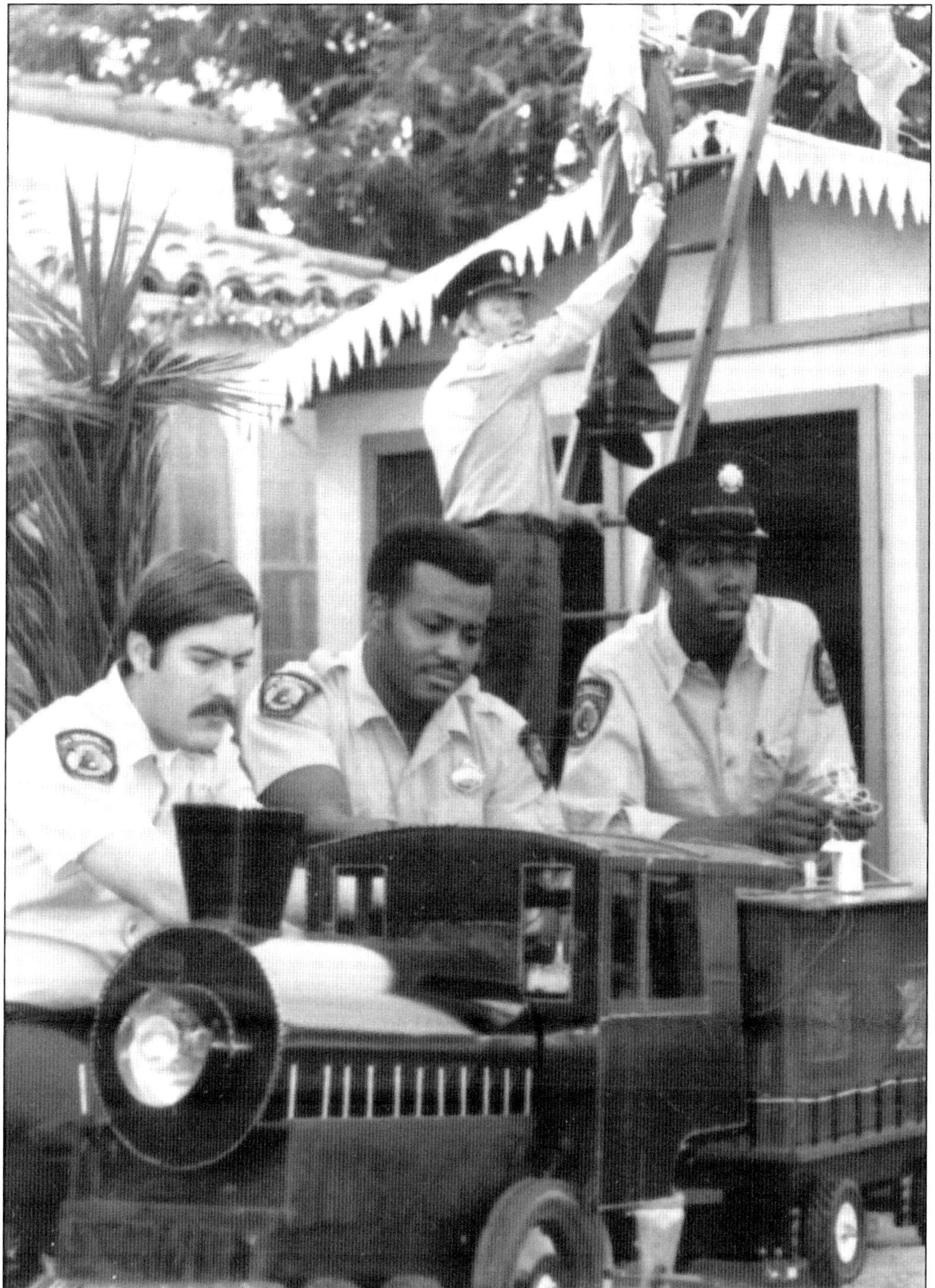

The late 1960s and early 1970s in Vallejo saw the hiring of several African American policemen and firefighters. In this 1970s photograph, Don Baxter (center) and Robin Mackbee are pictured with their colleagues preparing the old fire department at Maryland and Alameda Streets for Christmas. Mackbee, a lifelong resident of Vallejo, lost his life during a fire on July 28, 1980. (Courtesy of the Vallejo Naval and Historical Museum.)

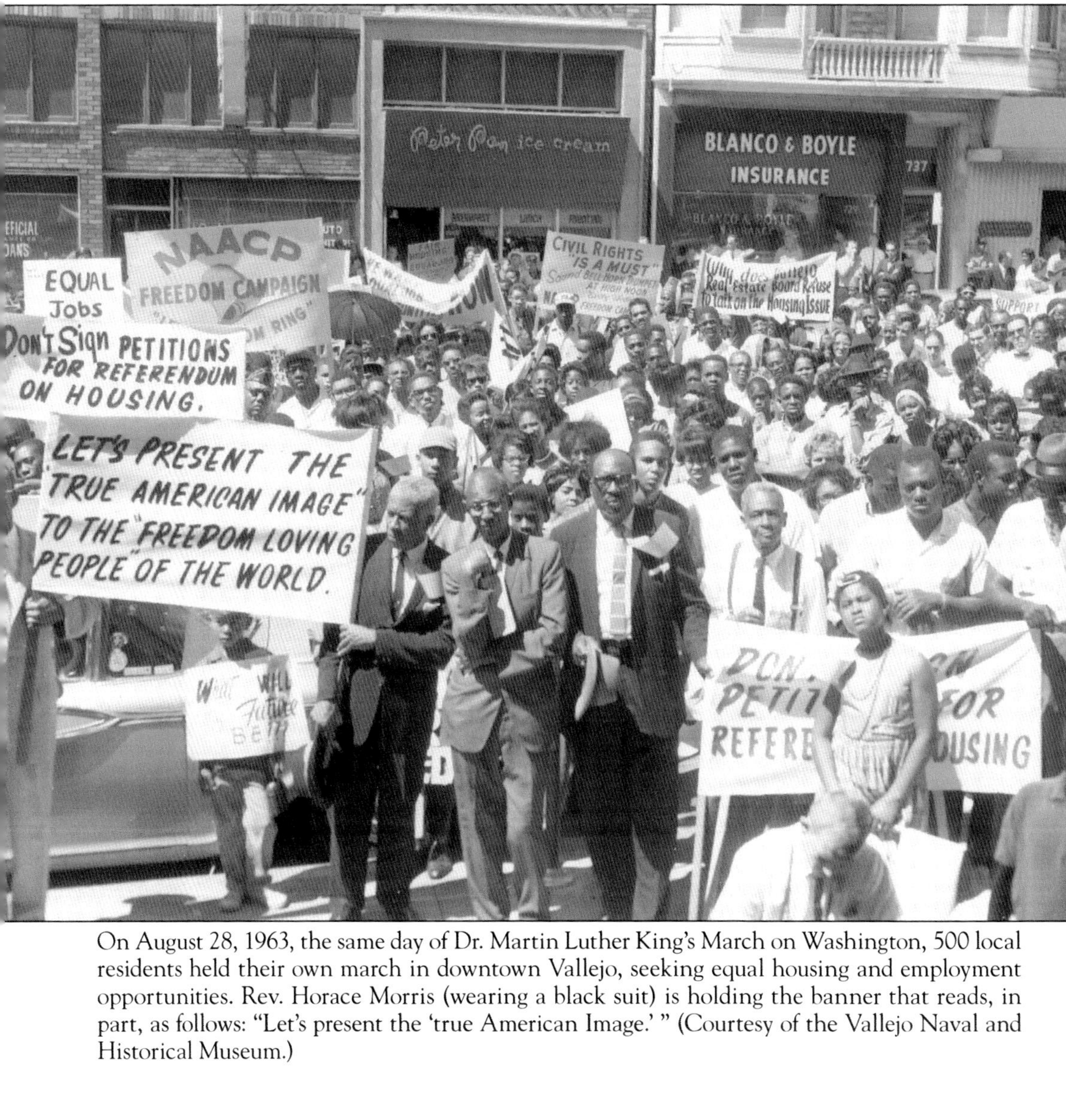

On August 28, 1963, the same day of Dr. Martin Luther King's March on Washington, 500 local residents held their own march in downtown Vallejo, seeking equal housing and employment opportunities. Rev. Horace Morris (wearing a black suit) is holding the banner that reads, in part, as follows: "Let's present the 'true American Image.' " (Courtesy of the Vallejo Naval and Historical Museum.)

Marchers proceed down Georgia Street in a peaceful march on August 28, 1963. By the early 1960s, African Americans nationwide were making their voices heard by marching, boycotting, and picketing for equal rights. The same was true in Vallejo. Several business in Vallejo—AGE was one—did not hire African Americans, though they shopped at the store by the hundreds. The Vallejo NAACP, with the slogan "Don't Buy Where You Can't Work," mounted a vigorous campaign against such bigotry and pushed for the boycott of any local store that refused to hire blacks. (Courtesy of the Vallejo Naval and Historical Museum.)

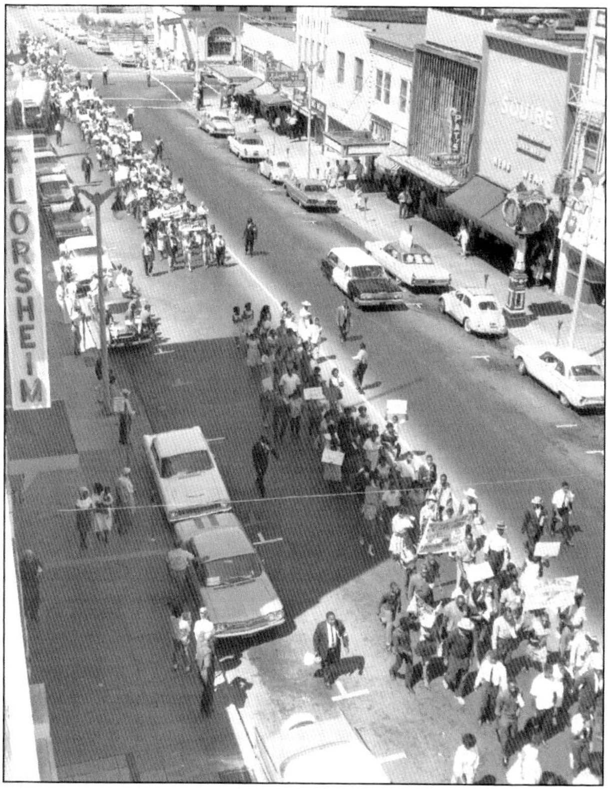

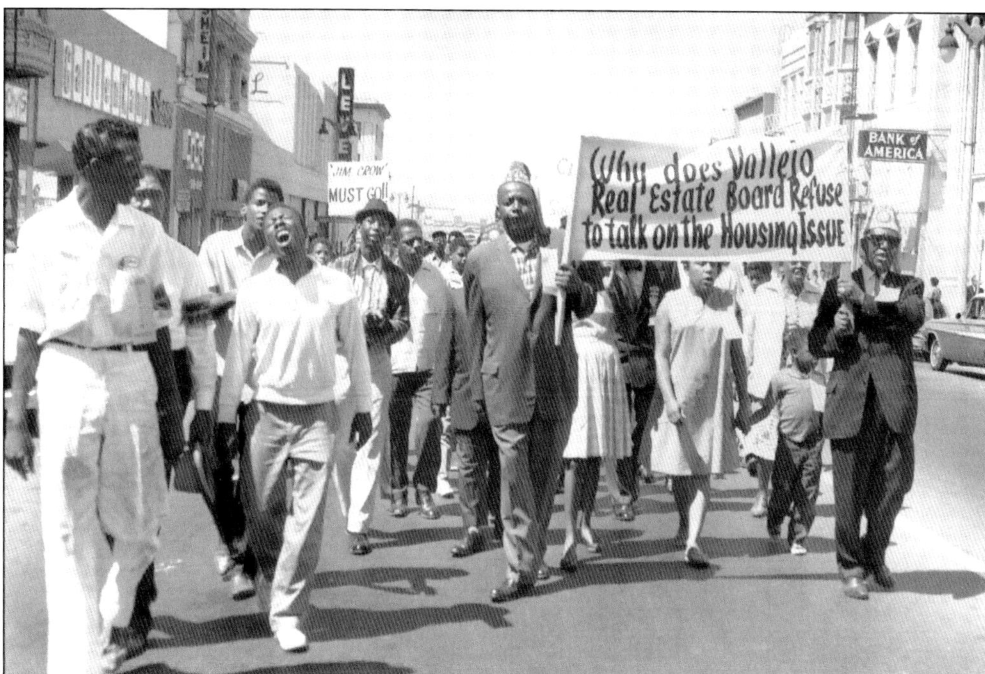

Dozens of youngsters joined the August 1963 protests. (Courtesy of the Vallejo Naval and Historical Museum.)

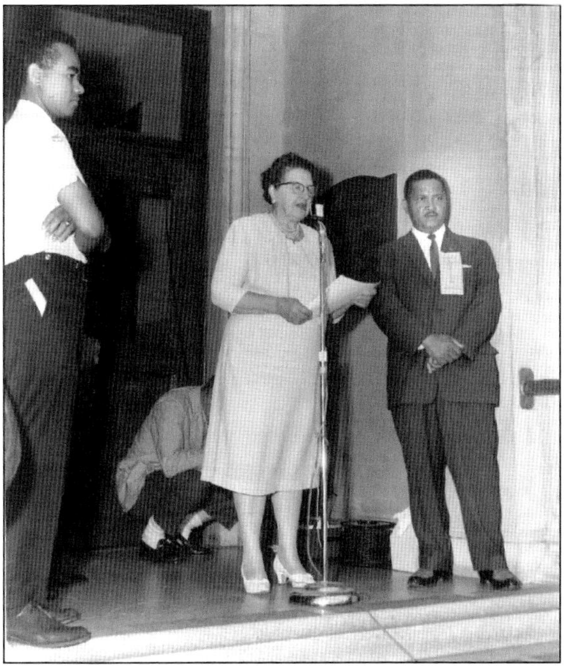

In this October 1963 photograph, Vallejo mayor Florence Douglas reads a proclamation in support of a rally organized by the local branch of the NAACP and the Vallejo Federated Leadership Council. Rally organizers included Bill Parrish (left) and Clarence Poche (right) of the NAACP. The rally was held at Vallejo's waterfront, and its aim was to support an ongoing boycott against local merchants who refused to employ African Americans.

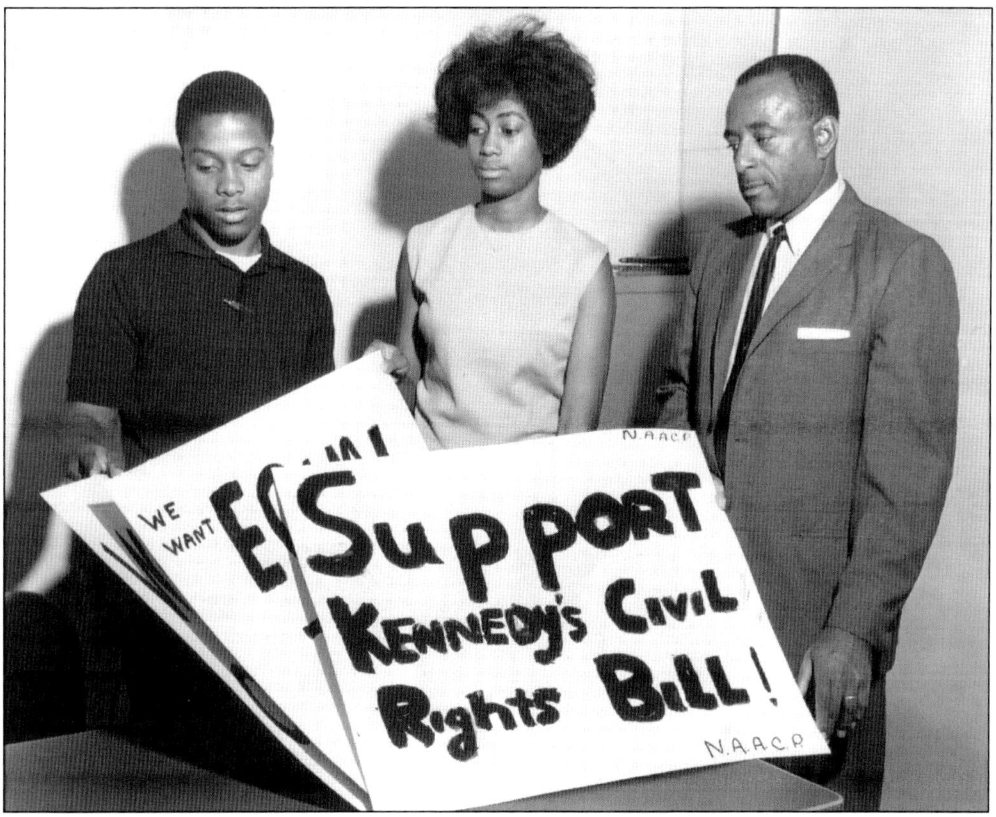

DuWane Hill, Vallejo NAACP president, looks on as students prepare for the August 1963 march in Vallejo. (Courtesy of the Vallejo Naval and Historical Museum.)

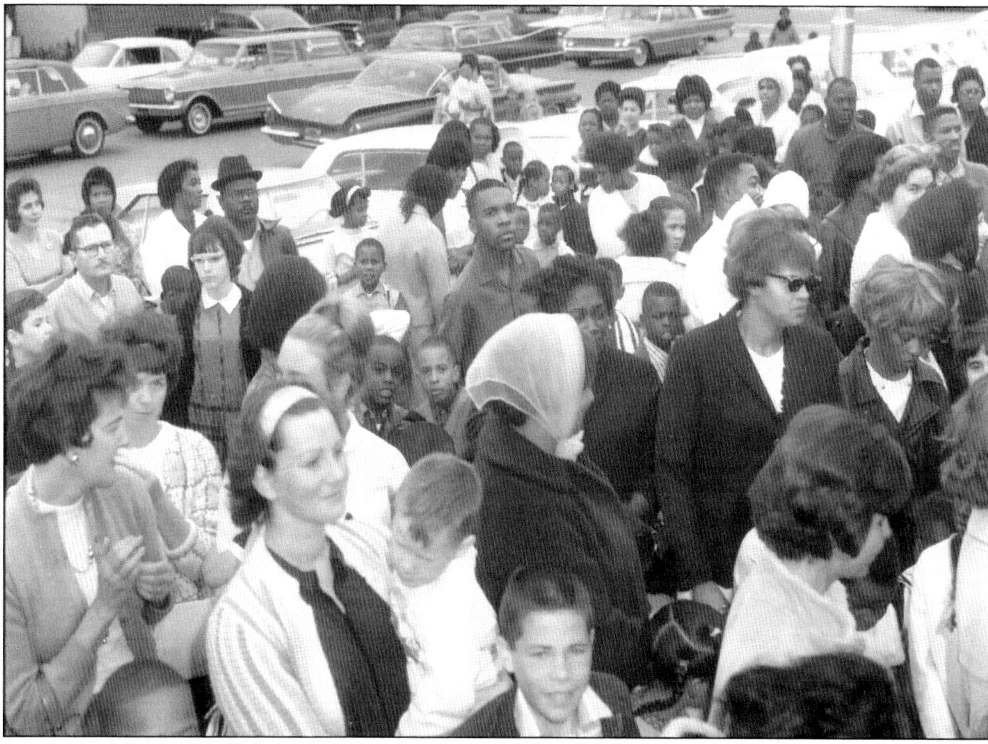

In September 1966, more than 250 parents in North Vallejo protested the doubling of classes at Olympic Elementary School. Built during the war years of the 1940s, Olympic was not equipped to accommodate the growing number of children who were moving to newly built subdivisions in the area. Just four years earlier, a group of African American leaders, including B.W. Williams and the Reverend Horace Morris, spoke of their fears that the area surround Olympic School would become segregated. Their fears were that children would not be adequately educated and city services to the area would suffer. (Courtesy of the Vallejo Naval and Historical Museum.)

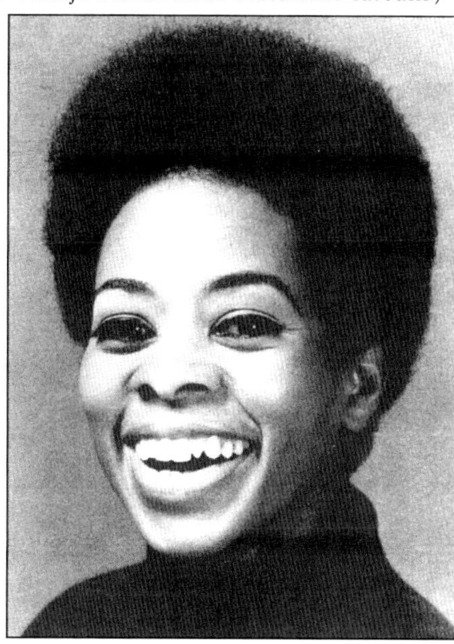

In the late 1970s, Kelly Marie Berry—dancer, actress, playwright, and innovator—launched Danse Uhuru, a multicultural enrichment program for young people in Vallejo. (Courtesy of the Vallejo Naval and Historical Museum.)

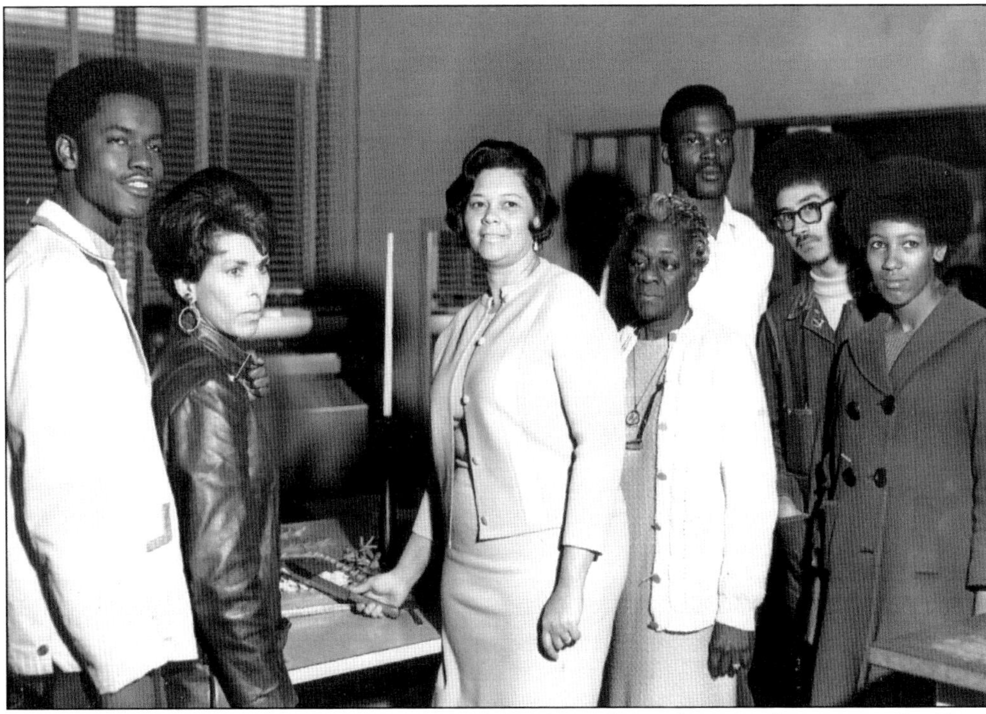

In this March 1969 photograph, students and faculty welcomed new college counselor Doris Higgins during a reception the Solano Community College Black Student Union (BSU). The college's BSU was formed in 1968. Higgins was one of several African Americans hired on the college's faculty, in large part, because of student protests on campus. Pictured with Higgins are, Michael Brown, Jere Faurea, Mamie Jefferson, Mike McGriff, Joe Tholmer, and Toni Davis. Mamie Jefferson was the first African American woman to run for the Solano Community College School Board. (Courtesy of the Vallejo Naval and Historical Museum.)

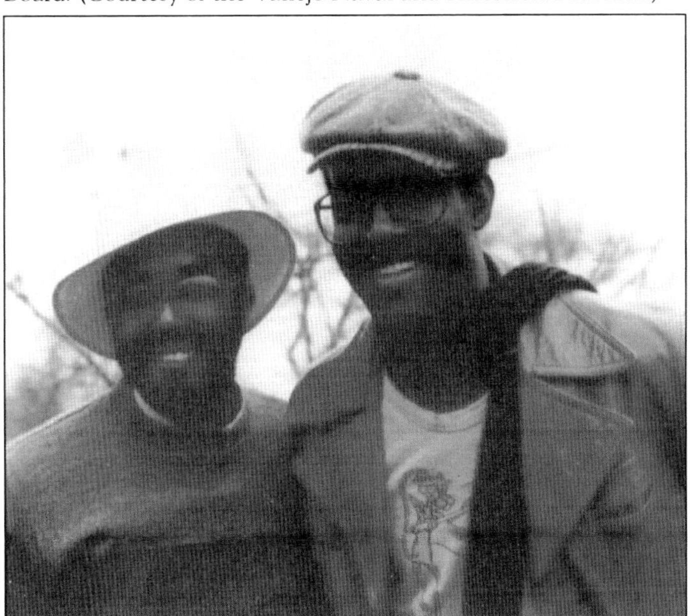

In 1968, Jerry Mobery and Michael McGriff were two of the founding members of the Solano Community College Black Student Union. The work of the BSU helped bring about numerous changes at the community college and in Vallejo, including the increased hiring of African American and other minority faculty and staff and the creation of an ethnic studies program. (Courtesy of the author.)

Jimmy Boyden, also known as "Jimbo Sudan," was actively involved in the protests at Solano Community College in the 1960s. He was one of 19 African American students who were arrested following a sit-in demonstration in November 1968 at Solano Community College. The students, including the author, were charged with trespassing after they refused to leave a classroom. (Courtesy of the Boyden collection.)

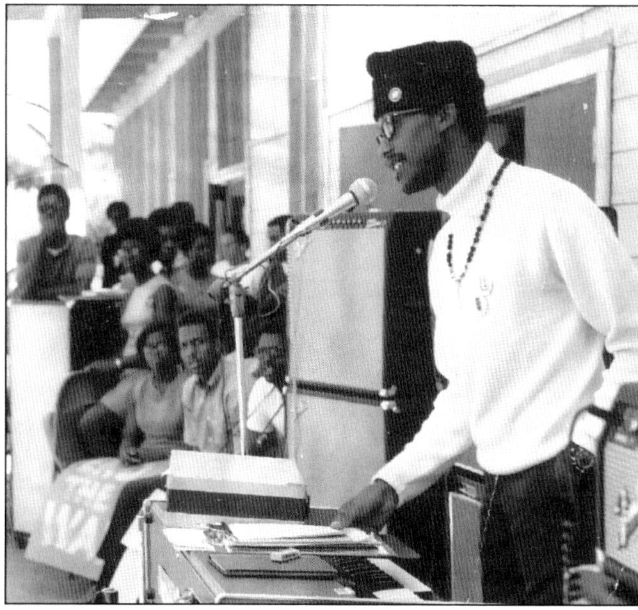

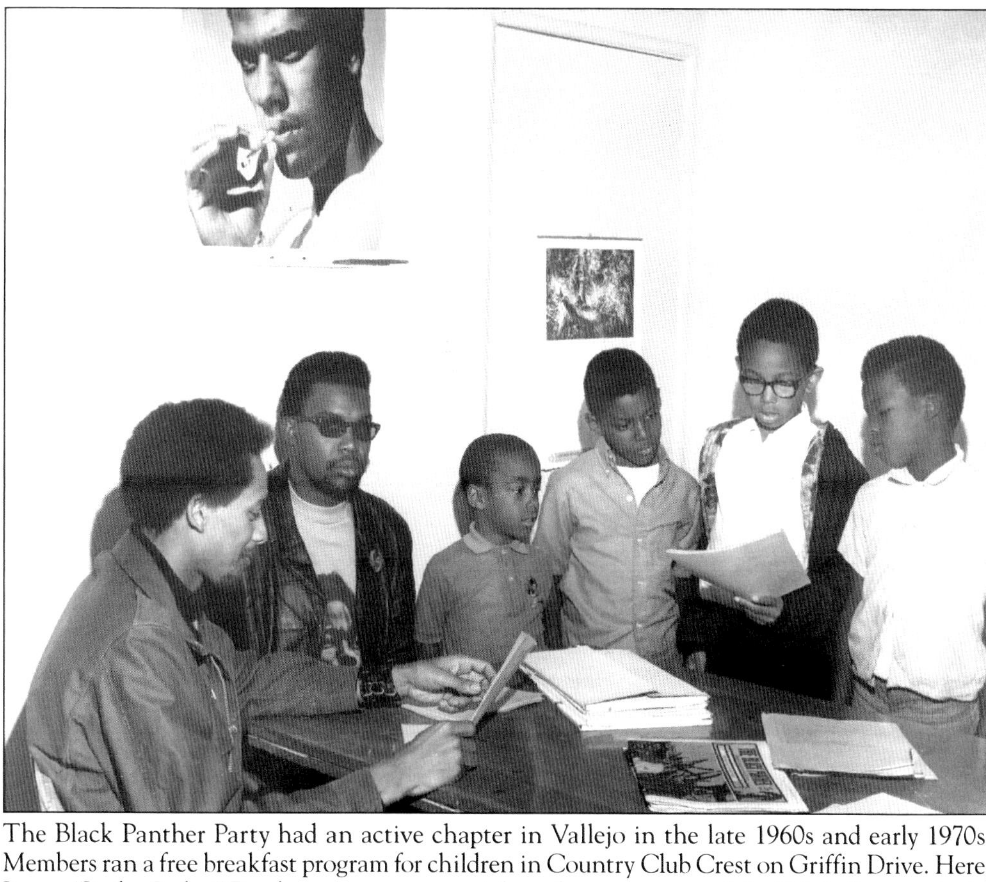

The Black Panther Party had an active chapter in Vallejo in the late 1960s and early 1970s. Members ran a free breakfast program for children in Country Club Crest on Griffin Drive. Here, Jimmy "Jimbo Sudan" Boyden passes out materials to the youngsters, while Calvin Bennett looks on. (Courtesy of the Vallejo Naval and Historical Museum.)

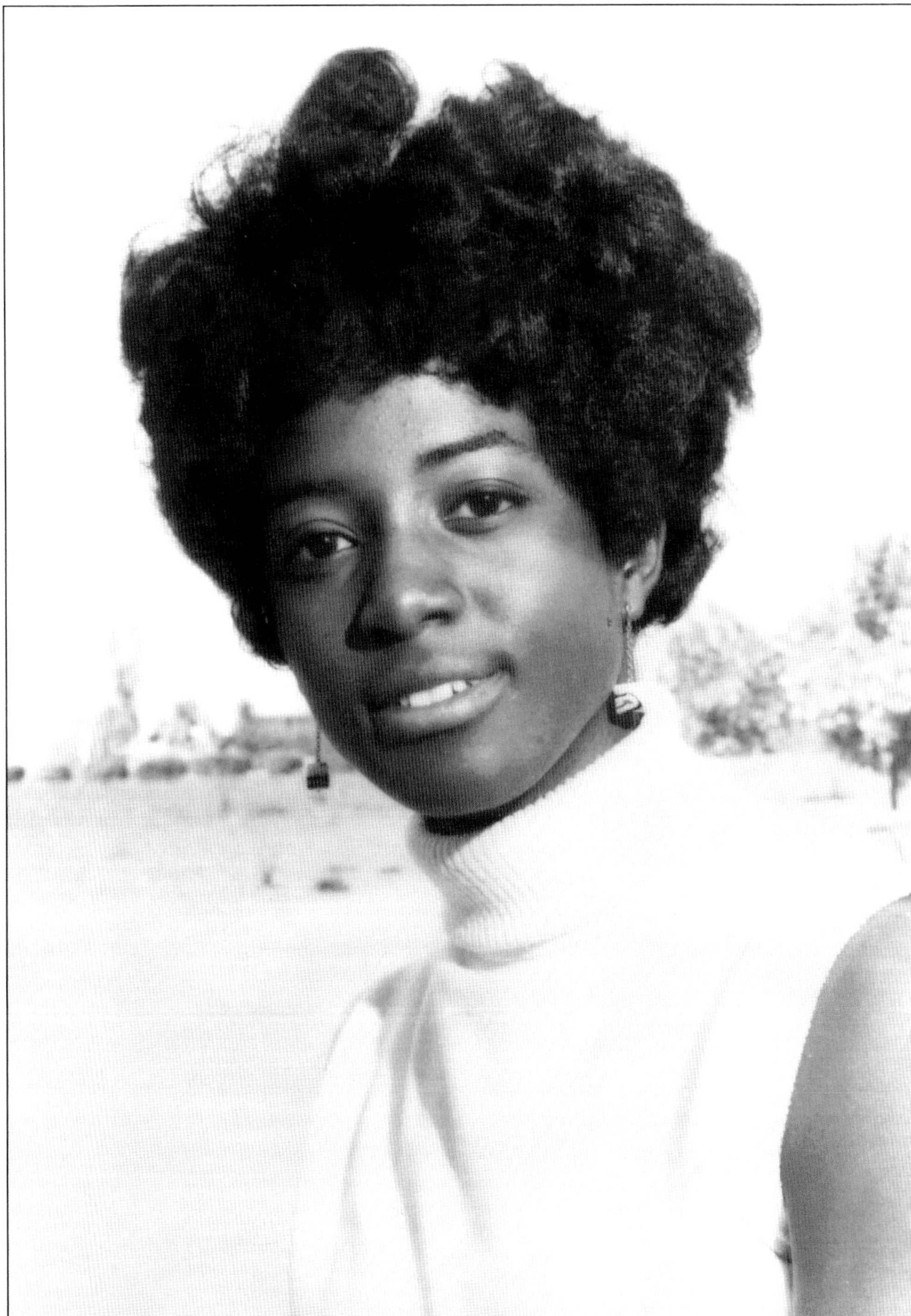

Barbra McCleod (Evans) was crowned homecoming queen of Solano Community College in 1968, making her the first African American homecoming queen in the college's history. (Courtesy of the author.)

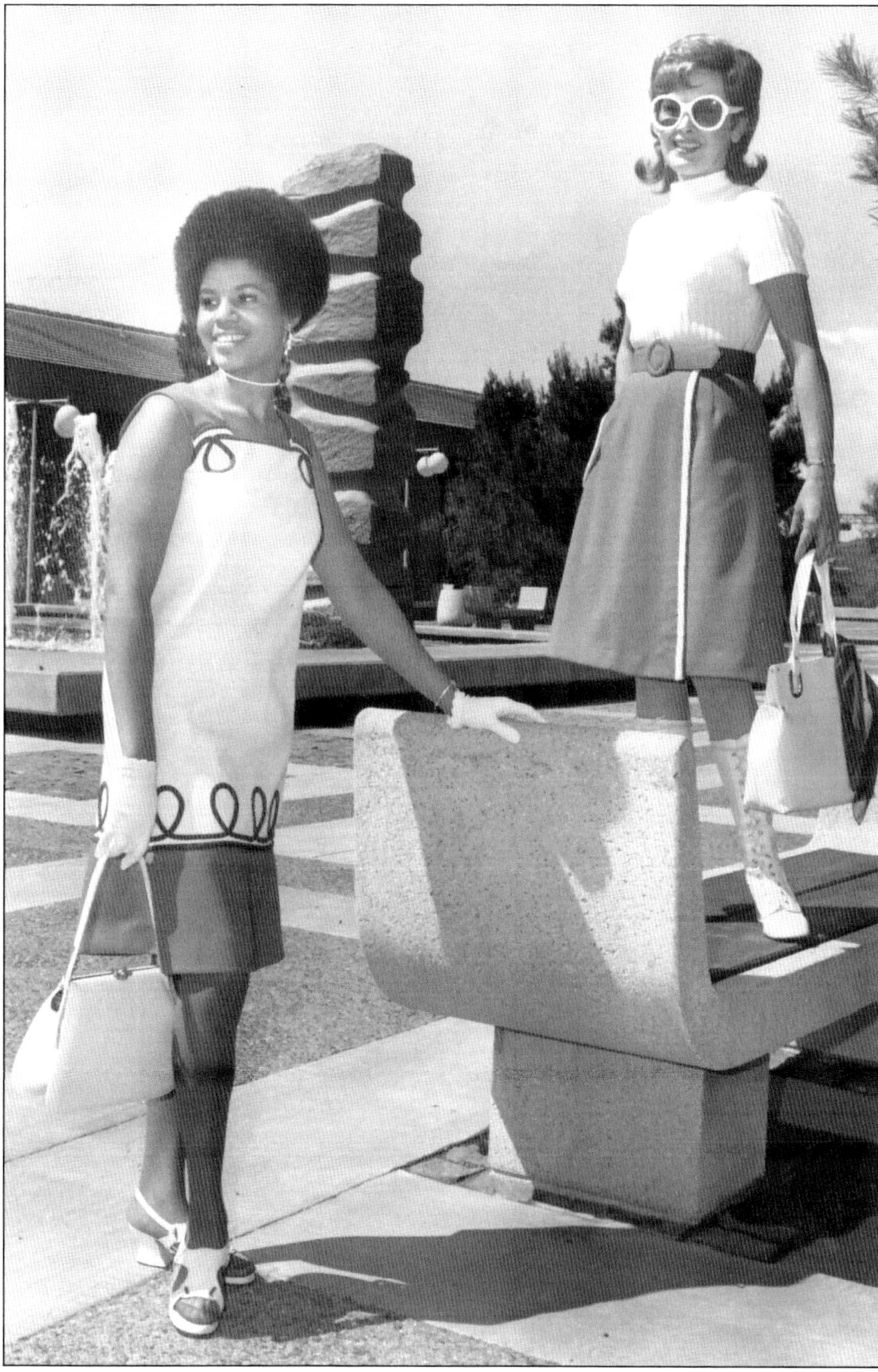

Linnie Bell Harris Joiner, left, was the first African American to work in sales at the Levee's Department in downtown Vallejo. She started working in Levee's during the holiday season before graduating from high school. Following her 1963 graduation, she started working full-time at the popular department store. In the early 1970s, Joiner became the first African American to work as a senior buyer for the company. (Courtesy of the Vallejo Naval and Historical Museum.)

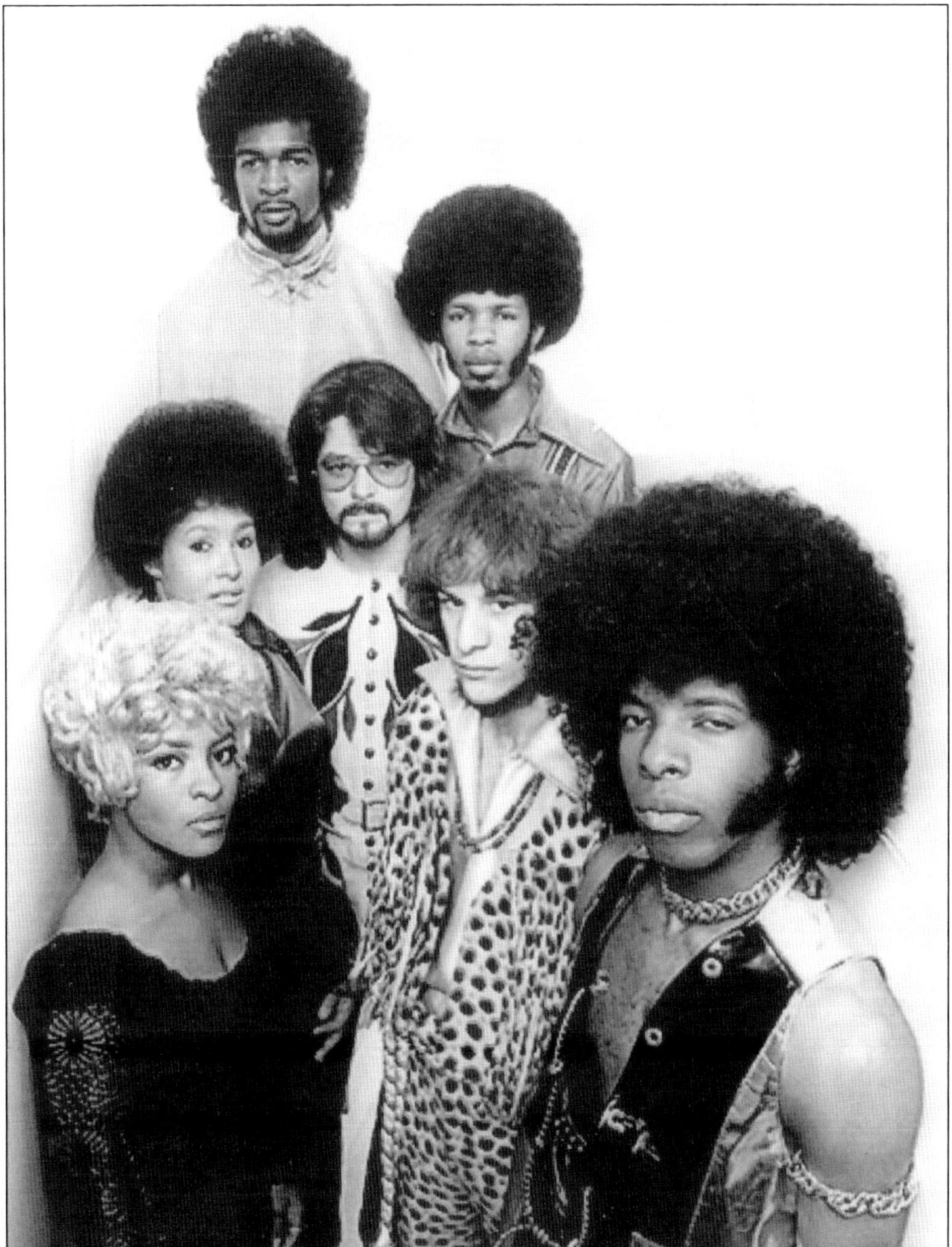

The main member of Sly and the Family Stone, Sylvester Stewart was raised in Vallejo. The Stewart family hailed from Texas and moved to Vallejo in the early 1950s. Sylvester Stewart's musical promise emerged early. As a youngster, he sang gospel with his family members, "The Stewart Four." While attending Vallejo High School, he joined up with local singing groups. Sly and the Family Stone, which burst on the national music scene in the late 1960s, included Sylvester, his sister Rosie, brother Freddie, and Bay Area musicians Larry Graham, Cynthia Robinson, Jerry Martini, and Greg Errico. (Courtesy of the author.)

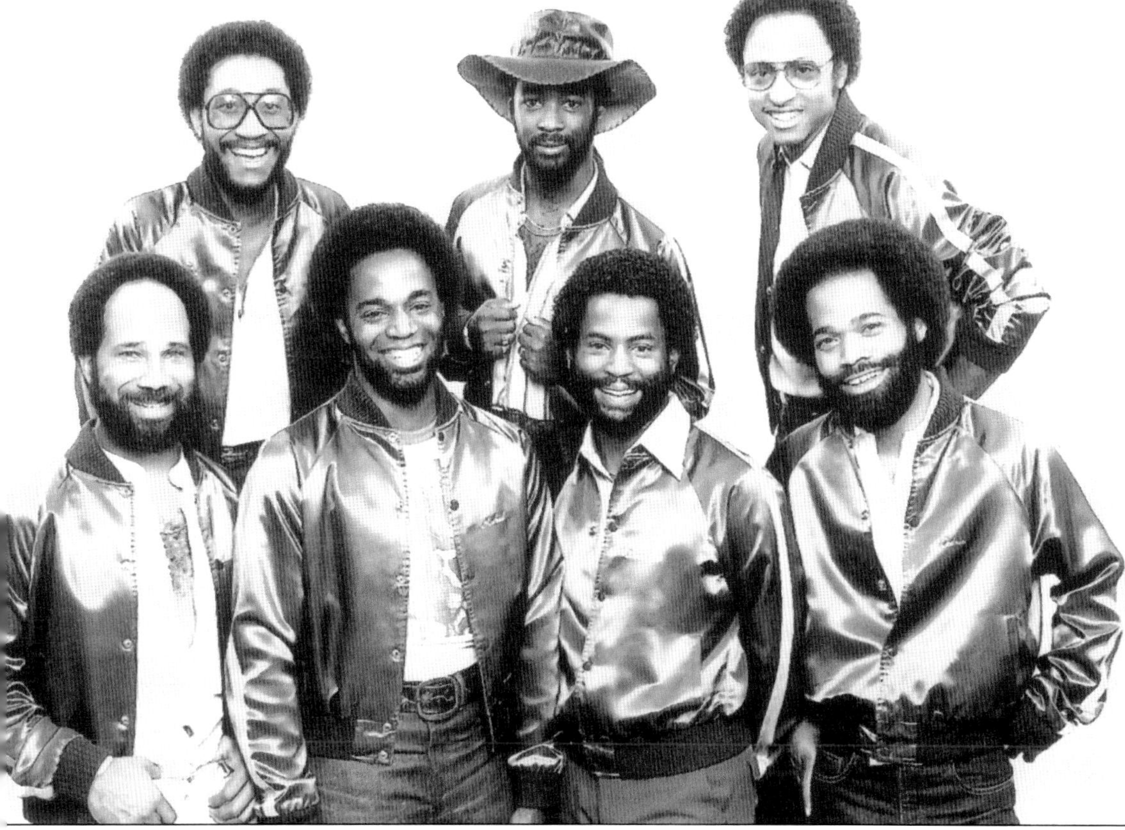

Con Funk Shun was yet another Vallejo musical phenomena that went national. Formed by Louis McCall and Michael Cooper while they were students at Vallejo High School in the late 1960s, the group was then known as Project Soul. Other Con Funk Shun members, most from Vallejo, include Karl Fuller, Felton Pilate, Danny Thomas, Paul Harrell, and Cedric Martin. During the 1970s and 1980s, Con Funk Shun had a number of hits, including "Loveship," "Candy," and "Spirit of Love." (Courtesy of the author.)

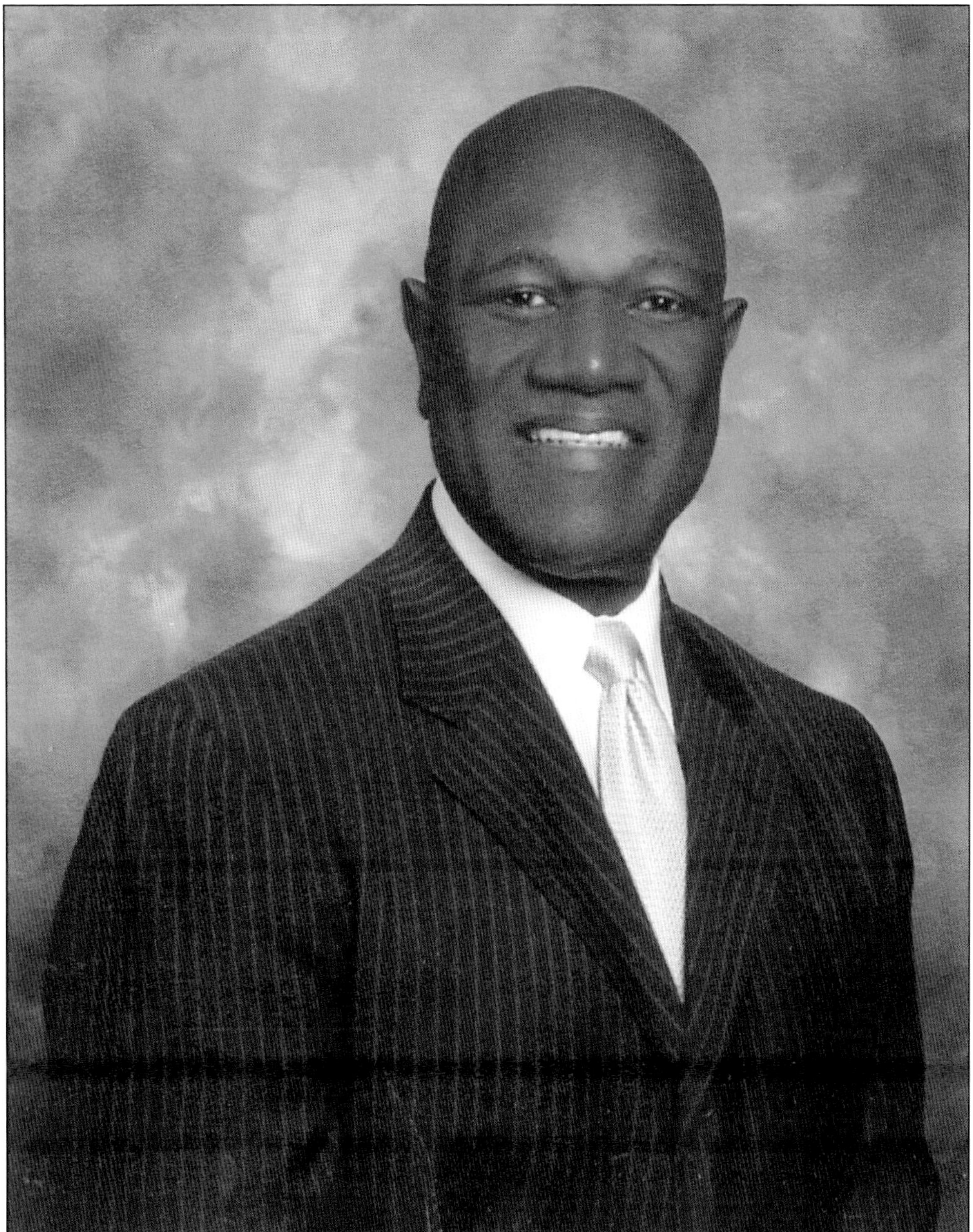

Joe Jones followed in the footsteps of Vallejo's first black Vallejo school board member, Jesse Bethel, when he was elected to the school board in the 1990s. Education and a lifelong love of learning were instilled in Jones by his parents, Addison and Theresa Jones. Jones's parents came to Vallejo from the South in 1951 for a better life. Jones built on his parents' values, working as a custodian to pay his way through college. He has served on numerous boards, including the Greater Vallejo Recreation District, and is executive director of the Willie B. Adkins Project, a program that prepares high school students for college. An executive with the Association of California School Administrators, Jones has received numerous awards including the prestigious Jefferson Award for public and community service. (Courtesy of Joe Jones.)

Foster Hicks became Vallejo's first African American city council member to be elected since Lewis Brown's historic election in 1964. Hicks, a political science teacher at Hogh High School, served two terms on the Vallejo City Council.

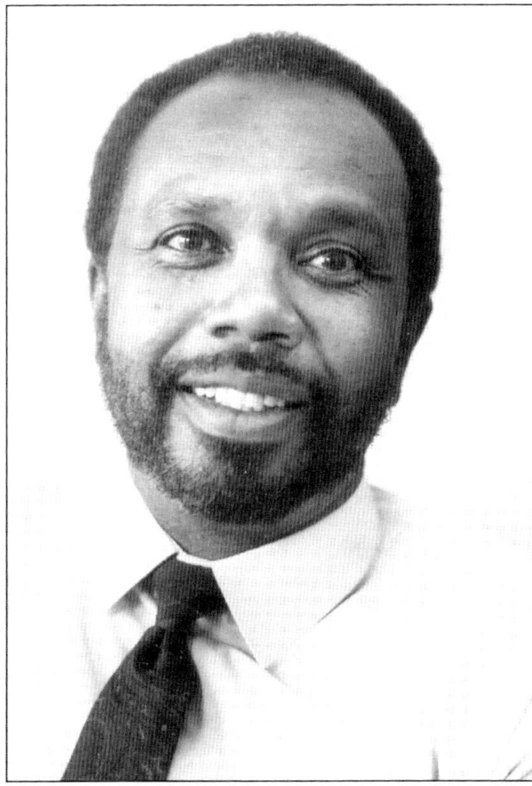

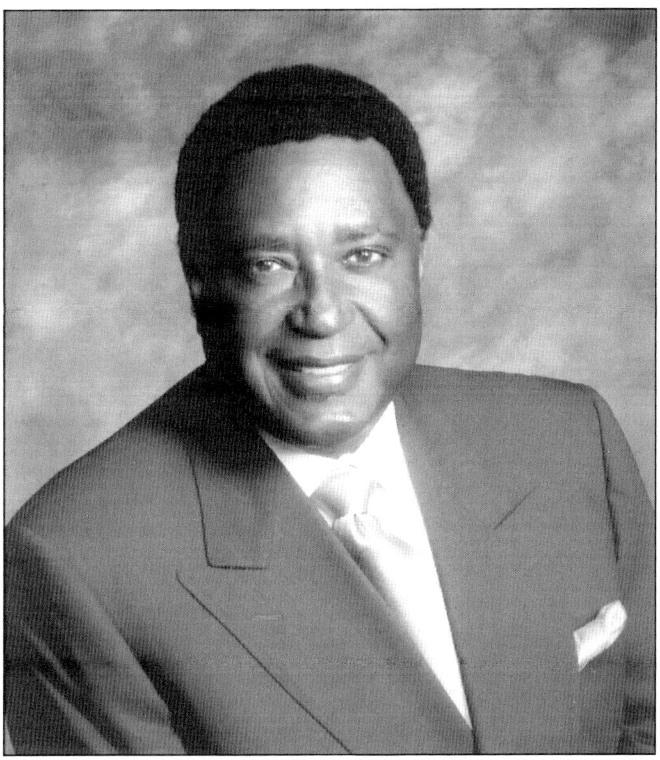

Famed attorney John L. Burris has deep Vallejo roots. Raised in Vallejo, he attended local public schools. A child of the Great Migration, the Burris family moved from Oklahoma to California in the 1940s. His law firm is based in Oakland. Burris is widely known for his civil rights work, especially in the area of police misconduct. (Courtesy of the author.)

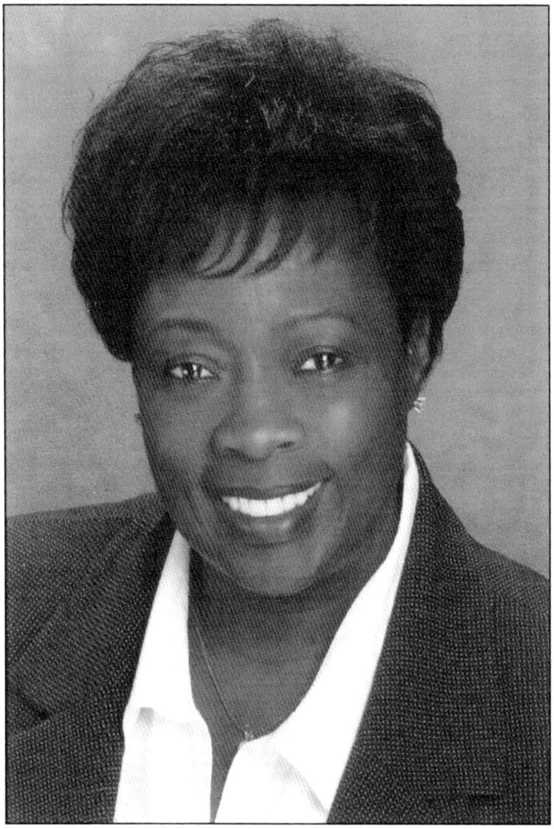

Pamela Pitts was Vallejo's first African American woman to serve on the Vallejo City Council when she was elected in 1998.

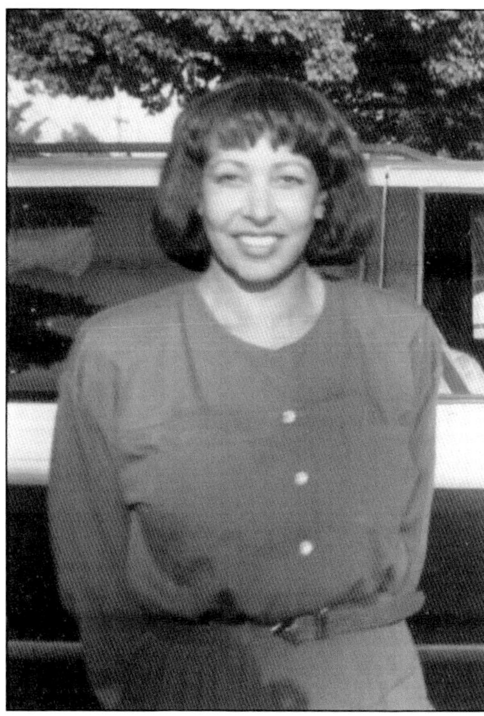

In the early 1990s, Jessica Mack-Viera made Vallejo history when she was elected as the first African American woman to serve on the Vallejo City Unified School District board of directors. A lifelong resident of Vallejo, Mack-Viera grew up on Vallejo's north side. In her 1991 candidate's statement, Mack-Viera said she was running for the school board to give voice to "parents struggling to be involved in their children's education." (Courtesy of the author.)

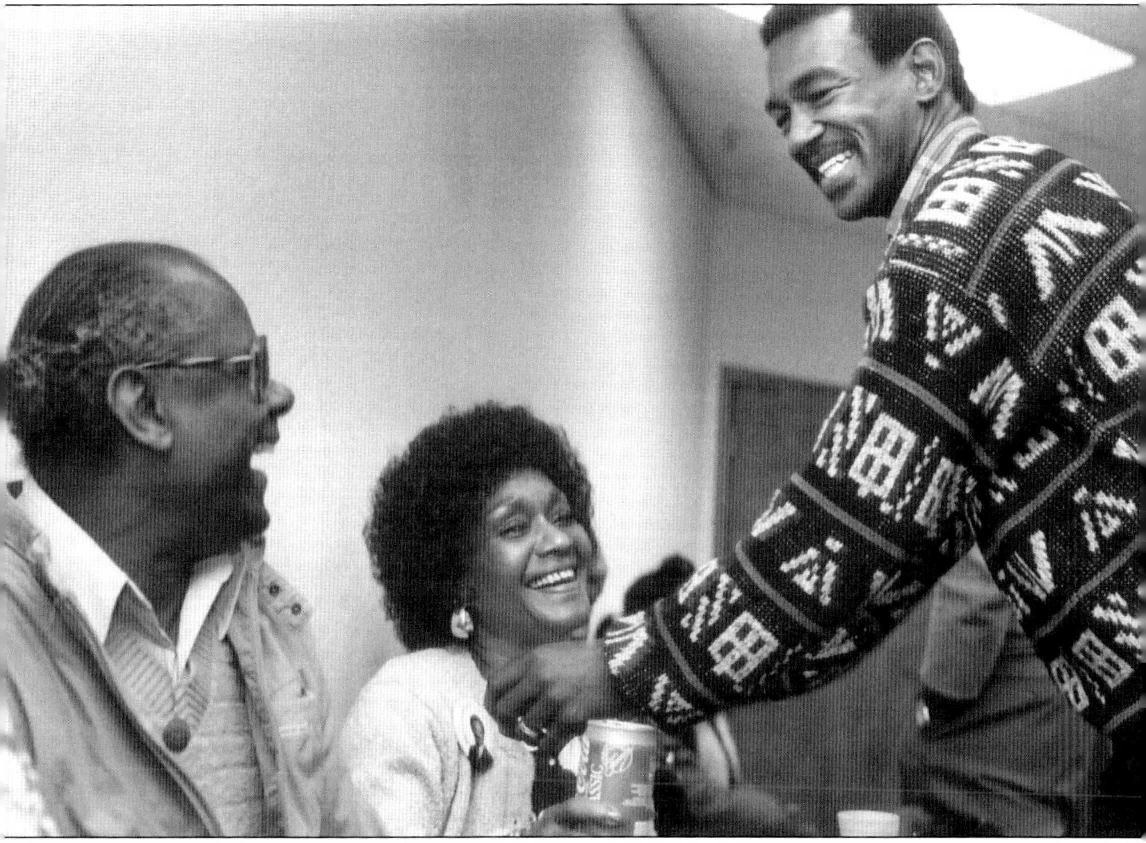

It is hard to measure the sacrifices made by the Great Migration generation who came west to settle in and forge new lives for themselves and their offspring. Just as the previous generations paved the way for them, the Great Migration generation provided leadership for those who followed them. In this photograph, the late James Williams and his wife, Ursula, who represent the Great Migration generation, share a light moment with attorney Osby Davis. In 2007, Davis, a child of the Great Migration, was elected mayor of Vallejo, making him the first African American to hold the post. In the early 1980s, Davis was elected to the Solano County Board of Supervisors, the first time an African American won a seat on that board. (Courtesy of the Vallejo Naval and Historical Museum.)